Inclusive Education: Diverse Perspectives

The companion volume in this series is:

Inclusive Education: Learners and Learning Contexts
Edited by: Melanie Nind, Kieron Sheehy and Katy Simmons

Both of these volumes are part of the second level Open University course E243 *Inclusive Education: Learning from each other*, which can be studied on its own or as part of an Open University undergraduate degree.

How to apply

If you would like to register for this course, or simply to find out more information about available courses, details can be obtained from the Course Reservations Centre, PO Box 724, The Open University, Walton Hall, Milton Keynes, MK7 6ZW, UK (Telephone 0 (0 44) 1908 653231). Details can also be viewed on our web page http://www.open.ac.uk.

Inclusive Education: Diverse Perspectives

**Edited by Melanie Nind, Jonathan Rix,
Keiron Sheehy and Katy Simmons**

 **David Fulton** Publishers

in association with

 The Open University

David Fulton Publishers Ltd
The Chiswick Centre, 414 Chiswick High Road, London W4 5TF

www.fultonpublishers.co.uk
www.onestopeducation.co.uk

First published 2003 by David Fulton Publishers
Reprinted 2005

10 9 8 7 6 5 4 3 2

David Fulton Publishers is a division of Granada Learning Limited, part of ITV plc.

British Library Cataloguing in Publication Data
A catalogue record for this book is available from the British Library.

ISBN 1 84312 065 8

Typeset by Pantek Arts Ltd, Maidstone, Kent
Printed and bound in Great Britain

Contents

Contents

About the Editors

Melanie Nind is best known for her work on Intensive Interaction, an interactive approach to teaching children and adults with severe learning difficulties (*Access to Communication: Interaction in Action; Implementing Intensive Interaction in Schools*, David Fulton Publishers). She has taught in special schools and co-ordinated learning support in further education colleges before teaching in higher education. Her research interests include, alongside teaching and learning, inclusive school cultures, mental health and profound learning difficulties and the politics of special education movements and interventions. She is a senior lecturer in inclusive and special education in the Faculty for Education and Language Studies at The Open University.

Jonathan Rix has worked as a language learning support teacher in a London comprehensive, and as a writer and facilitator in a wide variety of community, educational and theatrical settings. He has written over 50 basic language audio tours for people with learning difficulties. He is a parent representative on the National Portage Association Executive, and on the steering committee of his local playgroup. His current research is on the use of simplified materials and on access to cultural sites for people with learning disabilities. He is a lecturer in inclusive education in the Faculty for Education and Language Studies at The Open University.

Kieron Sheehy has worked in both education and health settings as a teacher, psychologist and lecturer. He has published in the areas of child development, learning and technology. His research is concerned with developing inclusive classroom practice through new technology and promoting mental health in people with profound learning difficulties. He is a lecturer in inclusive and special education in the Faculty for Education and Language Studies at The Open University.

Katy Simmons has taught in schools and higher education in the UK, USA and Australia, working with migrant groups, disadvantaged pupils and pupils with learning difficulties. She has acted as an advocate for parents and a campaigner on legal rights issues for young people with disabilities. She is a Trustee of the Advisory Centre for Education and chair of governors of a large secondary school. She has published on policy issues and is a lecturer in inclusive and special education in the Faculty for Education and Language Studies at The Open University.

Acknowledgements

We would like to thank all those who have contributed chapters to this Reader or who have approved their reprinting from other publications. Grateful acknowledgement is made to the following sources for permission to reproduce material in this book (chapters not listed have been newly written):

Chapter 2: Cooper, M. (1997) 'Mabel Cooper's life story', *Forgotten Lives: Exploring the History of Learning Disability*, ed. D. Atkinson, M. Jackson and J. Walmsley, Kidderminster: BILD.

Chapter 4: Giangreco, M. F. (1996) '"The stairs didn't go anywhere!": A self-advocate's reflections on specialized services and their impact on people with disabilities (an interview with Norman Kunc)', *Physical Disabilities: Education and Related Services (Journal of the Council for Exceptional Children, Division for Physical and Health Disabilities)* **14**(2), 1–12.

Chapter 5: Copeland, I. C. (2001) 'Integration versus segregation: the early struggle', *British Journal of Learning Disabilities* **29**, 5–11. Reproduced by permission of Blackwell Publishing Ltd.

Chapter 6: Barton, L. (1995) 'The politics of education for all', *Support for Learning* **10**(4), 156–60. Reproduced by permission of Blackwell Publishing Ltd.

Chapter 9: Almeida Diniz, F. and Usmani, K. (2001) 'Changing the discourse on "race" and special educational needs', *Multicultural Teaching* **20**(1), 25–8. Reproduced by permission of Trentham Books Ltd.

Chapter 10: McIntyre, D. (2000) 'Has classroom teaching served its day?', *Routledge International Companion to Education*, ed. B. Moon, M. Ben-Peretz and S. Brown, London: Routledge.

Chapter 12: Light, R. *Social model or unsociable muddle?*, www.daa.org.uk (accessed 19.7.02).

Chapter 13: Crow, L. (1996) 'Including all of our lives: renewing the social model of disability', *Encounters with Strangers: Feminism and Disability*, ed. J. Morris. London: The Women's Press Ltd.

Chapter 14: Swain, J. and French, S. (2000) 'Towards an affirmation model of disability', *Disability and Society* **15**(4), 569–82. Reproduced by permission of Taylor & Francis Ltd, http://www.tandf.co.uk/journals

Chapter 15: Morris, J. (2001) 'Having a say', *That Kind of Life: Social exclusion and young disabled people with high levels of support needs*. London: Scope.

Chapter 16: Rieser, R. (2001) 'The struggle for inclusion: the growth of a movement', *Disability, Politics and the Struggle for Change*, ed. L. Barton. London: David Fulton.

Chapter 17: Lewis, A. (2002) 'Accessing, through research interviews, the views of children with difficulties in learning', *Support for Learning* **17**(3), 110–16. Reproduced by permission of Blackwell Publishing Ltd.

Chapter 20: Hart, S. and Travers, P. (1999) 'Bilingual learners and the Code of Practice', *Multicultural Teaching* **17**(2), 37–42. Reproduced by permission of Trentham Books Ltd.

Chapter 21: Booth, T. (1999) 'Viewing inclusion from a distance: gaining perspective from comparative study', *Support for Learning* **14**(4), 164–8. Reproduced by permission of Blackwell Publishing Ltd.

Chapter 22: Holtermann, S. (1996) 'The impact of public expenditure and fiscal policies on Britain's children and young people', *Children and Society* **10**, 3–13. Reproduced by permission of John Wiley & Sons Limited.

Chapter 23: Dorries, B. and Haller, B. (2001) 'The news of inclusive education: a narrative analysis', *Disability and Society* **16**(6), 871–91. Reproduced by permission of Taylor & Francis Ltd, http://www.tandf.co.uk/journals

Chapter 24: Richardson, R. (1999) 'Unequivocal acceptance: lessons from the Stephen Lawrence Inquiry for education', *Multicultural Teaching* **17**(2), 7–11. Reproduced by permission of Trentham Books Ltd.

Every effort has been made to contact all the copyright holders of material included in the book. If any material has been included without permission, the publishers offer their apologies and will be happy to make acknowledgement in any future edition of the book.

CHAPTER 1

Introduction: From where you are

Jonathan Rix, Kieron Sheehy, Katy Simmons and Melanie Nind

Approaching from different angles

What are we looking at? There is a nearly empty mug of coffee on the desk. If you were to look and notice it, you would probably think, 'That's a nearly empty mug of coffee on the desk.' If you were to move your head a few millimetres and look again you would probably think the same thing.

But what if you were painting a picture of that mug? Maybe, you'd think about the light reflecting off its surface . . . after all, it is shiny. And what if you were allowed to drink only one cup of coffee a day? Maybe, you'd look at that mug and have a pang of disappointment that it was nearly empty, ignoring its 'mug' nature altogether. And how about if you couldn't see with your eyes but used your fingers instead? Would you know how much coffee was in it?

However simple something seems, it will always appear different if you approach it from a different angle.

What is a school? What is education? What are teachers? What are students? How do we develop learning in this culture? Who is responsible for the development of learning in this culture?

Every one of us will be looking at these questions from different angles . . . yet we'll probably assume that our answers would be much the same as most people's. After all, a mug of coffee is just a mug of coffee, isn't it?

Who made the mug? Who dug up the clay? Who shipped the clay? How much did they pay those mug makers? Where did the coffee come from? Why do people in the UK drink instant coffee anyway?

Each question can lead us in a multitude of directions.

Searching below the surface: is this education?

When we consider the development of inclusive education and practices, we need to remind ourselves that our communities are made up of billions of versions of the simple and obvious. Beneath each layer of understanding, however much it may seem to be common sense, are layers of socio-cultural and personal complexity. In an attempt to deal with this slightly terrifying (and potentially exhausting) factor of social living, people tend to agree to differ on many things. We tend to accept the generalisations to make life feel easier. It is at the point where the generalisations become the basis for judgements, decisions and beliefs that the problems multiply for us all. Inclusive education is, in our view, an attempt to make sure that generalisations are constantly tempered by questions; it is a call for us to step back from our certainties and listen to another perspective.

Richard Elmore (1995) asked us to imagine the first day of lessons in a school in which students have not been grouped, teachers have not defined their work according to such groups, no decisions have been made about how much time will be given to content, and no one has decided how student progress will be assessed. Imagine that first morning, imagine hundreds of people arriving, males and females, of all ages, some to learn, some to teach. Where would you put everybody? Do we put everybody in the hall, ask the teachers to stand on one side and the students to stand on the other? Do we divide the teachers up first or do we divide the students up? Do we expect teachers to teach everything they know or just something they know lots about? Do we expect students to study things which they already have some understanding of or of which they have no understanding? Are classes divided according to student interest or teacher interest? Are groups defined by number, by space available, by age, by height, by language spoken, by family group? Can students spend all day studying something they find interesting? Can teachers spend all day teaching something they find interesting? And how do we assess the ability of the teacher to teach and the learner to learn? Should we assess what the learner wants to learn or what the teacher wants the learner to learn?

> Certain solutions – the age-grade structure, the allocation of single teachers to classroom units, the allocation of specific content to specific periods of time, and so on – have become 'fixed' in the institutional structure of schools. They have become fixed, not necessarily because we know they work in some educational sense, although that may be true, but because ... they help us manage the demands and uncertainties of mass education. For the most part, we adhere to these regularities of schooling because we have seemingly always adhered to them and they have come to be identified in the minds of students, teachers, and parents with what it means to 'do school'.
>
> (Elmore 1995: 369)

Of course, underpinning Elmore's question are other assumptions. If you were presented with the problem of assisting large numbers of people to learn would you choose to send them all to the same building? Might you not decide that it was better to spread them amongst a community of people who had information that was needed? Maybe by taking such an approach we would separate ourselves from the notion that one group of people has something to learn and another group of people has something to teach. We may have decided in the first place that everyone has the ability to learn and everyone has the ability to assist others to learn. Maybe we would not perceive teaching and learning to be neatly definable, neatly assessable; maybe we would see them as hand-in-hand, that through teaching something we learn from it, and through learning something we become teachers.

Here we are then: asking questions of education

Of course, formal learning in the United Kingdom is considerably different from this last description and much closer to that described by Elmore. Our starting point is education within the classroom (or its close cousin the playgroup/church hall) and its end point is the examination. When considering many theories of communication and learning, as well as issues of human rights, we may feel that there is a certain amount of irony within this situation.

We place people in buildings that are generally poorly accessible, with varying quantities of facilities, and group them according to age (and often sex). We formally and informally identify and/or withdraw some people who do not achieve targets or are perceived to be inherently different according to relative physical, behavioural, emotional, cultural and cognitive parameters. We offer access to closely defined areas of information, which focus on the majority culture's traditional definitions of what needs to be learned. We present our information in one language, structuring learning within middle class norms of behaviour, and then require the people to demonstrate their knowledge within a variety of time constrained parameters, whilst informing them that their futures depend on it.

Nearly everything about the construction of this system is based on separation and segregation. It is ideally suited if one wishes to encourage individuality. Its design will suit the development of an understanding of socio-cultural and intellectual boundaries and one's position within a social structure. It will help in the development of specialists and elites. Yet these are not the only roles that we require of education. It is largely through this system that we expect people to become socially and culturally sensitive and responsible, to develop their individual and communal skills and intelligences. It is often education that is blamed when individuals fail to behave in a manner that is to the benefit of the whole.

Thinking about moving on

When considering the nature of human knowledge we must do so in relation to the society and culture in which it develops. We need to consider those socio-cultural conditions rather than examine the characteristics and aspects of that knowledge (Young 1971). We need to accept that the way in which we educate will have as much, if not more, impact than the information we want to teach. Equally, what we teach needs to be of relevance to the individual. Every communication that we interpret, all our thinking, hinges on an implicit expectation that the effort of processing will be worthwhile and meaningful to us (Sperber and Wilson 1986). As Ivor Goodson (1981) argues, school subjects have grown out of the ideas of various interest groups as they have sought to maintain and extend their own position and importance, rather than being self contained and rational units of meaning. Academic subjects have developed because of their relevance to the individuals creating the subject. They are not inherently relevant to people learning them; to those people the relevance may only develop over time. Similarly, the systems we operate are not always socio-culturally appropriate for all students. Shirley Brice Heath (1994) discusses the differences in the ways that working class black children and white children and middle class white children learn about reading at home. She explores how this affects their approaches to literacy and communication in general and subsequently their progress in schools designed around the middle class approach. Hardly surprisingly, the mismatch in approaches has a marked negative impact, not just on the development of literacy in the first two groups, but in wider participation and achievement too.

The examples mentioned above are just a few that demonstrate the link between the kinds of schools systems we have and their impact on the learning of the people within them. They demonstrate our need constantly and consistently to build and rebuild on the actual experiences of individuals so that their experiences, and the experiences of others, can be improved. They demonstrate our need to examine and question the structures and processes of our education system at every level if we are to make sure that all are learning rather than merely registered as being present for learning.

Our systems are inherited, of course. They have grown on the back of tradition. The changes that take place generally reflect the beliefs about education of those who have been educated within that system. They therefore echo what has come before. Clearly, it is difficult to make us change what we have always known. Yet change is supposedly something that education has had by the bureaucratic bucket-load during the last few years. It has been a constant and very stressful experience for many in schools, colleges and beyond. However, virtually none of the parameters described above have changed. The basic description of how we educate has, to all intents and purposes, remained the same.

Starting from somewhere else

The first real assault on the classic model of schooling is inclusion. In many ways the initial response has been entrenchment. Up have gone the numbers of pupils being put into special schools by many local education authorities. More determined have become many parents and schools about achieving 'statements of special educational needs' for their children. But there are many schools that are seeing the real value that inclusion brings to them, the broader experiences and learning opportunities for everyone within the system. These schools are doing their very best to move to a position where separation and segregation are reduced.

This drive for inclusive practice, however, still takes place in a system that is otherwise unchanged. At the start of the 21st century most schools only enable access for people who can walk and see and hear. Most Literacy and Numeracy classes (and many other subjects beside) involve streaming and setting. Teachers are almost entirely constrained by the time pressures and content requirements of the National Curriculum or other national edicts. Exclusionary action is taken far more often against individuals from minority ethnic groups than those from the ethnic majority. People with English as an Additional Language must still sit exams in English to gain any meaningful qualification. Boys are more likely to get special educational needs support than are girls. Children will only be marginal voices in defining and developing their schools and their learning.

Schools and school systems are not going to be changed completely or overnight. This is neither surprising nor something that we should demand. What they should change to and how they should change is open to debate. There is not a perfect system awaiting us on the shelf. What there is, instead, is a whole raft of best practice principles and processes from which we can choose. Applied research shows us many ways forward that can break down barriers to learning and increase the chances of inclusion for more. These best practice principles and processes are not going to lead us to one model of the school or classroom, either. They will allow schools to respond to the differing circumstances in which they operate in the manner most suitable to the people within them and served by them.

> It is possible, indeed highly likely, that there is no single best structural solution for any given set of principles of good practice. There may be instead a range of possible solutions that represent various adaptations of principles of good practice to particular conditions – students' backgrounds, the values and cultures of the communities in which schools operate, and the particular strengths and weaknesses of practitioners in a given setting.
>
> (Elmore 1995: 370)

Our chances of achieving structures and procedures that are responsive to the individuals operating with and within them means we must not be wedded to any aspects of the system as it presently stands. We must be prepared to adapt to the circumstances, but to do so in a way that takes account of its ongoing impact on those affected. To achieve such a state requires a great deal of flexibility. Our education systems need to be capable of adapting and continuing to be adaptive without diminishing their cohesiveness or accountability. This is a tall order, but one that we can move towards.

To achieve this requires that we become increasingly sensitive to those within the systems we operate. We need to consider and understand the perspectives of those who are affected by and who affect our educational structures and processes.

This book is an opportunity to explore some of those perspectives. It brings together the voices and ideas of some of those who have been or who are currently disabled by the education system and wider social structures. It incorporates the work of activists and researchers, theorists and practitioners. It presents personal experiences and reflections alongside socio-cultural analysis. It considers the development of ideas and beliefs and their application in the past, present and future; and it presents warnings and possibilities to guide and motivate both our thinking and the policies and actions we undertake in the delivery of education in the coming years.

A collection of perspectives

The book is divided into five sections. We begin with three writers (Mabel Cooper, Marjorie Chappell, and Norman Kunc talking to Michael F. Giangreco) *Looking back* at the systems and processes used to educate them in the not too distant past. We see how some aspects of the system supported a positive vision of the writers' individual identities, but more typically supported the negative. It is quite clear how systems constantly highlighted their 'disabilities', the differences by which they were typically defined and disabled. Our fourth writer, Ian Copeland, outlines the reasons why the segregated model, which caused so much dislocation for the first three authors, became the norm.

The second section, *Looking forward*, considers the need for a vision for the future of education and offers us some possibilities to bear in mind. The writers (Len Barton, Carol Boys, Jonathan Rix, Fernando Almeida Diniz and Khushi Usmani, Donald McIntyre, Kieron Sheehy) each look at issues of inclusion from a different standpoint and underline the inevitable struggle which will underpin the achievement of inclusive education in an inclusive society. They remind us that if we wish to develop inclusion we need to accept all individuals having control of their own lives, having a say in the running of organisations that represent them and affecting the processes of the institutions that dominate much that happens to them and around them. This section offers, too, some ways in which educational practices need to change to enable the development of inclusion. It also suggests the manner in which developments in communication technology may be used to assist in this and in providing a new platform for the voices of all.

The writers in the third section, *Looking from within*, share their perspectives as disabled people, or seek to hear the views of disabled learners. They explore the ways and means by which we describe our society and the practices and people within it. Richard Light, Liz Crow, John Swain and Sally French examine the development of the social model of disability, its future and its possible evolution; they consider too the development of ideas that underpin inclusion. Alongside them, the chapters by Jenny Morris, Ann Lewis, Joy Jarvis and Indra Sinka and Alessandra Iantaffi, force us to question how we should best come to understand individuals' attitudes towards differing models and ideas, and remind us that often the responses we hear may not be the ones which sit comfortably with our own notions of what is and what isn't inclusive. Richard Rieser reminds us too that often it takes just a few determined voices to make a real difference.

In the fourth section, *Looking from within classrooms and schools*, the writers highlight some means by which attitudes and procedures in the classroom can be developed to enhance learning. In Caroline Roaf's chapter, we are given an insight into how Learning Support Assistants view the roles they perform within schools and how they can be best utilised to improve the effectiveness and inclusivity of schools. Focusing on learning in context, Susan Hart and Penny Travers lead us to question the ways in which we define student learning 'needs'.

In the final section, the authors (Tony Booth, Sally Holtermann, Bruce Dorries, Beth Haller and Robin Richardson) are *Looking in from outside* to offer a different perspective. They consider how inclusion and inclusive practice are viewed by institutions, policy makers, and other agencies, as well as by the people within them. The chapters lead us to question the preparedness of many individuals and systems to adapt and change. Dorries and Haller highlight how we can present a case which will win widespread support, while Holtermann forces us to ask how much we are willing to pay to back up our words. In conclusion, Richardson challenges us to examine genuinely our practices and beliefs in all their forms and to act upon what we find.

This book is about perspectives. It is about learning from each other. It is telling us that if we wish to develop inclusivity we must take the time to explore our own views, to search out the views of others and to make sure that we listen and act upon the things that are said. These are essentials for developing inclusive education. Perhaps, even more importantly, this collection gives a clear reminder that we all have multiple social voices. Our roles in the social context change across time and within different situations. We need to take this into consideration, not only when we are evaluating ourselves, but also when we are trying to understand and empathise with the people who share our systems, processes and day-to-day lives.

References

Elmore, R. (1995) Teaching, learning, and school organisation: principles of practice and the regularities of schooling. *Educational Administration Quarterly*, **31**(3), 355–74.

Goodson, I. (1981) Becoming an academic subject: patterns of explanation and evolution. *British Journal of Sociology of Education*, **2**(2), 163–80.

Heath, S.B. (1994) What no bedtime story means: narrative skills at home and school, in Maybin, J. (ed.) *Language and Literacy in Social Practice*. Clevedon: Multilingual Matters.

Sperber, D. and Wilson, D. (1986) *Relevance: communication and cognition*. Oxford: Blackwell.

Young, M. (ed.) (1971) *Knowledge and Control*. London: Collier-Macmillan.

Part 1

Looking back

CHAPTER 2

Mabel Cooper's life story

Mabel Cooper

This is Mabel Cooper's autobiography, constructed from tape recorded
interviews. Her life reflects the changing policies and practices of the last
50 years. As a child she lived first in a children's home and later in a long-stay
hospital. Many years later she left hospital for a life in the community, where she
became involved in self-advocacy. The telling of her story is a major landmark in
Mabel's life. She hopes that it will inspire other people with learning difficulties to
find ways of telling their own life stories.

Family

I didn't know at that time that I had anybody. A lady called Mary Mason, she was a
nurse in St Lawrence's hospital, she helped me find my auntie. Auntie Edith. Then I
went visiting her. She's still alive and I still go and see her sometimes.

I've got five cousins as well which I searched for when my auntie was taken ill.
Auntie Edith gave me the number for them. One lives in Zimbabwe, in southern
Africa, one lives in Croydon and the others all live in Bedford. I go and visit them from
time to time.

It was a long time ago when I found my auntie. I was in the hospital then. She told
me my mother had died. She was my auntie's sister. I don't know my father. My
auntie doesn't know him. She said they were married.

My Gran lived in Croydon. My auntie moved and went to Bedford. My mother
lived outside Bedford.

Childhood

When I was little I lived in another place like St Lawrence's, but it was just for
children. This was in Bedford. It used to be run by nuns. And that had bars up at the
windows as well, because they used to call them places madhouses. It was in Bedford.
They haven't got it any more, they've vanished it.

I moved to St Lawrence's when I was seven, because they only took children what
went to school in this home. And I never went to school, so I had to move. In them

days they give you a test. You went to London or somewhere because they'd give you a test before they make you go anywhere. It used to be a big place, all full of offices and what-have-you. Because they said you should be able to read when you're seven or eight. I couldn't read, I hadn't been to school. That was 1952, I was seven years old.

The Hospital

First impressions

When I first went in there, even just getting out of the car you could hear the racket. You think you're going to a madhouse. When you first went there you could hear people screaming and shouting outside. It was very noisy but I think you do get used to them after a little while because it's like everywhere that's big. If there's a lot of people you get a lot of noise, and they had like big dormitories, didn't they? And the children were just as noisy, in the children's home, and they were all the same sort of people.

I went to St Lawrence's in 1952. I went to A2, that was the admissions ward. They didn't used to have many in there, they used to just take the new ones what came in. You were only there for about a week or two weeks. And they moved you on to another ward where there was all children. I stayed there till I was 15 and then I went to another ward where I was with adults.

There was bars on the windows when I first went to St Lawrence's, it was just like a prison. Of course it was called a nuthouse in them days, so it used to have bars on it. You couldn't open the windows. Well, you could, but not far enough to get out of them. You didn't have toys, no toys whatsoever. You couldn't have toys because they would just get broken and thrown through the bars in the window, and get caught in them.

It was big. There were lots and lots of wards. On the female side it was A to H. On the male side it was A to D. They all had about 75 people in. And then there was little houses on the grounds and they had about 50 people in.

School/work

There used to be children, there used to be two wards of children. One for little boys and one for girls. There was no school there, they only let you use your hands by making baskets and doing all that sort of thing. That's all you did. In them days they said you wasn't able enough to learn so you didn't go to school you went to like a big ward and they had tables. You just went there and made the baskets or what-have-you. Because in them days they said you wasn't capable enough to learn to do anything else, so that's what you did.

So in St Lawrence's they never went to school. They went and made baskets. If you didn't do that you went to one of the work places or in the laundry, or stayed in the ward and did nothing. As you got older you could stay doing baskets or you could go down the laundry or the work shops in the grounds. I made a friend of Eva and she did one of the workshops where I worked. I worked on the baskets. A lot of them used to stay on the ward, or go round and sit round on the field and didn't do anything. Because really, who wants to work in an old laundry? Not many people did that.

Some of them went out to work, where you'd go and try somewhere. Some of the people I used to be friends with did that. Gloria done it, my friend Gloria, because she was in hospital. She went to Purley Hospital and worked. She went out before me, she went out a long time before me. She stayed out, she never came back. If anything went wrong when they were out they used to go and pick them up, and bring them back.

Clothes

The worst thing was, I couldn't wear my own clothes, you had to wear other people's. Because you never, you never got your own because the beds were too close together, so you didn't have a locker or anything, you just went to this big cupboard and helped yourself. There might be six piles of dresses in this big cupboard. They had all the clothes in and you'd just go and help yourself to the clothes you want. I didn't like it, that you wasn't even allowed to wear your own clothes in them days.

St Lawrence's Hospital

Of course they had their own shoes, you couldn't wear your own shoes in them days, you had to wear their shoes and they were horrible. They made them there, in the hospital. You never went out for anything because they did everything in the hospital. The clothes were made in the hospital, in the sewing rooms.

They did everything there, they made their own bread and everything; they had a bakery. They had a farm. They used to have cows and sheep there.

Separation of men and women

On the male side you see they're different. The male side was different to the female side, there was more on the female side than there was on the male. There was a lot more on the female side. You couldn't mix with the men. You could go to a dance but you'd have men one side, women the other. You could dance with them, but they had to go back men one side, women the other side. Even in the dance hall there was two loads of staff in the middle, one full of women and one full of men, and you just danced around the staff in the middle.

The female staff were on one side, on one row and male on the other, and you just danced around them. You could go over and dance, and they had to go back to one side and I went back on the other.

Money

In them days you didn't have proper money. If they give you any money it's green, it's like little green coins. You can't use it outside, you can't buy anything outside, you could only use it in their canteen. You could just go down and spend it in the canteen. It was only for sweets.

Running away/hiding

If I got upset I'd just run away, for a couple of hours. You couldn't go out, so if I got upset I would just go off, and I would come back when I was ready. I wouldn't stay out the night or anything like that but l would come back when I was ready, and then I'd be all right. I would go round the field because their field is quite big at the back. And you could just sit there, there were seats and you could just sit and be on your own. And I'd come back when I was ready.

Life on the ward

Loads of people used to live in St Lawrence's. There were loads of them there. In a ward there was about 75, men or women – you couldn't get men with women. I was in a ward with 75 other women, and the beds were that small, they were that close to one another.

Of course they had some in the grounds as well, and they had fifty in those places.

Because there was too many in the hospital they did no cooking in the ward kitchen. If you think, 75 in one ward, they couldn't do cooking in the wards. They had a kitchen there but they did no cooking. They couldn't teach you to do anything because there wasn't enough time for the nurses. They used to go off at half one and another lot used to come on and used to stay till nine, and then they would go off and a night nurse would come on. During the day there would be three different lots of staff.

The ward was blocked off, there was doors. You weren't allowed to sit on your beds The beds were that close to one another, so you couldn't have anything private. I didn't have anything of my own, because they would get pinched, the other patients would pinch them.

Of course you wasn't allowed to stand on the corridors or do anything like that. If you didn't go into one of the workshops, or the laundry, or the basket making, or digging up gardens then you sat on the ward. Sometimes I did that, because it's all I knew. If that's all you know it's very difficult not to do anything else.

In the hospital you used to have to be in by eight, because of the night nurses at 9 o'clock. You had to be in bed by nine. If you wasn't in at 8 o'clock you'd have to go in one of the other wards and ask them to come and open the doors, especially if they haven't got a night nurse in one of the wards. In two of the wards they didn't have night nurses so if you wasn't in at 8 o'clock then you'd have to go and ask one of the other wards to open the door and let you in. You soon got told off in the morning if you did that. I never done that but it did use to happen. I stayed out of a lot of trouble, but some of the others did things what they shouldn't be doing, like staying out late. I don't think it's worth getting into trouble, you might just as well do what they want. And the day will come when you can go out and get about on your own.

You had to get up at half six, seven o'clock. In my time you didn't have choices. You just did as they said.

Meals

We all ate on the ward together, but not with the staff. The food was vile, I didn't like it. They used to bring the dinners up at 11 o'clock and they used to sit and talk till 12 or half past. The dinners were horrible. There was no choices. My friend Eva, she used to be one of the nurses, she used to heat it up for us.

Relationships

I made a friend and she used to work in one of the workshops in the hospital, and I used to go there. This was Eva. She was the staff, she was one of the nurses. Eva used to sit and talk to me sometimes but otherwise you don't get anybody because they'd say they hadn't got the time.

I made a few friends with some of the patients. There was Gloria, Gloria Ferris, I made friends with her. I still see her. I go out every Saturday with her.

A lot of them got married. I didn't have many men friends. I never had any visitors in the hospital, nobody at all, never.

I found my auntie because she wrote to me once or twice in the hospital. And I said I would like to visit this aunt and one of the nurses, Mary Mason, she said, 'Oh, I'll find out about it. I'll get a pass and I'll take you.' So she did. We phoned up, she phoned up auntie and I went to see her, and now I do go and see her regularly. She was living in Bedford then. She lived in London for a little while, and then she moved out of London and went to Bedford.

Trips out

You weren't allowed out of the hospital. You had to write up and ask could you leave the grounds. You had to ask the medical or write to the doctor and ask them. You couldn't just go across the road and look at the shops, it wasn't allowed not unless you wrote up and asked. I didn't go out because I got so used to not going out. You'd get lost if you're not used to it.

If you wanted to go out they would give you a card. And every time you went out, you could only go out from 2 o'clock till four. If you wasn't back by four then you would be in trouble. You could never go out on your own, you always had to go with somebody, like one of the staff. You could write up and get a pass for a Saturday afternoon, but you had to get permission every time. They would watch to see if you come in after four. If you didn't get back, they'd give you till six and if you weren't back then they would ring the police.

In the old days, you had to be very crafty, you had to be one ahead of them. You could get down the pipe. The pipes used to be very big and if you was on the third floor upstairs, and you went down on to the fire escape, there used to be a big pipe. You used to get down in that because it was wide, it was wide enough for you to fit. So they could get out of the bottom because the hole at the bottom was big enough for them to get out of. And it led you outside the gate which you couldn't get out of otherwise, because that was always locked.

You could go round the boundary. There used to be a big old church, it's not there any more they've built a school on there. You could go round the back of the church and by the fence there used to be an opening. We used to go out through that way and then get back in through that way. You could only get as far as the shop down the road, that was all. You could just go round and look, and come back again. At least it was something that you could do, till you got caught. I didn't do it much, I did it once or twice. Nobody else knew it was there.

In the hospital they used to have a church so you never went out of the hospital to go to church because they had one in there, on the corridor. I never went to church. I don't go now only because I can't read. And for me, it's ridiculous so I just don't go. In the hospital church the men sat on one side and the women sat on the other. They used to pass letters in through the church, underneath the seat the letters used to go. The women used to pass letters across. I never went to church so I never did that. You could go round the fields and, if there was no staff about, then you could do it that way but otherwise you couldn't.

If you went on holiday with the hospital you sat on the grass and didn't do anything. They just used to sit on the grass if it was a nice day. You didn't go on the beach or anything We went to like a holiday thing and they had green huts and they used to go to them. They didn't used to take anybody else. They just used to take people from hospitals. We never saw anybody else because they didn't encourage it.

Punishment

They had a ward up in the hospital G3 and they used to put people in there. They used to get locked up. I never was in G3 because I never run away or anything like that. They used to make you wear your bed slippers and then you couldn't run away. The door was locked, but you could get out. If you got out though you couldn't get back in so you had to ring the bell. G3 was for women, D3 was for men.

Reflections

In them days if you had learning difficulties or anything that's where they used to put you. They didn't say, 'Oh, you could go into a house and somebody would look after you.' They would just say `You, you've gotta go into a big hospital' and that's it. Years ago, if you wasn't married and you had a baby that was a disgrace and they would say, 'Oh the mother goes to a workhouse or a loony bin' as they had in them days, or the mother went into a workhouse or a loony bin and the child was put in care. I think that's why there was more women.

In the hospital if you wanted to do anything or to go anywhere it was so much of a bind because you had to keep asking someone to write for you, so a lot of the time I never did. I got used to the hospital. Not really because I wanted to be there, it was because that's what I knew. That's all you knew, you didn't know anything else not like I do now.

A lot of people, especially people like me, we always think if they didn't have enough money to keep us outside they would say, 'Right, you all have to go back in the hospital' and open them again. It's important they knock them down and then people like me and a lot more will know that won't happen. I think it worries a lot of people like me because they are still standing there because they could say 'OK, we're going to open all that again and all the people what were there go back up there.' Of course it saves them a lot of money. I know they have turned a lot of St Lawrence's off, they've built houses on there. Some of it's gone, but there's still a lot there[1].

Leaving hospital

Whyteleafe House

Whyteleafe House was the same as St Lawrence's, the only difference is that it was a house. It was still a big place. It was no different because they still had nurses and what-have-you. You still had 50 people. It was all women. I shared a room with six others.

Whyteleafe House used to be for people what used to go out to work, they didn't take anybody else. And then they said, 'Oh well, we haven't got enough people now what go out to work, we'll have to change it and put other people there.' That's how I got to go to Whyteleafe House.

The hospital used to bring me in the car and they used to take me back to Whyteleafe in the car. I lived at Whyteleafe House, they used to pick me up at the house and take me to the hospital for the day. At night time they used to take me back. I never went on the bus that we go on now. If you didn't go out, like me and a few of them, you still had to wait for someone to go with you. Eventually I just said could I go and try myself and they said I could. I went by myself but they don't like it.

I was about 31 when I went to Whyteleafe House. I've been out of St Lawrence's 16 years now. I asked to leave. My friend, Eva, she wrote and asked. She said I might be able to cope a bit. She got in touch with the social worker what used to be in the hospital. If you wanted to go to work or anything then they would just get in contact with one of the social workers.

First impressions of the outside world

When I first came out of there I thought the children were midgets. People have laughed because they said to me, `Was that the difficultist part of coming out of there and finding children are midgets?' I never saw children, only children in wheelchairs and what-have-you, not children running about and doing all the things they're doing. So really the children fascinated me, seeing them it really did fascinate me.

I 'd never been on a bus or on a train. Because you never went. These are all the things you didn't do. It's not like ordinary people going out and doing what they want to do. In them places, you didn't. So going on a train or going on the underground all them are new to me. In fact going on the underground and on the moving stairs and all that is quite new to me. I'm used to the bus now because I go so much. I don't have to buy a ticket, I've got a pass.

Early days in the community

I lived with a family in Caterham Valley but she used to keep having nervous breakdowns. She used to be ever so funny. And then, because there was nobody in the house when I went home one day, I got frightened and ran off. I went to Eva's house but I couldn't stay there so Eva phoned up and I went in where I worked, at the old people's home. I lived there, stayed there. I used to help look after the old people in Caterham. I used to help them do the cleaning. I lived there for a little while, and then they said, 'Oh, you can't live here any more.' They said, 'You know, it's not really for you.'

So I went to live with another lady, she had a Down's syndrome boy. A social worker, a man, decided this, but that was only supposed to have been for a short time. It was at Old Lodge Lane. I was there for a year and a half, then I went to Isabel's. I went because the other lady only wanted someone to play with her little boy and I didn't want to do that, not really. I don't want to keep somebody company.

When I first went to Isabel's she found me a morning job but they were again being a bit difficult because Isabel had to keep coming up and getting social workers to come and talk to them. I just gave it up. There was only me and Anne in the beginning at Isabel's. And then she said she was gonna have another one, and she had Gloria. Then they started to get more and more and more, till there was 13 living there.

I had my own front door key at Isabel's and she made sure always that you had money in your pocket. I had my own room and since I'd been at Isabel's I'd got my own telly and my own tape recorder. I stayed at Isabel's six years and a half and I thought, well, now it's time for me to adventure a bit more. Gloria got like me, she asked to move out of Isabel's because there was too many, like I did, and she went to live with two sisters.

I thought it was time I adventured. I got friendly with a lady called Anne Evans, one of the boarding-out ladies and a friend of Gloria's. I went to dinner one day with Gloria and Anne and I said to Anne 'Do you know I'm thinking of asking to move out of Isabel's? It's just too noisy.' There were 13 people then. I stayed as long as I thought I could stand it. And I said, right, this is enough, and I asked. I said to Anne, 'I am thinking of moving, definitely' and she said, 'Oh, leave it with me and I'll sort it out for you.' I went to a few places and I said no, and then I went to Mary's.

I've been at Mary's a year, gone a year now. I moved there in May 1992.

Life now

Mary is my carer now. She buys the clothes for me because I find that's difficult. Mary does it for me because my eyesight's not that brilliant and the writing's so small. I can't read the labels so Mary does it. Jean lives at Mary's, she's all right, she helped me write a letter last night. She can't walk very much but otherwise she's OK. So I've got Jean and I've got Mary, so there is people there.

Gloria lives in South Croydon with Nora. Nora is like Mary, a carer. So Gloria lives there and on Saturdays I go there to see her. We're good friends but I don't think I could live with Gloria. And I've got Flo, I've got quite a few friends what don't live, what hasn't been in hospital – but I've got some what have.

I go down the seaside, I go places. I just tell Mary I'm off and I go. Because when I first came out I had to learn to get on the bus and go to the places I want to do. I taught myself to go to Brighton. I had to. They showed me what train to get on. And then I didn't sit on the grass, I went to the fair because I like the fair. That was new to me as well. I even go to Margate. You have to go to Victoria and get a train from Victoria.

I joined People First two or three years ago, when Isabel asked me would I like to join. There were about ten people when it first started in Croydon, now there's loads. I didn't join in very much at the first time or for a couple of weeks, something like that. Then one of the men what was chairperson, he didn't turn up so they asked me would I take it on. So I said, 'Oh, all right, I'll take it on for one week.' And one week got more weeks than ever. This was last year sometime.

Because of being in the People First Group I went to Canada. That was the biggest conference yet, that was bigger than Mencap put together. That was good, Canada is one of the good ones. But I think I would have liked somebody else to come because it would have been more exciting with somebody else. Declan said it would have been nice for somebody else from Croydon to come as well. I do a few jobs for Declan, like going out talking to people, and help tidying their office, and doing all the little jobs they need to do on a Monday. Declan pays and keeps the money for me, so it pays for my trips and what-have-you.

The group I'm doing now is coming out in the community. Me and another fellow is going to do that, two days a week for three months. Two days every week, for three months. We've also been into one of the day centres in London but a lot of people, they don't understand. One of them we had to ask could they go out because she was making so much noise. But I said to them, `You know, she must be allowed to come back again,' I said, 'because she's out this time she mustn't stay out, she must come back and join in.' They said, 'Could the carers come in?' and I said, `No, not carers, just the people what's got the learning difficulty.' I said 'otherwise they're not going to talk.' So no carers. They talked about different things, they want more money to go to day centres.

Reflections on life now

Work

I had a job for a little while but I find outside work difficult. I don't think they understand really. I've had so much trouble with them I said I wouldn't work again. I just said I wouldn't do it again, I won't work, so I haven't worked since. I'm quite happy doing what I do.

Skills

At Isabel's there was too many to learn. I've learnt to do quite a lot with Isabel because of the cooking and that but I think because there's so many you don't get enough attention. It's just you might as well be back in the hospital. I think the smaller places are much better because I think the carer can help a bit more and she can teach you to do the things that you want, you should be able to do.

I can't fill in the forms yet. Mind you I'm going to the class and they're teaching me. I never learnt to read or write but I'm learning now. I think they should take people who've got learning difficulties in the proper school. I think they are starting to do that now.

Self-advocacy

I think being in a group teaches you you've got to learn to say what you want to say and not what everybody else wants you to say. The others feel the same. We've stopped the children, for starts. We've stopped them calling us names, the children don't do it so much. They used to call us horrible names, some of the names you would never dream of. They stopped it, even in Purley, and the teachers go with them now.

There's a little Down's syndrome boy, he comes off the bus to go home because he lives in Purley. And the children would not leave him alone, they used to tease him and everything, and he used to sit on the floor. They called him names, and they squirted water out of the window at me a few times and threw tins but they don't do it any more. That's because I told Keith and he said, 'Well, we'll write to the schools.'

It stops the children but then you don't stop the adults because they never learn. One Saturday I was with one of my friends and one of the women was so rude my friend was really shocked. This woman said, 'Bloody well get out of the way!' My friend was really shocked. It really did upset her because she said, 'You know, you have told me about it, that people are rude but I had to believe it to listen to it.' She had said, 'I'll come with you just to find out, to see what it's like.' And she said, 'It's damn disgusting that people ought to be allowed to do that.'

I'm more confident since I've been in the People First group. You do what you want to do and not get anybody else to do something for you.

I'm chairperson, but it's just the same as anybody else. You just help the people what can't do it for themselves.

Living in the community

It's hard for the ones what live out on their own mostly, the ones what have the flats. They do miss out. I think they get a bit frightened. Living out in the community, a lot of it, even for me, was new when I first started, so how must they feel? For people what's lived in the hospital for so many years, and then expect them to live on their own, it's wrong. If they've lived with their parents and that, and they go into a flat and they have a little support, they're OK. But for somebody what's lived in a hospital all their life and then to come out and go into a flat, that's murder. To me that is murder because that's just like putting somebody out in the street. They put them out on their own in a house, or by themselves in a flat, and they can't cope with it. I wouldn't do it, and I don't see why anybody else what's been in a long-stay hospital has to do it.

If they lived with their mum, OK, because their mum could watch over them. But if they come out of a big institution like I have, or a few of the others, they are not going to be able to do it. Because they've always had it, they've always had somebody there. They need support and somebody to teach them to do the things they should be able to do. To put them in a flat is murder. And you could find them dead one day, and then say, 'Oh, why, how did it happen?' Because somebody put them in a flat by themself and they've never been used to it. To live on one's own it's cruel. They shouldn't put people what's been in a long-stay hospital on their own. I think that's the worst cruelty ever.

I've been taught to cook and everything because the places I've been in they've taught me how to do that. But if I had to go into a flat and pay all the bills and what-have-you it would worry me to death, and I think it would worry anybody else as well. I don't think they should do it. I think I would worry just a little bit for the bills and that because I wouldn't know what to do. I quite like where I am, I think I'll stay for a little while. I don't want a flat, I think it would frighten me. I think it would upset me, and the least little thing upsets me.

A lot of people might not like it, some of them not at all, but I'm quite happy as I am.

Note

1. The rest of the hospital has subsequently been demolished. Mabel was guest of honour at the party held to mark the end of its life.

> Mabel Cooper's life story provides an important first hand account of a system that once segregated some children and adults from the rest of the community. It is inspiring for those concerned with inclusion as it shows that society's structures and practices can be changed, for the better, within one person's lifetime. As with other chapters in this book it highlights the importance of listening to, and learning from, those whose voices have often been silenced.

CHAPTER 3

Weaving a tale

Marjorie Chappell

This chapter is taken from Marjorie Chappell's unpublished autobiography. In it, she tells the story of her birth and infancy, and of her family's varied reactions to her disability. She goes on to recall her experiences as a disabled school-child in the 1930s, when, through the persistence and ingenuity of her mother, she attended her local village school. After that, her own persistence led to her being trained as a weaver. She brings her story up to date by recounting her experiences as a teacher and as an adult learner, who found the freedom to write through her computer.

'A bouncer' is born

My parents had been married for over two years when I arrived in 1929. No one ever wanted a daughter more than my father and mother. On March 28th, after a lot of struggling for hours on an iron bedstead I was eventually pulled out and I was here. My name was to be Marjorie Joan. Mother almost lost her life through my birth for I was twelve pounds, a bouncer as Father bragged that night in the pub. The nurse and doctor had put me on one side for dead, but my grandmother was there, and by the time the doctor returned, Grandma had washed and dressed me and, noticing I wasn't breathing very well, warmed me and I was soon asleep by the fire.

When the doctor returned, he ran upstairs and down again, and said to Grandma, 'I think she (Mother) will be alright if she lives until the morning.' Then he said, 'Shall I take it away?' Grandma said 'Take what away?' He said 'The dead baby, you don't want that left here, do you?' Grandma was horrified, and said, 'She's asleep.' With that the doctor went, without saying another word.

When Mother saw me, I was not a pretty sight, being rather bruised, with one eye pushed up into my head, but this quickly righted itself. I could not suck as I should and feeding me was a messy business but as time went on I did well, lost a bit of weight, then gained and just ate and slept the long hot summer away…

A dark and dreadful secret

One day when I was about nine months old, a neighbour remarked to Mother, that I was too good. None of her babies had ever stayed so still as I did, from feed to feed, and for so long. Mum asked the doctor about this. He said, 'Oh! Some babies take longer than others, to sit up and take notice. Nothing to worry about.' But time went on, and my arms and legs were jumping about, while Mother was trying to sit me up and stand me up on her lap.

No matter how often Mum asked for help and advice, there were no answers, nothing done or suggested as to how she could help me. I could not sit up or balance like others of my age and under were doing. No other girls of Mother's age who had their babies around the same time wanted to know us, and would walk by on the other side of the street. By this time, my father would not take me out or talk about me. It became a dark and dreadful secret, not to be mentioned or bragged about any more . . .

Then came the many years, when Mother took me around to many different hospitals and as many different specialists who all gave a different diagnosis, from rickets to mental troubles. She began to worry that I had something very rare, for there was never a name given to it. No one ever mentioned anything like 'spastic' (Cerebral Palsy) for that is what I am. Nor did she ever see another child like me in all those years when she took me from hospital to hospital.

(One day) eight doctors were waiting for her. They led her into a private room, sat her in front of them and told her that her baby, who was now about three, would never sit, stand, walk, talk, was blind, could not hear and was mental. Please note, she was always alone. Father never ever took me anywhere. She told them that I was trying with her help to do all this and she knew I could see and hear. She was just told coolly but firmly that this was just her maternal love and imagination. They made out forms for her to sign to have me put in a Home, forget she had ever had me and to go away and have more children as it could never happen again. Mother grabbed me up into her arms, cried and ran all the way home.

By this time we had moved to a village called Ferndown. This particular day Father wasn't indoors when she got home from the hospital. He would not come when mother called him as she was still crying. Father's reaction was always the same from that day on: when told they wanted to put me away, he agreed 'That is the best thing to do. Get rid of the little bugger,' he said . . .

Marjorie gets moving

Soon after we moved to Ferndown, Mother bought me my first tricycle which had a rounded back. She sat me on it, tied my feet to the pedals and my hands into a glove-like shield on the handle-bars. It had a furl on the back into which she could put the end of a walking stick and push me. It being a fixed wheel meant my legs had to work, going round and round with the pedals. Away we went and if I hadn't had that tricycle I believe that I would never have walked or done anything. I would have been the proverbial 'cabbage' and I have always been truly grateful to her.

Mother took me up to the village school, a Council School, right at the top of a long steep hill. In those dark ages, there were no Special Schools but a few Institution Schools, where remember I would have probably been put with mentally handicapped children years before, had the medics had their way. Going to this Council School was entirely up to the Headmaster and the teacher who was a Miss Durrant. Having got there on my tricycle, I would need help to get to my desk, toilet and if I stayed to dinner would need to be fed and washed afterwards. This was tried for half-days for a few weeks, but I remember it wasn't very long before I was going every day, and woe betide anyone who tried to keep me away from my beloved school.

There followed a few years of this, going everywhere and doing most things that every other child did, the only difference being, most went to school on foot, some had over a five-mile walk each way. A few went on bicycles on two wheels while I had three and a big basket to carry everything, including a very big cape for the many wet journeys. The foulest weather would never keep me away from school. Holidays were always far too long for me and I would have all the children around, playing school with my little desk and blackboard and easel, chalks and pencils.

Marjorie at school

When the three male teachers had to go off into the Army we had female teachers come from afar. They had never taught ordinary village children as we were, let alone gypsies and a disabled child like me with a speech problem and uncontrollable limbs. One awful day I will never forget it, I was sitting in a desk at the back of the classroom. It was something like silent reading and just before dinner break. The desk squeaked every time that I moved and this teacher asked, 'Whose desk is squeaking?' Up went my hand. I was told to stop doing it, but the more I tried to keep still, the more I moved and the squeaking went on. In the end, I was sent out of the classroom.

Nothing like this had ever happened to me before and I was about twelve. I burst into floods of tears, which brought the headmaster down the corridor just as the bell rang. I was sent off to dinner with all the others, and right through play-time the boys were jumping up to look into the very high windows. There they were, Headmaster Mr Allan and Miss Hall arguing away for the whole of the dinner hour. Neither had any dinner that day, but it never happened again. I recall that not long after this incident, the whole class were being very noisy for the same teacher. She had had enough and marched right round to every desk, whacking each child across the hand with a ruler, breaking two rulers as she went. When she got to me she walked on by; I was the only one not to get the wooden ruler – and I must have deserved it just as much as all the others.

I did not want to leave school. It wasn't until then that I realised that I was any different – being disabled had never come into it, except that I was left to pick up all the toys or was left to lie on the grass while they all had a run round or played football or some other game. I was always there with them and even if the ground was rough and bumpy, they would push me across. If it was kite-flying time, mine would be got up for me to hold. I must have enjoyed my childhood as well as any other child in the village.

Many, many years later I was talking to one of the girls I went to school with, who, I thought, paid me such a nice compliment. She suddenly said to me, 'We were very privileged to have you at our school.' She went on to say, that it had taught her how to treat disabled people and so she taught her children to do the same.

I finished school up in the 'Top class' with the very nice, understanding Miss Morgan, who did all she could to help me. When it came to our final examinations, I was allowed extra time to finish all the papers and came very near the top of the class overall. I was top for General Knowledge because I had always done more reading than anyone else. I always had a book on the go and could do extra reading during PT, art and dress-making lessons. Also during the last two or three years I had to lie on my stretcher for an hour after dinner so I passed the time reading. I was also interested in nature and everything around me. Every child helped me through those school days in their own way. I should have left school at Easter 1944, but managed to keep quiet. But I was advised to leave at the end of summer term, as Mr Allan said there were plans being made for me to go to Exeter.

Life begins in Exeter

Mr Allen, the headmaster, asked Mother to visit him, as he had been asked to send a report to St Loyes Rehabilitation College for disabled trainees at Exeter. He suggested I leave school at the end of the summer term for, as he said, 'If she stays at school, she will miss her turn of going there.' So very reluctantly I left my beloved school and Miss Durrant who had taught the infant children there for many, many years.

So away I went. Mother took me there by train and had to leave me there alone for the first time in my life. I was not yet fifteen years old and had left home with a suitcase and a tricycle. Life had really begun. The first day at St Loyes I shall never forget, and the following 21 months I shall also never forget for it really was tough. I was taken to an office in a workshop where there were women and girls learning dressmaking and one, Dorothy, making some most beautiful felt toys.

I met a Miss Molly Sable in the office, then before I knew it, ('horror of horrors') she was showing me how to make woolly balls on two rings of cardboard. This I had been doing all my life at home, along with embroidering little messages to my grandmothers. Mother through the years had done everything she could to help me steady my hands. But 'woolly balls' when I had been told I was going away to be trained? I was homesick and frightened of this woman.

Just in front of me sat a young woman who was in the big dormitory with me the night before. She was very like me and her name was Jenny. She told me that she rode a tricycle like mine and here she was very busy using a 'typewriter'. I had never even seen a typewriter before. I thought, if only I could have had one of those at school, how much easier it would have been. Writing so big, 'sprawling', slowly and painfully had always been my biggest handicap. I could never keep up with everyone else, but the teachers (God bless'em) had always marked my work with all the rest.

The next day, I asked if I could use a typewriter. Miss Sable said 'Yes' and I had to address some envelopes or do some other menial job. Somehow during the day I remember typing a letter to Mum. After that I informed the 'dragon' that I wanted to train to be a typist like Jenny over there. She laughed at me and told me to go and sew two woolly balls together and make a little doggy with them, with beads for eyes and two felt ears and a smaller ball as a tail.

The following weekend, Mother arrived, by train and bus, with a great big heavy German-made typewriter. She must have gone to work extra hours or made a dozen dresses to get the money to buy this. So having done nothing else but type all day Sunday, I must have got someone to take it to the work-room on Monday morning to present it to the 'dragon'. I can still hear her sneering at me. 'You will never be a typist,' she said. 'You can play with it in your spare time, but not in here. We have decided to put you in the dressmakers' workshop.' 'If I could have been a dressmaker,' I told her, 'I would not be here,' for my mother was a very good dressmaker whom I had watched and tried to copy all my life.

After being at St Loyes for about a month getting nowhere fast, I saw a doctor or specialist. The next day, I was told to get on my tricycle and go to Occupational Therapy. 'Where and what is it?' I asked. I was told where to go and found a very nice person waiting for me, with a foot-loom all threaded up and all I had to do was pedal away and thread a shuttle back and forth with a lot of pretty colours. How I enjoyed that and could not wait until the next morning to go again for the weaving was growing, even if I was pulling the edges in. I was supposed to be only going there in the mornings, but I used to shoot off up there in the afternoons. There was another typewriter there and the therapist took the trouble to show me a lot more as to what it could do. I was getting on well with my own typewriter, but no more was said about training me for typing or anything else. Then I found out what I had been doing. 'Weaving, Miss Sable, I want to be a weaver.' I was now weaving a floor rug. 'Nonsense,' she said, 'No one could make a living at that.' 'I can,' I said, 'and Mother is going to help me.' She would not listen.

I had to be at her office door first thing the next morning and she whisked me up to the Men's Department and into something called the Production Shop. Her orders were I could only go to Occupational Therapy in the afternoons. I sat at a bench with a lot of older men and I was shown how to pick up a little tiny golden object, put it under an electric machine and bore a tiny hole in it. With my wobbly spastic hands, it was a wonder I did not bore right through my fingers. I never like to use the word 'boring', but that was. What was it for? I never knew, something to do with watch and clock repairs, I think. That was what everyone else was doing in that shop. However, after a few days, I just refused to go there; I wanted to get on with my weaving and typing. So as not to give in to me, the 'dragon' had the machine and little gold bits brought down to the dressmaking work-room where she could keep an eye on me.

The battle went on until one day when she was supposed to be out all day, I took my knitting and did that. By the time I left home, I had just about conquered knitting and was making myself a jumper. It was now almost finished after many months of struggle. Miss Sable arrived back unexpectedly, walked straight up to me, and ripped every stitch out until the wool was just a heap on the floor.

After the knitting incident I took myself up to the Superintendent's Office. He was an ex-sea-captain, now in a wheelchair, and he understood through my tears that I was beginning to feel a failure, since I had been there some time, while others had been coming in and going out into the world. He asked me what I wanted to do. I said, 'Weaving.' 'Why not?' he replied. I was sent to Miss Osborne and told to stay there at the loom. She listened to me as I told what had happened. The rest of that day must have been a bit hot all round. The three of them were shut in together. The next day Dame Georgina Buller, who had founded the College for severely disabled people with her father's money, came to see me herself and between them all my future was sorted out.

A few days later, I remember being told that Dorset County Council had agreed that this is what I should do, and they would lend me the money to buy a loom. An advertisement was put into the paper and a loom was soon found for £10 and the Council agreed to pay. Miss Osborne and I had a day out. We went by train to Okehampton, where we found what to me was 'a little old lady' trying to sell wool on coupons and whose shop looked very bare and sparse. We were taken through to the back of the shop, where there were several looms for us to see. There was the loom that I needed, and we were left only to arrange transport for it. The next I knew was the loom arrived at the College with several other looms and weaving equipment and a note to say that she wanted me to have the loom as a gift as she felt that I would make very good use of it. All the other looms were a gift for the College.

Miss Osborne said that the £10 from the Council would buy the first lot of materials that I would need. The following week, Mother came and spent it with us, learning how to make and thread the warp on the loom, a mammoth task that I could never do. I stayed there a little longer, while Mother returned home, bought an old hen-house and converted it into a workshop. I and the loom arrived home. A few pounds of rug wool and warp came through the post and we were in business. The wool was three shillings a pound, I remember. I had been loaned £10 from Dorset County Council to buy a loom, not materials or workshop, and within six months of returning home to Ferndown, the Council requested £10 from Mother. No one ever inquired whether I had used it or not.

So began another era of my life, I was home again and in my own workshop, not yet 18. Mum was helping me not only to set up the loom but also to finish off and tidy up the rugs to make them saleable. A local ironmonger had offered to sell them for me in their shop and also from the van on their country runs. Mum was also going to work and trying to keep the family together.

A lot had happened to us all in those years; everything had changed, including Father. He and I could never get on – he still wanted to hide me and treat me as a child. 'That nipper!' he always called me. I rightly or wrongly fought back and defied him. Every time I went out on my tricycle to Guides or with friends, he would carry on at Mother, saying it wasn't right and he was sure no one wanted me with them. I was a damn nuisance in his eyes.

Secret ambitions

A teacher told me about the new local school for children aged from two to 16 with all kinds of learning difficulties. I said that one of my lifelong secret ambitions ever since I left school was to help others to read. I had realised from a very early age what being able to read had meant to me.

This teacher told me that this was a new school, and as they were badly in need of volunteers, would I like to have a go? She would arrange for me to meet the Headmaster, teachers and children the following week. So after a chat with the Head and a quick tour round the school (which was wheelchair accessible) it was decided to try it out for two weeks and see how we all got on. So I became a voluntary school teacher and returned to school again.

I stayed there five years, mainly helping fourteen- to sixteen-year-olds who could not even write their own names and addresses. Some were never able to get it right – they could not write out the months of the year or days of the week. Most of them 'would try' just to please me, because I was helping them not as a paid teacher but as their special friend. It was that one-to-one basis that really meant something to a lot of them. They were often waiting for me to arrive, paper and pencil in their hand and looking forward to their turn to come to me. I was left to work out how to help each child in my own way and I like to think it worked well. Not able to write very well myself, and as they would never be able to write, only print like a small child, it seemed as though we had something in common. I soon found boxes of letters on little square cardboard pieces, with capitals on one side and small letters on the other. They were just right for me and the children to work with.

I kept six letters (D.O.R.S.E.T.) separate in one box for all of them. The sweat and sometimes tears to make these look anything like Dorset was really heartbreaking to see, especially from these big 'almost-men' boys. Living in an area with names like Sturminster Newton (the school address), Gillingham, Shaftesbury and even Hazelbury Bryant, the reader can begin to visualise the literacy problems these pupils had. Sometimes I was a bit weary at the end of the day going over the same old things with them, but I really loved helping these children. I always got on well with all the teachers, who never resented me being there.

> Marjorie's life was changed when in the 1980s she moved with her mother to Milton Keynes. This final section brings her story up to the present.

The nearest thing to heaven

Now, after almost ten years of trying to help wherever I could, I am taking life more easily and enjoying the benefits. I am now living alone, which never seemed possible, and enjoying myself doing what I want. I've been swimming and sailing and been in an amateur dramatic group of disabled people. We met each week to read famous plays, putting on a production to an audience every few months. I have also dabbled in the arts and many other interesting outlets.

As far as I am concerned Milton Keynes is the nearest thing to heaven for all disabled people. My whole life has changed in every way. Moving here was the best thing that Mother and I ever did. She likes it here but of course would never have come here without me. Our vision of a future for me has certainly come true, far more than we visualised.

It was suggested that I should join the ACTIVE Group, which was a club for disabled people and parents of disabled children. At that time they got together every month to help each other understand computers, which at that time were beginning to be used in their children's education. I had never even seen a computer in my life but I was soon hooked; but I only got to use one on one evening a month and I think my fascination must have soon become apparent. The school where we met to use their equipment offered to lend me a computer, disc drive and printer during the Christmas holiday. My typewriter seemed very old hat after that and I had to get a computer somehow. I was hooked and could write easily for the first time in my life.

At the beginning of March right on our first anniversary of living here, I arrived at ACTIVE and a lady was waiting to be introduced to me. The lady spent the next two hours just talking to me asking me all sorts of questions, mainly about what I would do with a computer if I had one. I did not realise what was happening and where it would lead. As we parted she kissed me goodnight and I gave her my address, hoping we would meet again. Two days later a note arrived from her telling me to go out today and buy all the computer equipment I needed. It was just frightening. Mother was more upset than pleased. 'It was charity,' she said, and that she had never accepted. I felt there was also a little jealousy from the other members of ACTIVE. I was still an outsider and others needed computers too . . .

Weeks went by. I did nothing until the guardian angel rang me, for she was waiting to pay the cheque, and said 'You have to do something about getting it.' So the next day, I went and bought what I thought I needed. It was paid for, delivered and set up in the office we had prepared for it.

My life began all over again and I have never looked back, for writing is my life. The lady came to visit me once and had tea with Mother and me before looking around our specially designed bungalow and the little office I had made for myself. I had only bought a black and white monitor and she wasn't happy with that. She put it right the following year when she phoned telling me to buy a colour monitor.

What a difference it made to me. I got on so well, but nine years later I am still learning more about it and teaching others. Not only did a computer solve my writing problems, it helped me to become steadier and more confident in everything else I do; even my speech is a lot clearer. Using a computer led me, in 1989, to begin living on my own without always needing my mother around.

My 'live-in companion'

I have been having a go at an Internet computer course. I have completed one course and am deciding what to try next, as my computer is still my 'live-in companion', and now we, my computer and I, are on the Net and I am hooked, travelling from one thing to another without even thinking about it and wondering how I ever got on to that subject.

I gave a talk at a conference at the Open University about my life and achievements. I had written it out and it was read for me. Afterwards I could have sold 100 copies of my book if it had been printed.

The Open University now has a website that will show the kind of work they have undertaken about learning difficulties, as it is called now. I do not think that I really come under this heading. On the day before the conference, some of the speakers went along to the recording studio to make a video of themselves. Wow! My little bit came out well and I was congratulated. This is on the Internet website (www.open.ac.uk/shsw/research), and my whole story is there.

What a week to remember and to end this year on.

Marjorie Chappell, with her mother's support, struggled to resist the identity that others tried to impose on her. She has now discovered the identity with which she is most comfortable, that of autonomous learner and writer. As a writer, she is able to contribute her own perspective to the history that so far has been written by others. We might consider what we can learn from 'unofficial' sources such as Marjorie and how her account contrasts with more formal versions of history.

CHAPTER 4

'The stairs didn't go anywhere': a self-advocate's reflections on specialised services and their impact on people with disabilities[1]

Michael F. Giangreco

The information included in this article is based on a semi-structured interview conducted with Norman Kunc by Michael F. Giangreco on July 4, 1995 in Montreal, Quebec, Canada. The interview was tape recorded with Mr. Kunc's permission and was transcribed. The contents include selected portions of that interview and have been reviewed by Mr. Kunc to ensure that his opinions and ideas have been accurately presented in his own words.

Norman Kunc (pronounced Koontz) is a sought-after consultant and speaker on a wide range of educational, disability, and social justice issues. He was born with cerebral palsy and attended a segregated school for students with disabilities from the age of three until 13 when he was included in a general education school. Earning a Bachelor's Degree in Humanities and a Master's Degree in Family Therapy have augmented a lifetime of learning from his experiences of being labeled 'disabled' in North America. I have had the pleasure of being in the audience on a number of occasions when Norman has spoken, and each time I have come away with more to think about and act upon. His message is at times provocative and his insights are undeniable. Here is a bit of my afternoon with Norman Kunc.

Michael: Norman, thanks for taking time to sit down with me. Let's start by establishing what specialized services you received when you were in school.

Norman: Physiotherapy, occupational therapy, and speech therapy. Each specialist had her own room and they would pull me out of my classroom for a half an hour to an hour to get therapy, two to three times a week.

Michael: Could you tell me about some of your memories receiving those services?

Norman: First, I'd like to say that it's fitting that we are talking about rehabilitation issues on none other than Independence Day! To answer your question, I remember thinking that the physical therapy room was a very weird place.

---

1 Reprinted, with permission from Giangreco, F. (1996) '"The stairs didn't go anywhere!" A self-advocate's reflections on specialised services and their impact on people with disabilities.' *Physical Disabilities: Education and Related Services*, **14**(2), 1–12. © Council for Exceptional Children.

Michael: Why do you say that?

Norman: They had all this strange equipment and weights and mirrors and bars. But the weirdest part of the physical therapy room was the staircase. There was this staircase with a handrail on either side but the stairs didn't go anywhere – they went right into the wall! The physical therapist would come up to me and say, 'Walk up the stairs.' And I'd say, 'Why? They don't go anywhere.'
But she'd say, 'Never mind, walk up the stairs.' So, I'd walk up the stairs and nearly kill myself getting up there. When I got to the top the physical therapist would say, 'Good! Now walk back down the stairs.'
I'd say, 'Wait a minute! If you didn't want me up here in the first place, why did you ask me to walk up here?'

Michael: Did she give you a reason?

Norman: She would say, 'You want to walk better, don't you?' I didn't know any better, so I said, 'Yeah.' And what I learned at that moment in life was that it was not a good thing to be disabled and that the more I could reduce or minimize my disability the better off I would be. When I was in segregated school, I fundamentally saw myself as deficient and abnormal. I saw myself as inherently different from the rest of the human race. The implicit message that permeated all my therapy experiences was that if I wanted to live as a valued person, wanted a quality life, to have a good job, everything could be mine. All I had to do was overcome my disability No one comes up and says, 'Look, in order to live a good life you have to be normal,' but it's a powerful, implicit message. Receiving physical and occupational therapy were important contributors in terms of seeing myself as abnormal. Every part of my life, from the minute I was born, told me that I was abnormal, whether it was getting physical therapy, going to Easter Seal Camp, or wearing leg braces at night.

Michael: How did you react at the time?

Norman: Well I wanted all those things, to have a good life – so I ended up declaring war on my own body. It was me against my disability; and my disability was my enemy. I was bound and determined that I was going to conquer that disability.

Michael: How did you propose to do battle with yourself?

Norman: I turned into a kid that physiotherapists only see in their dreams. If they wanted me to do ten repetitions of a certain exercise, I did 20. If they wanted me to hold a precarious balance position to the count of ten, I held it to the count of 30. I was determined I was going to get to be a valued person. And if that meant conquering my disability, so be it.

Michael: These early experiences happened when you were in a segregated school. What happened when you went to a regular school?

Norman: I thought I could overcome my devalued status as a person with a disability by being in the regular school. At first the school administration wanted to send me to a special class for students with physical disabilities in a regular school about ten miles from my home. I said, 'The hell with that!' First of all, I wanted to go to the regular school in my neighborhood because, for me, I guess that represented being valued. Secondly, I was offended by the stigma of being in a special class. I didn't want all my non-disabled neighborhood friends to see me getting on that big blue bus for kids with disabilities. Why not just hang flowers around my neck with a sign that says 'crippled'. I wanted to avoid all of that.

Michael: From what you are saying it sounds like there were a lot of professionals who saw your disability but didn't see you as a person.

Norman: That's true. If I had to describe myself to you now I'd say that I have an undergraduate degree in humanities and Master's in family therapy. I got divorced, now I'm remarried and I live with Emma and two step kids. I like classical music and jazz. Having cerebral palsy is one small aspect of who I am: it's part of who I am, but it's not the defining characteristic that makes me who I am.

Michael: When people disproportionately focus on your disability, how have they treated you?

Norman: People make unwarranted assumptions about who I am as a person because of my disability. People in airports sometimes think I have a mental disability or treat me like a child. Sometimes they assume that I need their help. People sometimes assume that people with disabilities are asexual, have unresolved anger, are in denial, or that all of us must be lonely or sad, that our lives are filled with frustration. The fact is that a very small part of my life gets blown up into a very big part. Unfortunately, too many people see me as nine-tenths disability, one-tenth person.

Michael: What has been the impact of these assumptions on your life and the lives of other people with disabilities?

Norman: It makes you feel that you are not quite human. Almost like you have to earn your right to be human. In earning your right to be human, what do you get? Human rights! So when you are perceived as less than fully human, what typically are rights for non-disabled people become privileges for people with disabilities. It's like if you have a disability they are doing you a favor by letting you live in the community. As soon as I demonstrate I am mentally capable then I have earned my right into the community. I see this going on not only with people with disabilities but also around the whole issue of poverty. You have to demonstrate your merit It's categorizing people as producers versus non-producers. When people see that I am intelligent and articulate, the message is, 'Even though this guy has a disability, he can make a contribution to society. Therefore we'll let him in!'

Michael: It sounds like what you have experienced is a classic example of what Marc Gold called the 'competency/deviancy hypothesis' where the more competent the person is perceived to be, the more others will tolerate deviance in him. Of course, even that language, the term 'deviance', is so loaded with negative connotations.

Norman: I prefer to think of my disability as type of diversity rather than deviance or deficiency; my disability is just one characteristic or attribute among many that make me who I am. People do not need to prove their worthiness. Obviously, what we are talking about here is a human rights issue. We need to establish the unconditional and inherent worthiness of people regardless of what combinations of diverse characteristics they present.

Michael: When did you start feeling as though your disability was a characteristic of your personal diversity rather than a deficiency?

Norman: Let me tell you a story from when I was a university student. One night I was at this pub with a bunch of my friends. At one point, one of the guys started imitating my voice. It surprised me and I didn't like that he was doing it. So, afterwards I went up to him and said, 'Why did you imitate my voice?'
He said, 'Because that's how you talk.'
I told him, 'Hey, I'm articulating my words. I'm using my voice clearly. I'm not drooling. You imitate my voice and my whole show goes out the window.'
And he said, 'Norman, why are you trying to be non-handicapped?' And that caused a categorical shift in my thinking. We talked for a long time that night and went through a lot of beer. Finally it dawned on me that I had *the right to be disabled*. And rather than seeing my disability as a deficiency, I began to see it as part of the inherent differentness among people; it was simply a characteristic. I came to understand that it really was no different from any other characteristic like height or weight or race or gender. So to say it another way, prior to that incident in the bar, I saw myself as abnormal. You were the normal people, I was abnormal. You are all non-disabled, I'm disabled. I saw myself as categorically different from most of the human population. I was part of a group with all the other abnormal, deficient, broken, disabled people. Once that shift happened to me I said, 'Wait a minute, I'm part of the normal diversity of the human community. I'm normal in that I am

diverse.' I began to think, 'Wait! Why has this small characteristic of who I am been used as a criterion to put me in a segregated school, to do this to me, to do that to me?' Everything that happened to me suddenly came up for evaluation.

Michael: Let me back up for a moment and ask you about your experiences receiving therapy services when you went to regular school. Did you continue to receive the same types of services to the same extent?

Norman: No, it pretty much stopped.

Michael: Who made that decision?

Norman: Well, I think the therapists actually made the decision because they thought I could do a lot of things, plus I wanted to stop anyway. Ironically, my speech improved the most the year I quit speech therapy.

Michael: It sounds like by high school you had strong ideas about what you wanted for yourself. Did those coincide with what your therapists thought was best for you?

Norman: I believe they *thought* they knew the best destination for me, but they were mistaken. The therapists usually saw the destination as one of two things. The more naive therapist often perceived the destination as being one of normalcy; to make me more valuable in society's eyes. So that was one destination. This may not even have been conscious to the therapists; I think it may have been unconscious.

Michael: Do you think people in special education and rehabilitation fields are professionally socialized and trained to think that way?

Norman: Yes, absolutely, but it goes beyond that. I think the field of rehabilitation is to people with disabilities what the diet industry is to women. We live in a society that idolizes a full and completely artificial conception of bodily perfection. This view of the 'normal' body tyrannizes most, if not all, women so that far too many women in our culture grow up believing that their bodies are inadequate in some way. The issue here is that I want professionals to think about the whole parallel between dieting and rehabilitation. That's why I always tell people with disabilities, 'Never do physical therapy with a therapist who is on a diet!' If she hates her own body, she'll inevitably hate yours!

Michael: You said there were two views. You talked about people who want to strive toward 'normalcy', whatever that is. What is the second view you alluded to earlier?

Norman: Now there may be some therapists who say, 'Wait a minute, I don't want to make people more normal. I want to help them function better so that they can do more things.' Although that seems to be a far more enlightened perspective, I still have serious concerns about it because professionals mistakenly equate functioning level with quality of life and that may not be what's going on for some folks. Professionals say, 'If I can help you function better, then your quality of life will improve.'

Michael: This is a very mainstream view. What are your concerns with that way of thinking?

Norman: If you think about it, non-disabled people often don't equate the quality of their own lives with their ability to function in a certain way, so why apply it differently to people with disabilities? Rather than functioning level, I think most people would agree that the quality of life has to do with important personal experiences, feelings, and events, like relationships, having fun, and making contributions to the lives of other people. If you think about the most meaningful moments in life, they probably don't have to do with your functioning level. I'd bet they have more to do with other things like getting married, the birth of your first child, your friendships, or maybe going on a spiritual retreat; they probably don't have to do with your functioning level. Ironically, developing relationships, the opportunity to make contributions to your community, even fun itself is taken away from people with disabilities in the name of trying to get them to function better to improve, presumably, the quality of their lives. So I didn't get to go to regular school and then I missed the opportunity to make friends. Why? Because professionals were trying to improve my quality of life by putting me in a special school where I am supposed to learn to function better. So they take away the opportunity for me to have friends and subsequently they actually interfere with the quality of my life.

Michael: Are you saying that people with disabilities don't need to learn to function better?

Norman: No. For me I guess the key is the difference between what I call 'ease of living' and quality of life; many people confuse the two. Ease of living would be something to minimize the physical struggle, time, or energy that has to be expended in daily tasks. But just because life gets easier doesn't necessarily mean that my quality of life has improved.

Michael: Could you elaborate on what you mean?

Norman: Sure. In our society I think that many people assume that if they make their life 'easy enough' that the quality of their life will naturally follow. So they focus on making their lives easier through earning more money, or getting a better house, whatever, assuming that this ease will bring about quality. Now, while I see ease of living as partially contributing to quality of life, I believe it's overly simplistic to assume that quality comes from ease. Instead, I think many things contribute to a quality life, like relationships, having a sense of belonging, fun, making a contribution, and to some degree, struggle itself.

Michael: In your presentations I have heard you talk about some very sensitive personal experiences you had receiving physical therapy and the impact it had on your life. Could you share some of those experiences?

Norman: When I was doing my Master's Degree program in family therapy, we did a section on sex therapy. We did exercises involving touch, comparing our reactions to those of people with sexual dysfunctions. Jokingly I said to my sex therapy professor, 'I can teach it, just don't ask me to believe it.'
He said, 'What do you mean?'
I replied, 'I hate being touched.' At that time I was involved in a sexual relationship where I could touch the other person, but I did not like to be touched. About four months later we were studying the side effects of post traumatic stress disorder, specifically how it related to victims of rape and sexual assault. As we reviewed the symptoms, like resistance of touch, lack of trust, and all things they were talking about, I kept thinking, 'Yep, that's me.' Then I thought, 'Wait a minute? Why do I fit all these categories?' That's when I first made the association between sexual assault and my own life. My body carried the memory, and these discussions triggered me to think back to physical therapy.

Michael: Are you saying that you were sexually assaulted by a therapist as a child?

Norman: It depends on how you define sexuality. If you define sexuality as in a forced sexual act, then no. But if you define sexuality as it is being defined today, in terms of physical space, in terms of your own control over your own body, then yes, it was sexual assault because the ramifications for me were sexual around the whole issue of touch. What I am saying is that the very practice of physical therapy in some of its historically common forms can have abusive outcomes.

Michael: Could you elaborate on what you mean?

Norman: If you think about it, from the age of three until the age of twelve, three times a week, women who were older than I was, who were more powerful than I was, who had more authority than I had, brought me in to their room, their space, their turf. They took off some of my clothes. They invaded my personal space. They gripped me and touched me, manipulating my body in ways that were painful – it hurt. Some of the exercises that were done in physical therapy were very painful, others were threatening. For example, there was the one where you are sitting or kneeling on the floor and the therapist kneels behind you and pushes you in different directions forward, sideways. The stated purpose of that activity is to improve reactive balance responses, but when I do this with non-disabled people as a training activity they find it enormously threatening when a person behind them is shoving them, especially when they never know what direction they were going to get pushed. When I was in school, I didn't know I had any other choice than to go along with it. So when you think of it, what did I have from the age of three up? People, women, who had more power than I did, took me in to their space, they took some of my clothes off, touched me in ways that were painful, and I felt that I had no choice in it. To me it's a form of sexual assault even though it was completely asexual. It's the power and domination that is part of the abuse. It's important for professionals to understand and acknowledge the power differential that exists between themselves and the children with disabilities they are supposed to be serving.

Michael: Norman, I am sure you realize that their are many people reading this who would say that the therapy procedures you describe are done to people with disabilities for their own good, after all it has a medical basis and it's considered a 'helping profession'. How do you respond to people who say that there is nothing abusive about what therapists do, that they obviously have only the best of intentions for people with disabilities?

Norman: I am only speaking of my own experience, but my response has to do with the whole issue of intent. Sometimes people get hung up on my ideas because obviously the therapist does not have the same intent as a rapist. Obviously their intent is different, its positive, but there still can be a similarity of action and a similarity of consequence. My problem is that we can minimize the significance of the similarity of the action and consequences simply because the intent was positive.

Michael: So is part of your purpose to have professionals rethink what their intent really is and whether it matches their actions and the consequences that follow?

Norman: There is a difference between caring and competence. Many human service professionals assume that because they care for people their actions are inevitably competent. As soon as you challenge the competence of their actions, you're seen as questioning their caring for the person. It seems that competence, in their mind, is inextricably interwoven with caring. And they say, 'But how could you say I'm sexually abusing this little boy? I like this little boy. I would never do a thing to harm him.' You say, 'Yes, I know you care for him and your actions may be cruel.'

Michael: So what do you say to well-intentioned professionals who want to be of service to people with disabilities?

Norman: We've got to slow down. First of all, very often the temptation of many professionals is to ask, 'Tell me how to do it differently,' rather than saying, 'Help me think about this.' I hope people come to understand the complexity of the issues. That's what I'm concerned about.

Michael: Is there other advice you would offer to people who want to reflect on their practice to improve it?

Norman: I tell teachers and therapists all the time, 'If you really want to work on professional development, keep a journal.' Spend a half hour every night and write about what your students are doing. You don't gain the ability to deal with the complexity of people just by acquiring an abundance of strategies. You gain the ability to deal with the complexity of people from the depth of thought. And many people avoid seeking depth of thought because they are too busy acquiring this endless library of disjointed strategies.

Michael: We certainly have a lot of strategies out there. Can you suggest any actions people can take to put them in some sort of perspective?

Norman: Read the stories of people with disabilities. Read the self-advocacy and disability rights literature.

Michael: If I am hearing you correctly, you are saying that there are no cookbooks, no easy answers about what is the 'right' thing to do.

Norman: That's right. It's the same as being a man in our male dominated society. At some point, as a man, I have to enter the world with fear and trembling knowing that I will, through my functions of power and privilege, do damage to women. I try not to, but I will. There is no recipe for me to say, 'If I do this, this, and this, I will be fine.' It would be nice, but it's not the way it is.

Michael: What do you hope professionals gain from hearing this perspective?

Norman: I hope professionals will recognize that the very nature of their role is an oppressor because of the massive power differential between themselves and the children they work with, or should I say 'work on'? The good news is there are things we can do.

Michael: Like what?

Norman: Everyone can start with themselves and draw on their own experiences. For example, as a man I need to listen to the stories of women. Not with my own arguments going on in my head, 'Yes, but, yes, but . . .' Instead, I need to listen to what it feels like to be a women who fears for her own safety when getting out of a car alone in an underground parking garage. I need to really listen to that. I need to really hear that story rather than beating myself up with guilt or shame because men historically have dominated women in our society. I need to listen to that story in a way that overlaps with my own experience with fear as a person with disabilities. When a woman listens to my story about airline agents being overly condescending to me, rather than her feeling guilty and saying, 'Oh my God, I've done things like that to people with disabilities,' I would like her to listen to that story and remember a time when a car salesman or an auto mechanic was condescending to her: 'Yes dear, you wouldn't understand that.' Relating people's stories to your own experience is part of developing that depth of thought and reflection.

Michael: So how does one avoid being oppressive when providing specialized services?

Norman: First of all, I think all advocates have to be self-advocates. On Monday morning, the professional may not always do the best thing, but that is not the point. I think the question is not so much how can I guarantee not to do damage; the question is to recognize oppression, recognize the issues, and be willing to struggle with them.

Michael: What kinds actions can you envision as an outgrowth of recognition of the issues, reflection, and struggle?

Norman: I can envision three different therapists reading this interview and in the most positive ways having different ways of coming at therapy. One may talk about it with her colleagues; another might change the nature of how she does certain exercises with a child; another might keep a journal to help her reflect on her work. All are relevant, but the important part is that they have listened to it and in some way tied it to their experience and then decided to take actions based on who they are as people, not as professionals, as people. I hope they will move forward conditionally, continuing to be cognizant that other stories may come up that will challenge them again; this is an ongoing struggle. Reflection, personal commitment, and the beauty of struggling with ambiguity is where real connections get made between people that raise them above the oppressor/oppressed scenario.

Michael: In that way will these professionals become better advocates for people with disabilities?

Norman: Let me back up a moment. My point was that all advocates need to be self-advocates. What I meant by that was I don't want professionals to advocate on my behalf believing that they now have this new found knowledge about what people with disabilities want. I don't want therapists to say, 'I've read ten issues of the *Disability Rag*' and then spout out all the politically correct jargon. No! I want therapists to tap into her experience as a woman, to tap into her experiences of being in a position of less power, to pull that whole experience of women's rights and their own oppression into that therapy room. So when a case conference comes up where there is some issue being raised around intervention, around touch, or whatever, I want her to tie it to her own experience and challenge things not just from the stories of other people, but from her own experiences.

Michael: Does that mean only people who have had some significant level of personal experience being oppressed can relate to the stories they hear from people who have been oppressed in other ways?

Norman: Do you mean, what do I recommend to you, Mike, as an able-bodied, straight, white, middle-class male? Listen well. I think people don't need to be members of an oppressed group in order to listen. I have met people of an oppressed group who can't listen. I think you are listening to my story more intently than many women have listened to my story. Sometimes I think I can get a short-cut with women or with African-Americans. I can use analogies about used car salesmen, diets, or racial discrimination.

Michael: Any final thoughts?

Norman: Just listen.

We chose to include this interview for its powerful and challenging ideas, particularly about the personal impact of accepting diversity, rather than striving towards and enforcing standards of an artificial perfection. As with other chapters in the book, this chapter illustrates the damaging outcomes of seeing a person in terms of a single attribute or characteristic. Importantly, Norman Kunc calls for professionals to listen to the voices of others, and reflect on their own practice in order to transform it.

CHAPTER 5

Integration versus segregation: the early struggle

Ian C. Copeland

> This chapter outlines the first educational provision for pupils in the UK who were considered dull, backward and defective towards the end of the nineteenth century. Ian Copeland compares early examples of integrated and segregated education and suggests why the latter approach prevailed and become dominant.

Introduction

Karl Marx presented the powerful argument concerning the relationship between events in the past and those in the present in a cryptic (if also sexist) way:

> Men make their own history, but they do not make it just as they please; they do not make it under circumstances chosen by themselves, but under circumstances directly encountered, given, and transmitted from the past. The tradition of all the dead generations weighs like a nightmare on the brain of the living. (Feuer 1969: 360)

A more recent analyst has argued that tradition takes on a heightened importance within social conventions based upon so-called expert judgements such as legal and judiciary customs, medicine, and the treatment of mental disability and educational practices (Foucault 1977: 37, 140).

Prior to Forster's Act of 1870, elementary education was largely the concern of the different religious bodies who based what was taught in their schools upon their different religious beliefs. School attendance was voluntary and less than half the population, particularly in rural districts, bothered to attend since the young could potentially supplement family income through their labour. This was particularly the case amongst the poor.

Education for the disabled child was largely dependent upon the efforts of charitable organizations which had concern for the deaf and/or blind child. (Throughout the present historical analysis, descriptive terms then in vogue to describe the disabled are employed to preserve authenticity. No offence to the modern reader is intended.)

Wealth provided access to education for some children. Thomas Braidwood's Academy for the Deaf and Dumb founded towards the end of the eighteenth century is an example. However, such an enterprise was primarily intended to be the basis for a profitable business. Hence, in a climate of competition, control over teaching personnel was rigid and teaching methods were guarded jealously.

For those lacking wealth, there was some institutional provision for the education of blind and/or deaf children, but standards were very variable. [. . .] What follows examines the first educational provision for pupils considered dull, backward and defective.

Elementary education and the establishment of two Royal Commissions

The general background to the establishment of the Royal Commissions was: (1) Forster's Education Act of 1870, which permitted non-denominational school boards to found schools to supplement the existing places provided by church schools; and (2) Mundela's Education Act of 1880, which compelled children to attend school. Thus, elementary education became comprehensive, and for the first time schools contained children who had previously received no formal teaching and who came from families whose members had not attended school. As a consequence, 'the lower classes [in schools] were thronged . . . by unwilling and ignorant victims' (Smith 1931: 307). The number of pupils in elementary schools expanded rapidly from 1.7 million in 1870 to 4.8 million in 1891 (BoE 1901: 104). The class sizes were also very large; if pupil teachers who had recently completed their own school lessons and were subsequently apprenticed to teaching are included in the calculations, then there was a pupil:teacher ratio of 60:1 in 1870 and 48:1 in 1891 (BoE 1901: 105). In addition, the teaching regime in elementary schools was policed by Robert Lowe's Revised Code of Practice with its central principle of payment by results. In accordance with this principle, the amount of grant which a school was paid was determined in small part by each pupil's general merit and attendance rate, but in larger part by the pupil's performance in examinations of 'the three Rs'. Thus, classes were large, and teaching methods were mechanical and primarily directed towards preparing the pupil for the examination (cf. Smith 1931: 254–61; Wardle 1976: 68–89).

The state of elementary education did not escape the attention of politicians. In January 1886, a Royal Commission to examine the working of the Elementary Education Acts under the chairmanship of Lord Cross was announced (RCEEAs 1886: 3–4). A few days later, a Royal Commission to examine the education of the Blind, Deaf and Dumb, etc. under the chairmanship of Lord Egerton was also announced (RCBDD 1889: 2). The establishment of this latter Commission had been tortuous and incremental. In 1885, a Royal Commission had been set up to inquire into the education of blind children. However, some few months later, and following a lobby on behalf of the deaf and dumb by Lord Egerton, its terms of reference 'were extended by the inclusion of the deaf and dumb and of such other cases as from special circumstances would seem to require exceptional methods of education' (RCBDD 1889: xi).

The consequence of the coexistence of the two Royal Commissions

The coexistence of the two Royal Commissions was a profound historical conjuncture. The prime consequence was the division of the school population in terms of theory and planning into two unequal groups. Early on, the Cross Commission determined that 'exceptional children', i.e. 'the dull and deficient' in the words of a Senior Inspector of Schools (RCEEAs 1886: 131), should be the concern of the Egerton Commission. The latter accepted this proposal and observed that 'there are a great many backward children in our Elementary schools who require a different treatment to that of the ordinary children' (RCBDD 1889: 104). Thus, the school population was divided into the ordinary and normal on the one hand, and the abnormal or subnormal on the other.

Egerton's terms of reference conjoined physical and mental categories, uniting blind, deaf and dumb children with those with other learning difficulties. That decision had at least two profound genealogical consequences for pupils with learning difficulties: (1) the physical and mental categories together became a part of the domain supervised by the medical profession; and (2) this conflation tended to limit the quest for an educationally based solution.

The definition of intellect

One hundred and forty-three witnesses presented evidence to the Egerton Commission on the education of blind, deaf and dumb children. In contrast, only seven presented evidence on children in the 'exceptional' section. However, in the report on the latter section, very nearly half of the references draw upon the evidence presented by Dr George Shuttleworth, then Medical Superintendent of the Royal Asylum for Idiots and Imbeciles at Lancaster. ('Exceptional' children were conceived as being imbeciles or idiots in the language of the time.) In his evidence, Shuttleworth presented a definition of exceptional children that the report subsequently reiterated. Shuttleworth's opinion was that a distinction between idiots and imbeciles could not be made simply because it was a distinction of degree and not of kind. Thus, he stated that 'idiocy means a lower degradation of intellect, a greater deficiency of intellect, and imbecility means a lesser degree of such deficiency' (RCBDD 1889: 705 cf. 95). While Shuttleworth offered no explanation of what was meant by intellect, nor was he asked to, it is clear that intellect was the norm that first distinguished this group of exceptional children from their peers and then organized the group internally in terms of degrees of deficiency. The definition was both relativistic and decontextualized in so far as it lacked external references. The efficacy of the definition was 'proved' by Shuttleworth's case notes which, in his own words, 'contained accurate histories' of several thousand patients treated at the Royal Albert Asylum (RCBDD 1889: 706 cf. Alston 1992: 30–2). Thus, the diagnosis confirms the condition and the condition the diagnosis. The science is securely circular because the diagnosis is the proof of the condition and the condition is proof of the diagnosis.

However, another witness openly acknowledged the definition as an organizing principle, stating that:

> In other words, idiocy is a deeper mental defect than imbecility. This view meets all requirements whether for scientific purposes or for purposes of medical treatment, or for practical purposes connected with care, management and education.
>
> (RCBDD 1889: 670).

However, the Commission had also received evidence which was in disagreement with Shuttleworth's at least in terms of aetiology. Francis Warner was a professor of physiology and a paediatrician in a London hospital. He submitted evidence regarding physically and mentally defective children on the basis of case notes collected over a period of 12 years. Warner estimated that some one in 20 or 5% of children in large urban areas were unable to cope with elementary education in its then current state. He cited surveys to back up the estimate and among the reasons he put forward were: irregular development in hearing and eyesight; diseases of the heart and lungs; being orphaned; the large classes in schools; mechanical teaching and examination; and the sometimes cruel and brutal methods of correction (RCBDD 1889: 698–9). While the detail of the differences between Shuttleworth's and Warner's positions has been set out (Copeland 1995: 187–99), it is clear that there were alternative routes for the provision of education for the exceptional group of children available to the Commission to recommend, in accordance with the contrasting opinions of Shuttleworth and Warner.

The Commission's recommendations left the issues surrounding provision for exceptional children unresolved because there were no directions regarding the responsibility for their education or its length, unlike those for the blind, and the deaf and dumb. The question was taken up some 10 years later in a special committee of the Education Department (DCDEC 1898). Shuttleworth was a member of that committee and presented the very first piece of evidence on 'the definition of terms' (DCDEC 1898: Vol. II, 1). He reiterated the definitions of idiots and imbeciles which he had presented to the previous Commission (DCDEC 1898: Vol. II, 2) and also linked educational provision very firmly with a prior medical examination. This definition and the attendant medical examination figured in the ensuing permissive legislation [1899, 62 & 63, George V, Chapter 32, 1 (1)], and also in that which required local authorities to make assessments of exceptional children in 1913 [3 & 4, George V,

Chapter 28, 1 (1); HM Government 1913] and in 1914 [4 & 5, George V, Chapter 45, 1 (1); HM Government 1914]. The definition proved an enduring genealogical pillar in the educational provision for these exceptional children.

The social and political context of the period of time in which these deliberations took place is also an important background factor. In the final three decades of the nineteenth century, the phenomenon of declining birth rates appeared across Europe. Between 1870 and 1930, the birth rate declined by almost half from 3.4% to 1.5% of the population (Soloway 1990: xi). However, the phenomenon was manifest differently in different social groups, with the steepest decline in middle class families. Hence, alarm arose that the middle classes might be swamped by the size of the working class. The cult of Social Darwinism, a precursor of the eugenicist movement, held that mental capabilities were, for the most part, inherited and that there was a struggle for the survival of the fittest (Thomson 1998: 10–32). In the period between 1886 and 1899, a major feature of the intellectual disposition of members of the middle classes was a fear of the impact of differential birth rates, which could lead to national degeneration, and to an increase in promiscuity and crime. The eugenicist's preferred solution to this perceived problem was the segregation of those deemed unfit in special schools and colonies.

Just as the Egerton Commission had set out the definition of exceptional children in 1889, so it presented the blueprint for the location of the provision of education. The Commission categorized that segment of the idiots and imbeciles which was considered educable as the 'feeble-minded'. On this basis, the Commission stated that, 'We recommend that feeble-minded children should be separated from ordinary scholars in public elementary schools in order that they may receive special instruction' (RCBDD 1889: 106). The recommendation was ambiguous: while it encouraged the separation of exceptional pupils, it failed to identify where their education was to take place. Was it to be in public elementary schools or in special schools?

The first practical scheme for inclusive education

The Leicester School Board opened the first special class in April 1892. It occupied a room which had been vacated in an existing elementary school in the middle of the town. The principles upon which the class was based and the organization of classes in the Board's schools were developed by the Board's Inspector, Henry Major.

The Inspector had graduated in medical science 'in the London University' (DCDEC 1898: Vol. II, 136), but treated the science of the intellect with caution and rejected divisive practices as far as was possible. Major made it clear in his evidence that he did not categorize members of the special class as idiots (DCDEC 1898; Vol. II, 137) because:

We have only the narrow margin between a greater inefficiency on the one hand and ordinary dullness on the other. I do not think it would be right to take children out of the ordinary school if they are at all fit, notwithstanding dullness and want of knowledge.

(DCDEC 1898: Vol. II, 136)

In addition, Major argued that there were instances where:

[The pupil] would not be deficient in all directions. We find some cases . . . where a lad will do his elementary science work well, but he cannot read well or he is deficient in number.

(DCDEC 1898: Vol. II, 139)

The test for admission to the class was primarily educational and administered by the Inspector himself:

I examine them from a reading book, not to see whether they can read, but to see whether they have a certain amount of intelligence in the interpretation of pictures and in the answering of social questions limited to their own surroundings.

(DCDEC 1898; Vol. II, 133)

He subsequently elaborated upon this to include counting using simple numbers.

While the hours of the class were very similar to the elementary school, 'the lessons are very much shorter'. The curriculum was described as 'educative and recreational' with an emphasis on manual tasks. The room itself was made as bright as possible with places for flowers and pets. The desks were arranged around the edges rather than a central block. There were 12 pupils in the class and two teachers 'chosen from the infant school as [. . .] very clever in Kindergarten and very sympathetic in the treatment of infants' (DCDEC 1898: Vol. II, 134). Although there may be 12 pupils 'en gros, . . . the teachers individualize themselves' (DCDEC 1898: Vol. II, 137).

This special class operated in parallel with a system of Standard 'O' classes which existed in all the Leicester Board's schools. Elementary schools were conventionally organized on the basis of six Standards or classes which consisted of age cohorts. Standard 1' was so designated because it contained the class of pupils who were entered for the first examination for grant purposes (cf. Smith 1931: 254–5; Wardle 1976: 68–70). The Leicester Board devised a system of Standard 'O' classes which contained those pupils considered unlikely to be successful in the examination at their first attempt, and, consequently, were kept back for a year. Every school had such a class that varied in accordance:

. . . with the character of the school. There are some schools that are in almost a middle class neighbourhood where there are very few of them indeed – only 3 or

4 [pupils] out of 600 . . . and we have other schools in the slums, where there is quite a fair class – 15 or 20.

(DCDEC 1898: Vol. II, 136).

The chairman of the Committee was surprised by this information and sought clarification to confirm that a single teacher could be responsible for a class of pupils so small in size. The Inspector confirmed that each was 'a special class of a different character from what we call specifically our "special class" (DCDEC 1898: Vol. II, 136). Major added that the pupils in these classes were often the children of railway navvies or migrants from rural areas. Both sets were likely to be badly housed and poorly looked after. Other cases arose from arrested development springing from specific diseases. These background factors echoed the arguments which Francis Warner had presented to the Egerton Commission.

Thus, the Leicester Inspector and School Board treated the science of exceptional children with caution and eschewed divisive practices. Selection and admission to the special class were based on educational criteria. The classroom, curriculum and teaching were adapted to accommodate individual pupils. The emphasis lay upon the characteristics which all pupils had in common, albeit to differing degrees, and upon the aim of inclusion. This was vividly illustrated in the case of pupils with physical disabilities. Here schools were given special apparatus such as 'a little chair' to carry a pupil upstairs (DCDEC 1898: Vol. II, 137).

The blueprint for segregated special schools

The School Board for London developed its policy for provision for exceptional children within the arena of the Board's own Subcommittee who originally had been concerned with blind and deaf children, but whose title was changed to the 'Special Schools Subcommittee' in 1891 when their brief was extended to embrace the exceptional children (SBL 1904: 178). Thus, the Board's Subcommittee was a reflection of the Egerton Commission's conjoining of physical and mental conditions. Major-General Francis Moberly was Chairman of that Subcommittee and Vice-Chairman of the Board itself when he presented evidence to the Departmental Committee. In October 1891, London had appointed its Superintendent of Schools for Special Instruction, Mrs Elizabeth Burgwin, who had been an enterprising head teacher in a school in one of the East End's poorest districts for almost 20 years (cf. Horn 1990: 48–53). In August 1892, two special schools were opened.

The Special Schools Subcommittee developed the policy for a system of schools for special instruction which the Board adopted. The Subcommittee readily accepted the medical science formulation of the exceptional child, and within a few years, Shuttleworth was appointed as the Board's examiner for admission to the special classes. At the heart of the Subcommittee's thinking, planning and establishment of these schools was the principle of classification. As the Board's Vice-Chairman stated, 'my idea . . . was to classify as much as we could' (DCDEC 1898: Vol. II, 101; cf. Burgwin 1900: 255). So that classification could be achieved efficiently, the policy was adopted that there should be normally at least three classes on any one site with a minimum of two and a maximum of five (Burgwin 1900: 256).

The system of Schools for Special Instruction was supervised and operated separately from the system of elementary schools in the capital. Each school had its own head teacher, who was responsible for the organization of classes and teachers in the school. Each head teacher was under the supervision of the Superintendent of Schools for Special Instruction. The Superintendent, in turn, was responsible to the Chairman of the Board's Special School Subcommittee.

A pupil's admission to a School of Special Instruction was made on the basis of an examination. In all cases, the Board's Medical Officer and Superintendent of Schools of Special Instruction were present (Burgwin 1900: 256). The local schools' inspector was also present. At a very early stage in the development of the system, the head teacher of the elementary school which proposed the pupil's entry was excluded from the examination. There was also an unsuccessful proposal by the Subcommittee to exclude parents from the examination on the grounds that there were too many people in attendance.

The Subcommittee also devised a series of documents which had to be completed before and after the examination. The first required comments from elementary school teachers on the pupil's abilities and disposition. The second was an account of the pupil's familial background and history. The third was an annual record of the pupil's progress (cf. DCDEC 1898: Vol. I, 11–14).

The curriculum in the special schools consisted of:

Scripture, reading, writing, arithmetic, singing by the Tonic Sol-Fa method, drawing, colouring, modelling in clay, basket weaving and needlework. Great attention is paid to physical exercises.

(Burgwin 1900: 256–7)

The reification of science and segregation

The London Board accepted the relativistic and decontextualized definition of intellect in its policies for educational provision for feeble-minded pupils. This is evident from the fact that the terms in which their planning proposals are couched are redolent of the terms in the Egerton Commission (cf. SBL 1891: 497,1904: 183). The organizing principle of classification itself derives cognately from the definition and suffers from the same shortcomings.

The genealogical basis for the policy of separate, segregated schools springs from the German auxiliary schools scheme. In 1880, the German Minister of Education instructed all towns of more than 20 000 inhabitants to provide auxiliary schools for 'children who, after two years at a State Elementary school, have proved themselves incapable of doing the work' (DCDEC 1898: Vol. II, 249). However, children with sensory defects were excluded, as were epileptics, juvenile criminals, and those backward through irregular attendance or illness. Thirty such schools quickly came into being. In 1890, the London Board considered a report on the organization of one such school and instructed the Subcommittee 'to prepare a scheme for special classes' (SBL 1904: 183). However, early in 1891, the instruction was changed to a scheme for 'special schools . . . for those children who by reason of . . . mental defect, could not be taught "in ordinary standards or by ordinary methods."' (SBL 1904: 183).

The abstract theory or thinking which underpinned the definition of intellect became a factual reality in London's segregated special schools. These grew from two schools with five teachers and 208 pupils on the roll in 1892 to 53 schools, 199 teachers and 2154 pupils on the roll in 1900 (SBL 1904: 163; Burgwin 1900: 256).

The London Board regarded itself as a catalyst and pioneer in this area of policy. It also sought to involve the Education Department in its efforts, and specifically drew the Department's attention to the desirability of legislation in 1894 and again in 1896 (SBL 1904: 184). The Department's Committee on Defective and Epileptic Children was established in December 1896. There were seven members: three Senior Inspectors or Examiners of schools, a member of the Council of the Association for Promoting the Welfare of the Feeble-Minded, George Shuttleworth, and the London Board's Medical Officer and its superintendent of Special Schools. Shuttleworth was shortly to join the London Board as its Examiner for Admission to the Schools for Special Instruction. The London Board's influence is evident from the Committee's composition.

The growth of London's special schools has been presented above. These also became the model, and as an Education Department Report for 1895–1896 observed, 'the example is being followed in other large centres of population' (quoted in SBL 1904: 184). In addition, the other boards which established special classes before 1899 routinely dispatched their intending teachers for extended observation of the working and organization of London's special centres.

The presence of Shuttleworth and the two London Board members on the Committee gave scope for the celebration and elaboration of the science underpinning the divisive practices. London's special schools verified and represented the divisive practices in the real world. Thus, the science of the dividing practices and the divisive practices themselves were mutually reinforcing. The science and the practices made the child their subject. The process of examination and the completion of admission forms transformed the subject into a case. In this way, the science, the divisive practices and the case make a precise exemplification of Foucault's modes of 'objectification which transforms human beings into subjects' (Foucault 1982: 208).

Foucault maintained that the prime focus of his work was to trace the manner in which social processes shape individual identities. These processes involve a mixture of ideas or ideology, and social practices. Some of these processes are structural features of society which coerce individuals to a degree; for example, the different employment experiences of men and women. However, other processes find their willing subjects; for example, music or football fans. Foucault also wrote a history of the transformation of punishment from something inflicted upon the criminal's body to an intention to rehabilitate the criminal's mind. He described this as 'a history of the present' (Foucault 1977: 31). By this, he meant that the events of the present day take place in the context of the pre-existence of past events, thoughts and actions.

Conclusion

What then are the important features of the early struggle between integration and segregation, as witnessed in Leicester and London, respectively, which manifest themselves in the present?

The first is the division of the population to be educated into a group considered ordinary or normal, and a group regarded as unusual or abnormal. In this context, the difference between Shuttleworth and Warner is crucial: the former considered the problem to be the property of the child which needed special treatment, while the latter perceived the influence of social factors such as poverty and unemployment. The preference for Shuttleworth's opinion laid the emphasis upon the special nature of treatment rather than factors which may by manipulation facilitate educational experience.

The second factor is London's drive to establish segregated special schools for pupils with learning difficulties. The city adopted this policy with the opening of its first special schools in 1892. London's special schools increased rapidly from three in 1892 to 21 in 1896 and 53 in 1900 (DCDEC 1898: Vol. II, 48, 101). These schools acted as the model that other education authorities imitated either through their agreement or through lack of reflection. Teachers were routinely dispatched to the London special schools to observe and to train. The concrete existence of the schools was the foundation of the justification for their existence.

The third factor was that there arose from the existence of special schools a body of people who wished to enhance the status and difference of the special school from that of mainstream schools. This involved both administrators and teachers. The National Special Schools Union held its first national conference in Manchester in 1903. Elizabeth Burgwin, London's superintendent of special schools, was a vice-president and George Shuttleworth a member of the committee. The National Council encouraged the formation of local branches of the Union. An explicitly declared object of the Union was 'to promote the interests of Special School Teachers'. The existence of the Union continues to emphasize what makes special children different rather than what they share with all children. This is still evident in the work of the Special Educational Needs National Advisory Council, and bolsters the stance of teachers' unions such as the National Union of Teachers and the National Association of School Masters and Union of Women Teachers on the question of inclusion.

[. . .] More recently, integration has taken the form of the inclusive education movement (Daniels & Garner 1999). However, the practical elements of the early struggle which are still present relate to special school ideology, personnel and concrete buildings as recent research confirms (Croll & Moses 2000).

References

Alston, J. (1992) *The Royal Albert: chronicles of an era*. Lancaster. University of Lancaster, Centre for North-West Regional Studies.

Board of Education (BoE) (1901) *Report of the Board of Education 1899–1900*, **Vol. III**. London: HMSO.

Burgwin, E.M. (1900) The physically and mentally defective. In Spalding, T.A., ed. *The work of the London School Board*. London: P. S. King and Son: 125–31.

Copeland, I.C. (1995) The establishment of models of education for disabled children. *British Journal of Educational Studies*, **43** (2): 179–200.

Croll, P. & Moses, D. (2000) Ideologies and utopias: educational professionals' views of inclusion. *European Journal of Special Needs Education*, **15**: 1.

Daniels, H. and Garner, P. (1999) *Inclusive education: world yearbook of education*. London: Kogan Page.

Departmental Committee on Defective and Epileptic Children (DCDEC) (1898) *Departmental Committee on Defective and Epileptic Children, 2 Vols*. London: HMSO.

Feuer, L.S. (1969) *Marx and Engels: basic writings on politics and philosophy*. London: Fontana.

Foucault, M. (1977) *Discipline and punish: the birth of the prison*. London: Allen Lane.

Foucault, M. (1982) The subject and power. In Dreyfus, H.L., Rabinow, P., eds. *Michel Foucault: beyond structuralism and hermeneutics*. Brighton: Harvester: 186–201.

HM Government (1913) *Mental Deficiency Act, 3 and 4, George V, Chapter 28*. London: HMSO.

HM Government (1914) *Elementary Education (Defective and Epileptic) Children Act, 4 & 5, George V, Chapter 45*. London: HMSO.

Horn, P. (1990) Elizabeth Miriam Burgwin: child welfare pioneer and union activist. *Journal of History Education*, **14** (3): 48–60.

Royal Commission on the Blind, Deaf and Dumb, etc. of the United Kingdom (1889) *RCBDDUK*. London: HMSO.

Royal Commission on the Elementary Education Acts (RCEEAs) (1886) *Elementary Education Acts: report of the Royal Commission, etc*. London: HMSO.

School Board for London (SBL) (1904) *Final report of the London School Board, 1870–1904*. London: P. S. King and Son.

School Board for London (SBL) (1891) *SBL Minutes*, **Vol. 23**.1. London: P. S. King and Son.

Smith, F. (1931) *A history of English elementary education, 1760–1902*. London: University of London Press.

Soloway, R.A. (1990) *Demography and degeneration: eugenics and the declining birth rate in twentieth century Britain*. Chapel Hill, NC: University of North Carolina Press.

Thomson, M. (1998) *The problem of mental deficiency: eugenics, democracy and social policy in Britain 1870–1959*. Oxford: Clarendon Press.

Wardle, D. (1976) *English popular education 1780–1975*. Cambridge: Cambridge University Press.

Ian Copeland suggests that the elements of the early struggle he describes continue to exert a powerful influence on the current context in which inclusive education is being developed. These elements include the creation of a group requiring special treatment, the promotion and imitation of a special school model and the growth of a professional body of special educators.

Part 2

Looking forward

CHAPTER 6

The politics of education for all

Len Barton

This chapter is taken from a published conference paper that Len Barton presented at the International Special Education Congress in Birmingham in 1995 on the theme of Education for All. At this time he looked forward, from a political perspective, to significant challenges integral to the process of change and these retain their relevance in the early part of the twenty-first century. We must have a vision, he argues, and we must struggle to achieve it, and this includes tackling assumptions about education as a market place.

'Education for All' is one of the most important and urgent issues facing all societies concerned with the education of their future citizens. The pursuit of 'Education for All' will entail engaging with questions of social justice, equity and participatory democracy. It is thus part of a human-rights approach to education and living, one in which the barriers to the empowerment of *all* pupils must be removed.

It is essential, therefore, that we do not underestimate the serious, complex and contentious nature of the issues involved in the pursuit of inclusive policies and practice. The process will be challenging and disturbing, necessitating fundamental changes to the social and economic conditions and relations of a given society. This will include changes to the values informing the prioritisation and distribution of resources, how society views difference, how schools are organised, how teachers view their work, the styles of their teaching and the nature of the curriculum.

This paper will maintain that a fundamental barrier to the realisation of education for all is the growing emergence and implementation of policies and practices informed by a market ideology. The concept of the 'market' and its applicability to education will be explored and the paper will highlight the political nature of these developments.

The politics of education for all

All governments are concerned with controlling human service provision. This includes the issue of funding and the extent to which investment in particular institutions results in the sorts of economic and cultural reforms that are viewed as worthwhile.

Government priorities and decisions, and the values informing them, are all part of the public manifestation of the intentions and vision they hold with regard to the form of society they wish to see develop and continue. Thus, the allocation of human and material resources are fundamentally political decisions. Their significance is much more crucial in a social context in which there are both limited resources and extensive inequalities arising from the existing economic and structural relations. Questions of politics, power and control are central in this situation. The nature of discrimination and its impact on the lives of different groups must be carefully explored and exposed. This will be particularly important where a 'blaming the victim' mentality represents the official discourse used to explain these conditions and experiences (Ryan 1976).

Educational issues are complex and contentious and often involve passionately held beliefs and values. These entail making connections between schools and the wider society of which they are a part. This involves the capacity to range from the microcontexts of biographical and school life to the wider social and economic conditions and relations in which the former are embedded. One of the leading analysts of school change and improvement, Fullan (1993), has advocated that if schools and teachers are to make a difference then:

> Making a difference must be explicitly recast in broader social and moral terms. It must be seen that one cannot make a difference at the interpersonal level unless the problem and solution are enlarged to encompass the conditions that surround teaching . . . and the skills and actions that would be needed to make a difference. Without this attitude and broader dimension the best of teachers will end up as moral martyrs. In brief, care must be linked to a broader, social, public purpose . . . (p. 11)

Any serious consideration of education for all must therefore engage with questions of politics and power and encapsulate socio-economic conditions and relations.

Within the context of 'special education', this engagement is very underdeveloped. There are several reasons as to why this is so. First, special education has been dominated by a form of reductionism which gives a privileged status to individualistic explanations. Within-the-child factors are emphasised, encouraging 'special needs' to be viewed as a personal trouble and not a public issue (Mills 1970). In particular, medical and psychological ideas have powerfully informed policy and practice. This has had the effect of depoliticising the issues involved. Secondly, given the restrictive nature of this approach, attempts to introduce complex questions – for example, of power, politics, class, gender and race – into the analysis can be seen as unnecessary and unhelpful. This will be particularly so where the 'special' quality of such provision is justified on the grounds that all children are treated equally. Lastly, the strong traditional belief that professionals involved in special education provision are caring, patient and loving, and that politics should be kept separate from education, make it difficult to raise such questions.

The politics of disability

Disability is a significant means of social differentiation in modern societies. The level of esteem and social standing of disabled people is derived from their position in relation to the wider social conditions and relations of a given society. Particular institutions have a very crucial influence on social status. This includes the level and nature of employment, education and economic well-being (Equality Studies Centre 1994).

Status is influenced by the cultural images which, for example, the media portray about particular groups, the legal rights and protection afforded them and the quality and duration of educational experiences. How a society excludes particular groups or individuals involves the process of categorisation, in which the inabilities and unacceptable and inferior aspects of a person's make-up are legitimated. Through the act of the 'individualised gaze', problems are located within the individual resulting in a view of them as 'other' or negatively different.

A crucial feature of the oppression of disabled people has been the extent to which their voice has been excluded. Overcoming disabling barriers will include listening to the voice of disabled people and their organisations, especially as they struggle for choice, rights and participation. Jenny Morris (1992) has captured the concerns of disabled people in a booklet concerned with the issue of rights. The voice is unmistakably clear: 'Our vision is of a society which recognises our rights and our value as equal citizens rather than merely treating us as the recipient of other people's good will' (p. 10).

This must be the context within which the question of inclusive education needs to be explored. It is crucial, given the general unwillingness of national governments 'to think in terms of a national comprehensive plan to meet the needs of disabled people' (Daunt 1991: 174), as well as the difficulties a market approach to educational policy, planning and practice are beginning to generate with regard to issues of social justice, equity and entitlement.

Inclusive education

Inclusive education is part of a human rights approach to social relations and conditions. The intentions and values involved relate to a vision of the whole society of which education is a part. Issues of social justice, equity and choice are central to the demands for inclusive education. Disablist assumptions and practices need to be identified and challenged in order to promote positive views of others.

Inclusive education is concerned with the well-being of *all* pupils, and schools should be welcoming institutions. Special education entails a discourse of exclusion and this is seen as a particularly offensive aspect of such provision. This is clearly demonstrated in the concerns of a group of non-disabled parents over the education of their disabled children. In the introduction to a forthcoming book of the stories of their children, the editors (parents) maintain:

For us the concept of segregation is completely unjustifiable – it is morally offensive – it contradicts any notion of civil liberties and human rights. Whoever it is done to, wherever it appears, the discrimination is damaging for our children, for our families and for our communities. We do not want our children to be sent to segregated schools or any other form of segregated provision. We do not want our children and our families to be damaged in this way. Our communities should not be impoverished by the loss of our children.

(Murray and Penman 1995)

From this perspective, the goal is not to leave anyone out of school. Inclusive experience is about learning to live with one another. This raises the question of what schools are for. They must not be about assimilation in which a process of accommodation leaves the school remaining essentially unchanged (Wolfe 1994).

It is essential that the demand for inclusive education does not result in a critique of special schooling which becomes an end in itself. We are not advocating that these developments are merely in terms of the existing conditions and relations in mainstream schools. They too will need to change and there are certain features that are unacceptable, including the plant, organisation, ethos, pedagogy and curriculum. It will demand the transfer of resources, careful planning and continual monitoring. We are not advocating a dumping practice into existing provision.

Inclusive education needs to be part of a whole-school equal opportunities policy. If we are to resist complacency and recognise the degree of struggle still to be engaged with, and if official rhetoric is to be translated into reality in substantive terms in the lives of *all* pupils, then the question of inclusive education needs to be an integral part of a well-thought-through, adequately resourced and carefully monitored equal opportunities policy. By being an integral part of an equal opportunities approach, it will provide a basis for the identification of those features of the existing society, including policy and practices within specific institutions and contexts, that are offensive, unacceptable and thus must be challenged and changed.

The transition from segregated special schools to inclusive provision and practice will demand careful planning and sensitive implementation. In the current context, some parents prefer their children to attend a special day or residential school. From the perspective adopted in this paper, such choices should not be viewed as a defence for the continuation of special schools, but rather, as Dessent (1987) has forcefully argued:

Special schools do not have a right to exist. *They exist because of the limitations of ordinary schools in providing for the full range of abilities and disabilities amongst children.* It is not primarily a question of the quality or adequacy of what is offered in a special school. Even a superbly well organised special school offering the highest quality curriculum and educational input to its children has no right to exist if that same education can be provided in a mainstream school.

(p. 97; my emphasis)

The marketisation of education

The demand for education for all needs to be set within the wider context of the attempts by successive Conservative governments to restructure the welfare state. [...]

A powerful programme of change has been directed at the governance, content and outcomes of schooling, post-school and higher educational provision.

The ideological force behind such developments has become known as the 'New Right'. [...] The fundamental features of the new economic policy became those of efficiency and modernisation and, as Gamble (1994) also notes, the market was depicted as the 'best way of allocating resources, providing incentives and stimulating growth' (p. 42). [...] In this process, notions of 'citizenship', 'freedom' and 'equality' are invested with new meaning and informed by market assumptions. [...]

Under the guise of reducing state control, the role and powers of local educational authorities (LEAs) have been radically reduced, local management of schools (LMS) has been introduced and the working conditions and definition of teachers' work has been changed. A new form of language has been introduced by which we both think about and evaluate education – it is the language of business. Thus, 'quality', 'accountability', 'cost-efficiency', 'effectiveness', 'performance indicators', 'development plans', 'mission statements', 'targets', and 'appraisal' are key concepts in this discourse. Pupils are now viewed as 'units of resource'.

Within a market-driven system of provision, there will be winners and losers. The market is not a neutral mechanism: it involves socialising individuals into a new value system. Gewirtz, Ball and Bowe (1993) maintain that: 'the market rewards shrewdness rather than principles and encourages commercial rather than educational decision-making' (p. 252). [...]

One of the fundamental features of the marketisation of education has been the intensification of competitiveness. The emphasis on competitiveness supports the celebration of individualism and the development of an increasingly hierarchically organised system of provision. In this context the question of access to particular schools raises the issue of selection and the existing 'cultural capital' of pupils entering particular schools (Walford 1992). One analyst has called this 'the rise of parentocracy' (Brown 1990). We already have indications that these policies and their implementation are leading to a more socially and divisive system of education (Ball 1993). [...]

Vincent et al. (1994) maintain that LEAs are finding it less possible to resist the influx of a more market-created culture. This is viewed as fragmenting and atomising educational provision. Legislative restrictions, the fragile financial climate and reduction in the amounts of reserves LEAs are permitted to hold have combined to decrease their ability to meet their general tasks, and special needs functions in particular. They conclude that a market-oriented discourse: 'encourages an emphasis on individualism which is antithetical to the concept of a planned and pervasive approach to provision for "vulnerable children"' (p. 275).

In terms of the pursuit of education for all, the impact of market-led decision making on educational provision and practice raises serious concerns about the establishment of national policies supported by the political will of governments. Indeed, Bines (1995) contends that the marketisation of education is now resulting in the influx of a strong form of managerialism. […] Managers within schools increasingly face the dilemma that 'giving too high a profile to SEN work may not match with concerns to promote a market image based on a high level of pupil achievement.'

Some key questions can be identified as emerging from the analysis provided in this paper. They include:

- What view of 'difference' is enshrined within a market discourse?
- To what extent is the marketisation of education leading to an increase in special educational provision?
- To what extent does the populace discourse of 'parental choice' mask existing stubborn inequalities?
- How far will the marketisation of education reduce collaboration between schools?

Conclusion

In presenting this notion of the 'market', I am aware of reservations being expressed over its applicability to education. Clearly, education is not a 'free market' and has contradictory features resulting from explicit political interventions by government. These include the introduction of the National Curriculum and the use of various undemocratically elected 'quangos'. What we have, as Bottery (1992) so shrewdly notes, is 'a paradoxical mixture of a free market liberalism and centralist autocracy' (p. 4). Thus, it may be more appropriate to work with the notion of a quasi-market (Ranson 1994). This in no way detracts from the necessity of situating any discussion of education for all within a wider sociopolitical framework.

In the World Conference on Special Needs in Education (1994) held in Salamanca, Spain, a framework for action was adopted which will hopefully inform policy and practice on an international scale. Confirming a human rights approach and attempting to develop new thinking on this issue, the document states:

The trend in social policy during the past two decades has been to promote integration and participation and to combat exclusion. Inclusion and participation are essential to human dignity and to the enjoyment and exercise of human rights. Within the field of education, this is reflected in the development of strategies that seek to bring about a genuine equalisation of opportunity. Experience in many countries demonstrates that the integration of children and youth with special educational needs is best achieved within inclusive schools that serve all children within a community. It is within this context that those with special education needs can achieve the fullest educational progress and social integration. While inclusive schools provide a favourable setting for achieving equal opportunity and full participation, their success requires a concerted effort, not only by teachers and school staff, but also by peers, parents, families and volunteers. The reform of social institutions is not only a technical task; it depends, above all, upon the conviction, commitment and good will of the individuals who constitute society.

If we are to see the fundamental changes required in order for us to realise a truly inclusive society, then it will necessarily involve us addressing questions of politics and power.

What we are ultimately concerned with when we allude to the issue of education for all is determining what constitutes the 'good society': how is it to be achieved and what is the role of education in this task? We have no room for complacency but every reason to intensify our commitment to struggle for the removal of all disabling barriers

in this instance, an uncritical acceptance that a marketisation of education will lead to a better society for *all* citizens.

We need to dream, to have a vision, but one which arises from an informed understanding of the discriminatory factors of the material world we now live in.

References

Ball, S. J. (1993) Education markets, choice and social class. The market as a class strategy in the UK and US. *British Journal of Sociology of Education*, **14**(1), 3–19.

Bines, H. (1995) Special educational needs in the market place. *Journal of Educational Policy*, **10**(2), 157–72.

Bottery, M. (1992) *The Ethics of Educational Management.* London: Cassell.

Brown, P. (1990) The 'third wave': Education and the ideology of parentocracy. *British Journal of Sociology of Education*, **11**(1), 65–86.

Daunt, P. (1991) *Meeting Disability: A European response.* London: Cassell.

Dessent, T. (1987) *Making the Ordinary School Special.* Lewes: Falmer Press.

Equality Studies Centre (1994) *Equality, Status and Disability.* University College Dublin.

Fullan, M. (1993) *Change Forces: Probing the depths of educational reform.* Lewes: Falmer Press.

Gamble, A. (1994) *The Free Economy and the Strong State.* Basingstoke: Macmillan.

Gewirtz, S., Ball, S. J. and Bowe, R. (1993) Values and ethics in the education market place: The case of Northwark Park. *International Studies in Sociology of Education*, **3**(2), 233–54.

Mills, C. W. (1970) *The Sociological Imagination.* Harmondsworth: Penguin.

Morris, J. (1992) *Disabled Lives: Many voices, one message.* London: BBC.

Murray, P. and Penman, J. (1995) Draft Introduction, Sheffield.

Ranson, S. (1994) Public institutions for co-operative action: A reply to James Tooley. *British Journal of Educational Studies*, **43**(1), 35–42.

Ryan, W. (1976) *Blaming the Victim*. New York:Vintage Books.

Vincent, C., Evans, J., Lunt, I. and Young, P. (1994) The market forces? The effect of local management of schools on special educational needs provision. *British Educational Research Journal*, **20**(3), 261–77.

Walford, G. (1992) *Selection for Secondary Schooling*. Briefing Paper No. 7, London: National Commission on Education.

Wolfe, J. (1994) Beyond difference: Toward inclusion and equity. In F. Pignatelli and S. Pflaum (eds) *Experiencing Diversity: Toward educational equity*. California: Corwin Press.

World Conference on Special Needs Education (1994) Framework for action on special needs education. *International Review of Education*, **40** (6), 495–507.

This chapter has provided a broad context for the discussions in the following chapters of what we might envisage and want from inclusive education in the coming years. It has illustrated the policy tensions under which we currently operate and shown that seeing our way through the maze of mixed messages must be an important first step in thinking through our wish-list for inclusion and making it happen.

CHAPTER 7

Inclusion – looking forward

Carol Boys

Carol Boys is the Chief Executive of the Down's Syndrome Association. She is also the parent of Alex, a young person with Down's syndrome. In this chapter Carol looks back at the changes that have given young people a much stronger right to mainstream education. She shows that, even with the emergence of new rights, inclusion can often depend on attitudes, of an LEA, a school or of an individual teacher. For Carol and Alex, inclusion has been a process of problem solving, though the solutions they hoped for were not always there. As she looks forward to Alex's adult life, Carol reflects on the changes that are affecting both him and the DSA. As a young adult, Alex, like his peers, wants a say in his own life. The DSA is moving from being an organisation 'for' people with Down's syndrome, to one where people with Down's syndrome serve as trustees and take part in decision making. Carol observes the strength and support that people with Down's syndrome increasingly choose to draw from one another. She argues that adult services will need to change, if they are to meet the changed aspirations of young people who have experienced inclusive schooling.

Celebrating achievements

Since it was founded over thirty years ago, the Down's Syndrome Association (DSA) has been at the forefront of the fight for inclusion for people with Down's Syndrome. Driven by pressure from parents and other voluntary organisations the DSA helped to bring about major change in legislation in the form of the 1981 and 1993 Education Acts. It also played a very important role in the consultation process for the 1997 Green Paper, *Excellence for All Children: Meeting Special Educational Needs*, which resulted in an even greater push for inclusion.

Even though the law now makes it much easier for a child with Down's syndrome to take their place alongside their peers at the school of their parents' choice, there is still a steady stream of families who need the services of the DSA educational advocacy worker to guide them through the complicated statementing process and to help them to achieve what they are entitled to in law. More and more children with Down's syndrome are now attending their local school and research shows that socially and academically they do better when working alongside their peers in an inclusive setting.

Inclusion in education has already been shown to be the key to breaking down some of the barriers of discrimination towards people with learning disabilities. We know that students in ordinary schools who have had the experience of learning alongside their peers with Down's syndrome have a much greater understanding of their peers' potential to be included in society. The whole school has to go through a learning process from the moment a pupil with Down's syndrome arrives in the class. Inevitably, teachers and other members of staff are daunted by the extra work that they fear will need to be done. Parents of other pupils in the school may be anxious that the child with Down's syndrome will take up too much of the teacher's time and their child's education will suffer as a result. At the DSA, we have even heard anecdotal stories of parents of other children who have been concerned that their child might 'catch' something. Experience has shown that if the staff team are given information and support right from the start, most of them will very quickly realise that they do have the skills to teach a child with Down's syndrome and there is no 'magic formula' to be discovered. Inclusion can and does work. The case has been made.

There is no doubt that it is becoming much easier for children with Down's syndrome to be able to attend their local school and there have been some encouraging success stories with many young people obtaining GCSE passes, some of them in academic subjects and with good grades. But what next? What happens after school? That is the burning question. It is one that I face as a parent and also as a part of the decision-making team at the DSA.

Alex's story

My own experiences of inclusion began 19 years ago when my son Alex was born with Down's syndrome, a great shock to our whole family. When the dust settled I was very quickly making plans for Alex to go to our local primary school with his brother who was then six years old and already well established in the reception class. My friends and neighbours with children in the school just took it for granted that Alex would go along with the other children when the time came. It never occurred to me, or them, that there might be a problem with the local LEA and funding. Why would he need funding? Funding for what? I put his name down for the local school and although everyone there knew Alex had Down's syndrome it didn't seem to be an issue.

Alex went off to playgroup with his friends and, apart from a tendency to try to make for the door and discover the outside world on his tricycle at every given opportunity, everything went well. Alex was always very popular with the other children. He went to all the parties and quite often got invited to lunch after a playgroup session. During that period, Alex kept up very well with the other children; he was physically very strong and well coordinated, his language was slower but it nevertheless developed very well. Everything seemed to be going swimmingly.

The first inkling that there might be a problem with a move to the primary school nursery came at a coffee morning with a throwaway comment from an educational psychologist taking time out from Berkshire LEA to have her children. 'Did you know that Berkshire have only ever had one child with Down's syndrome in a mainstream school. It was a complete failure and the family left the county.' I took absolutely no notice of her comments because I was still naive enough to assume that because the school had accepted the registration, everything would just fall into place. I couldn't have been more wrong!

Alex did in fact start at the primary school nursery, but only because the head teacher would not take no for an answer from the LEA; she insisted that he be given a chance even if it meant taking him without support. The worst part about that period in Alex's school career was the army of 'experts' that appeared on the scene making assumptions about what Alex might or might not be able to achieve. The school couldn't just be left to get on with it. The nursery teacher had many years of experience of teaching children with special needs, including children with very little language and those from families where English was not spoken at home. She was constantly having her confidence eroded by the interference of the so-called 'experts' from the LEA with their protestations that 'children with Down's are much better off being taught in special school.' Despite this interference Alex continued to make good progress, and although we didn't see a speech and language therapist in the school until he moved up to the juniors, Alex's language improved. His schoolmates would ask him a question and if they didn't understand his response, they would get him to repeat himself until they did understood what he was saying.

The leap from nursery class to infants didn't seem to worry Alex either – so long as he was with his friends he was happy. He continued to be a very popular member of the class and, although there was sometimes a tendency for other children to do things for Alex instead of letting him do them for himself (he would take his coat off and hold it out for another child to hang up if allowed to), generally speaking, things went well. I did have to spend quite a lot of time in school myself with teachers, reassuring them and constantly trying to share more information about techniques for teaching children with Down's syndrome. As he moved from year to year, his progress depended very much on the attitude of the class teacher and his or her ability to cope with Alex's emerging needs as the gap widened between him and his peers. I remember one teacher in particular, who, although initially not very happy to take Alex into her class, reluctantly agreed and vowed to try her best to embrace the idea of inclusion. All seemed well until one day, I went to collect him from her class and, to my horror, one whole corner of the classroom had been designated 'Alex's Corner' – complete with large sign. This corner was where Alex sat with his LSA and all his work was on display around him. The worst of it was that the teacher did not see a problem with what she had done. Needless to say, the corner went and Alex was moved to another class in that year.

Considering that this was very early days for inclusion, there were surprisingly few major problems in the infants and Alex moved up to juniors alongside his friends. By this time we had managed to negotiate a reasonable amount of classroom support for Alex, but once again the ability to use that support effectively varied from teacher to teacher. Alex himself quite often resented what he saw as interference from the LSA, he hated being seen as different from the other children and this would often manifest itself in the form of abusive language directed at the poor LSA. His growing band of admirers found his lack of inhibitions and outspokenness highly amusing and would often encourage him in his efforts to humiliate his long-suffering companion. The immediate solution was to change the LSA – it worked!

By the time Alex entered year 6, local politics were becoming an important issue in Berkshire and, although we didn't know it at the time, they would interfere quite dramatically with his choice of secondary school. The break-up of Berkshire County Council, the fact that many of Alex's friends were taking the grammar school entrance exam, and that others were destined to go to the huge local comprehensive with no interest whatsoever in taking a child with Down's syndrome, meant that we were left with no choice but to consider other options. We were told that although there were plans afoot to put more resources for statemented children into one of the smaller comprehensive schools on the other side of town eventually, nothing was going to happen until the political situation had been sorted out. It was decided that Alex would repeat year 6 in the hope that the problem would be resolved. This was a disaster! Alex became seriously depressed. He did not understand why he couldn't go to school with his friends and although he had some friends in the year below, he saw having to join them in their class as a retrograde step.

The whole of that year was spent trying to find a suitable placement for Alex with a peer group that he could relate to. Although academically he was way behind his peers, socially he was and always had been extremely able and very aware of the importance of 'street credibility'. We looked at almost every school in the county, but because the LEA had invested very heavily in large campus special schools during the 80s, not one of the special schools seemed to be appropriate for Alex, who had been used to his mainstream school peer group. His expectations and aspirations were very different from the other pupils we came across. Finally, a solution seemed to have been found. A visit to a school in Dorset on the advice of a very experienced special needs advisor found a peer group that Alex immediately related to. After much soul-searching and agonising about the idea of Alex going away to residential school, we agreed to let him go and he has enjoyed most of his time there. Although he has been happy at school, he has constantly asked the question 'why couldn't I go to school with my old friends from primary school? Is it because I have Down's syndrome?' and of course the answer to that question is 'yes'.

Steps into the future

Alex will be leaving school this year and he is about to take his biggest step yet towards independence. Although he has spent the latter end of his school career in a special school (albeit quite an unusual special school) Alex still regards himself as very much a part of our local community. His dreams and expectations are that he will have a flat, a job, get married and do all the things that other people do. The question is, will he be allowed to make those choices for himself? Will the support services be flexible enough to enable him to fulfil his expectations? Or will he have to make do with what's available in our area, whatever that might be?

The fact that we have been fortunate enough to live in a very supportive community has made all the difference to our family's experience of inclusion with Alex. When he was younger there were always children in the house and he was treated very much as one of the gang. He was included in everything: it just never occurred to anyone to leave him out. However, such a high level of local inclusion made it all the more difficult for Alex when he had to go off to a different school. The realisation that he had Down's syndrome and that somehow that made him different from his friends came as a real shock to him. We had always talked about Down's syndrome with Alex, he'd heard family and friends talk about it and he had regularly come into contact with people with Down's syndrome. Nonetheless, I don't think it had ever occurred to him what it might mean until it became obvious that he wouldn't be able to go to the same school as his friends.

Although he has been away at school in Dorset, Alex has kept in contact with some of his close friends from primary school. Many of them have moved on to universities, colleges and employment. Some of them are the sons and daughters of my friends, which makes it easier for him to keep in contact, but they are all busy with their lives and although they like to see Alex occasionally to catch up with news, their relationships with him are very different from the way it was when they were all much younger. Alex is looking for a peer group to relate to in his local community. Like so many other people with learning disabilities he is anxious about the future, wondering where he is going to live and, more importantly, who he is going to live with. Will he be able to get a job? If so how? He is once again asking 'Why do I have to have Down's syndrome?' or, 'If I didn't have Down's syndrome I could get a job and a flat in London like my brother.' The so-called 'experts' are back again, this time with different titles and from different departments, all claiming to know what is best for Alex. He is totally confused and of course worried about the future.

Wanting a say

Alex is not alone in his struggle to realise his dreams and aspirations; we hear many similar stories every day at the DSA. The increase in the numbers of people with

Down's syndrome reaching adulthood has had a great influence on the development of the work of the Association over the last few years. Details of population breakdown of people with Down's syndrome are sketchy, but in Northern Ireland there are quite robust figures available and these suggest that the majority of people with the condition are now over age 16. It is probable that this is the picture for the whole of the UK. The DSA has had to adapt and extend its range of work to respond to the emerging needs of adults with Down's syndrome. For so many years the Association concentrated its work on issues for children with Down's syndrome and their families; then, gradually, enquiries began to come into the organisation from adults with Down's syndrome themselves. As new issues emerged, new strategies had to be developed to deal with them.

It is nearly four years since a group of people with Down's syndrome came together with a facilitator to make a video and an accessible booklet about Down's syndrome for people with Down's syndrome. At their first meeting the group decided to call themselves the 'Down to Earth' group because they felt that the materials that they were working on would bring their audience 'down to earth'. They hoped that the video would reassure people with Down's syndrome that they weren't different or special and that it would emphasise the aspirations and needs that we all have in common. They also wanted to explain to the viewer that people with Down's syndrome do not always have an easy time because of prejudice and discrimination, but that shouldn't mean that their expectations need not be met. The content of the video was very much the group's own work and the result is a very powerful insight into how people with Down's syndrome view themselves and what they feel about society's attitudes towards them.

Down to Earth has become a concept at the DSA rather than just a name for an individual group. The development of accessible information for people with Down's syndrome now forms an important part of what the DSA does. The recent production of accessible health materials is probably one of our most important pieces of work since the publication of *He'll Never Join the Army*, a report about discrimination towards people with Down's syndrome in the health service. The report heralded the start of the Association's highly successful 'Health Alert' campaign. The accessible health materials have been written in consultation with a group of people with Down's syndrome who meet regularly in the London area. The materials aim to empower people with Down's syndrome by making them aware of the sort of health problems that they might encounter. But more importantly the material helps them prevent some of those problems occurring in the first place by telling them how to access regular health screening. It also includes checklists and information for people with Down's syndrome, their carers and professionals.

The *Down to Earth* magazine is also beginning to develop as a publication in its own right. This is a magazine for people with Down's syndrome compiled and edited by people with Down's syndrome. At the moment it is a place for sharing feelings and an opportunity to publish the many letters and poems that are received at the DSA from people with Down's syndrome. It started out as very much a fun publication to be included with each edition of the Association's regular *Journal*, but gradually more and more people are starting to write to us raising important issues that are beginning to present new challenges for the DSA.

Probably one of the greatest challenges for the Association has been the need to adapt to meet the expectations of people with Down's syndrome, expectations which can quite often be at odds with the views of their parents and carers. Discussions about relationships, sexuality and marriage can often be quite difficult for families to deal with, and the recent election of the first two people with Down's syndrome to the board of trustees has been an eye-opener for us all. Until recently the board was entirely made up of parents of people with Down's syndrome. Planning strategy and discussions about issues have taken on a whole new perspective.

There have been two very successful residential conferences for people with Down's syndrome, involving delegates from all over the UK, in a 'Share and Exchange' programme and many support groups have set themselves up around the country calling themselves 'Down to Earth'. Some of the members of the original Down to Earth group have now gone on to do other things: Ailsa Pearcey has become a public speaker and television presenter, Kate Powell is the editor of the *Down to Earth* magazine and Andrew Roebuck is now a trustee of the DSA as well as holding down a job and living in a flat with his wife, Sarah, another member of the original group.

'Keeping us strong'

Many of us have been surprised that despite our extreme efforts over the years fighting for people with Down's syndrome to be included, we should now find many of them wanting to come together and meet as a segregated group. One possible reason is that they see the Down to Earth movement as a powerful self-advocacy group where individuals can discuss their problems in an environment where they can be sure that others in the group will understand the issues. One member from a group said 'We have certain things in common, mostly the extra chromosome, but you will find that we look more like our families than we do each other.' Another said 'It's good to talk to people who can understand – it helps us keep strong.' The fact that people with Down's syndrome are easily identifiable can make them an easy target for prejudice and discrimination, even from other people with learning disabilities. Meeting together allows them to give each other immense support to tackle the issues that they face as a group.

Self-advocacy and decision making is becoming more and more important for people with learning disabilities. The Government's White Paper, *Valuing People – A New Strategy for Learning Disability*, sets out to promote choice, opportunity and better services for everyone with a learning disability. It is an amazingly ambitious agenda for change to current practices and delivery of services to people with a learning disability, giving them much a greater say in what happens in their lives. It promises greater social inclusion and independence.

However, so far, very little real change has happened in the two years since publication and many learning disability organisations are encouraging their members to campaign now for better support to ensure that all the promises made by *Valuing People* will be fulfilled. There has never been a more important time for self-advocacy groups to truly develop their own voices and bring about major change in the services and choices that are available to them. Why shouldn't someone with a learning disability be able to choose where they live and who they live with, have a job, get married and have all the aspirations that we all share? There is a need for greater imaginative thinking. It's not acceptable any more for local authorities to say that they don't have the resources to provide for the needs of individuals. 'Person-centred planning', we are told, is the way forward, with the needs of the individual being of paramount importance.

The reality does, however, seem to be different. Better housing and support packages are urgently needed to enable people with learning disabilities to own their own home or share with the people of their choice. No more having to live at home with aged parents and no alternative. More opportunities to work and enjoy meaningful activities are required and day services need radical modernisation to meet the expectations of the users. People with learning disabilities who have had the benefit of good inclusive education will not be content to spend their time sitting around doing soul-destroying activities at the local day centre. The Learning Disability Partnership Boards (LDPBs) were set up to drive *Valuing People* forward. They were meant to give people with learning disabilities the opportunity to take part in the decision-making process and give them a greater opportunity to have their say. Some authorities have gone to great lengths to make their meetings accessible but others have done very little. Very few local authorities are including the partnerships in full decision making or facilitating them in doing so. There are even examples of authorities using modernisation as an excuse to make reductions in the amount of money that they spend on services for people with learning disabilities without even consulting the LDPBs.

There is no doubt that opportunities for greater inclusion in education have brought about change in the expectations of people with learning disabilities. The influence of role models in ordinary schools has led to pressure for improvement and change to the opportunities available for adults. The Down to Earth project has already done much to promote the idea that people with Down's syndrome can and do want to be involved in making their own choices. The DSA is making a concerted effort to rise to the challenge of promoting and facilitating greater self-advocacy for people with Down's syndrome and there are other learning disability organisations across the country attempting to do the same. *Valuing People* can make a real difference towards achieving the reality of better choices for people with learning disabilities. There has already been a great deal of progress with including them in the planning and implementation processes but we still have a long way to go.

Where next?

What now for the DSA? How can people with Down's syndrome be encouraged to have more meaningful involvement in the work of the Association?

There are many ways that this could be achieved. Members with Down's syndrome could make a real difference to their own lives. It is very important to build on the successes of 'Down to Earth', making it possible for people with Down's syndrome to become spokespeople for the Association. With support, they could give talks to politicians and decision makers about issues such as employment and housing. They could be given the training to act as media spokespeople on television and radio and to make comment in the newspapers, which would of course be much more powerful than someone commenting on their behalf. More people with Down's syndrome should be employed by the Association as permanent members of the staff team. There should be more people with Down's syndrome on the board of trustees of the Association making decisions about policy and shaping the work of the DSA. Who knows? In twenty years' time someone with Down's syndrome could be doing my job.

Carol Boys leaves us thinking about how the Down's Syndrome Association might change over the coming years to reflect increased participation from its members. We might consider more broadly what future we see for organisations run 'for' people with disabilities or for the voluntary sector as a whole. Would guaranteed civil rights mean that such organisations became redundant? Or will there be an increasing role for organisations offering strength and support through shared experience?

CHAPTER 8

A parent's wish-list

Jonathan Rix

Jonathan Rix describes in this chapter the complexity of his responses to his son, Robbie, who has Down[1] syndrome. He looks at where his responses come from and how they influence his hopes for Robbie's future education. Some of his responses are at odds with one another and he charts the struggle and often the impossibility of reconciling one view with another. Underlying the complexity, however, is his simple conviction that Robbie's own voice must be heard. An inclusive school, and an inclusive society, will value Robbie and be willing to learn from him.

Here is a chapter
On wishes
For a child
By a parent
('You can write this')
(Should I say No?)
In a category
For people
Interested
in
Inclusion

Here is another voice
One more
Whispering
A message

Can you hear it?

Among the many
Trying to drown out the roar
of
So much denial

[1] There is a growing internatonal trend towards using the term Down Syndrome as opposed to Down's Syndrome. Like many changes in labelling, the process is slow and faces opposition.

I am Robbie's dad
I am Robbie's dad
I am Robbie's dad
(Need I wish for more?)

Voices of experience

Like everybody else I have a multitude of experiences that define me and affect me in different ways. When I think about my son's education I am faced with the conflicting insights, beliefs, needs and hopes that arise from those different experiences. I struggle to identify and prioritise these conflicting voices. Some people may be able to put them aside: I have always found it difficult not to listen to them all.

So which voices dominate my thinking most frequently? There's the father's voice. I am a father of two children. I am the father of a person with Down syndrome. Coincidentally, I am the younger brother of a person with Down syndrome. My sister was born in 1951. This means I am the son of parents of a person with Down syndrome.

I'm also a teacher – I spent 13 years teaching in a girls' comprehensive in Hackney; I have worked with people with learning difficulties and written numerous texts for this group. I'm a researcher and an activist – I have carried out formal research into people with Down syndrome, and been involved with pressure groups and non-governmental organisations working to improve the lives of disabled people.

I'm also an interpreter of the other voices from people around me – my partner, my daughter, my family, my colleagues, my local community, our support services and our wider society.

And Robbie's voice?

As I write this, he is 19 months old, but his is the voice that I want to hear most of all. (Actually, as I write this, I can hear that voice screaming . . . and I want him to be a bit quieter.)

Isn't that what this is all about?

In this chapter I try to trace the impact of some of these voices on my hopes and desires for Robbie's education.

Listening to different voices

As a father, I wish my son to have his basic needs met, and to be happy, fulfilled, well balanced, and socially involved and responsible. But, inexplicably, I have a far greater urge to protect Robbie, and I feel, rightly or wrongly, that my actions will have greater long-term significance in his life than in my daughter's.

As the youngest brother, I have only ever known a family that includes a person with Down syndrome, and so have never not known loving a person who is disabled. But since my sister was born more than 50 years ago, she was part of a generation who were almost instantly placed in institutions. This segregation of my sister confused me and left me with a feeling that I was party to an injustice.

As a son of parents who were persuaded to put their child in an institution, I believe I understand the guilt that they have felt, and their refusal to wallow in that guilt. I see how this has driven them to make the life of their irredeemably institutionalised daughter as complete as possible, and to work for the rights of all people who are disabled. While I do not share the guilt they said all parents feel if they are genetically responsible for their child's impairment, I do, however, share their drive to shape the wider world.

As a teacher, I know the pressures of the classroom and of the educational system in this country. I know it is hard to give time to students when it is needed rather than when it may be available. I understand the need for systems and consistency within those systems despite individuals needing to work outside those structures. I understand the difficulties of differentiating curricula and overcoming the pressures within institutional settings.

As an individual working formally and informally in many different community settings I know what exclusion feels like. I have also experienced an initial heavy sense of despair when a group of intellectually disabled people joined a well-established, enabled group of which I was a member, forcing a complete change of practice. As a consequence of forced change I have also learned more than I ever thought I would.

As a researcher I can recite the characteristics defining Down syndrome: that 50 per cent of affected people will be short-sighted, 20 per cent will be long-sighted, and many will have additional focus problems; 40 per cent will have mild hearing loss, 15 per cent will have severe hearing loss, 20 per cent will have atlantoaxial instability and so on and so on and so on . . .

As a husband I know I must shut up. I am in danger of being the know-it-all. Clearly, I am just one of two parents, one of many people who know my son. I am no more an expert in him than any parent is about their child; though I might need to ask questions, and discuss issues in a way that many parents would not.

So where does this leave me?

Making sense of it all

A few months ago I was acting as parent-helper at my daughter's playgroup, which is the playgroup Robbie is likely to attend. All the children were sitting on the mat and reciting the nursery rhyme 'Incy Wincy Spider' with associated hand movements. As I watched this hugely enjoyable activity unfolding I found myself worrying about Robbie's interaction in this same setting in a few months' time. The playgroup leader was using gestures for 'Incy Wincy Spider' that were different from those which Robbie had learnt. Her hand gesture for the spider was actually the sign for a butterfly; and her delivery and the overlap with hand gestures were at a speed that would probably mean Robbie wouldn't have time to produce the appropriate gestures himself. What should I do in that situation? Were my concerns justified or creating a self-fulfilling prophecy? Should I have gone and spoken to the class teacher or just got on with joining in with 'Incy Wincy Spider' and accepted that I was over-obsessing?

I lie awake at night thinking about this sort of stuff. I think about the minutiae of it all.

And that, I think, is what underpins any wish-list I may have for Robbie's education. I want him to be surrounded by people who are thinking about the minutiae, but know when they are being unnecessarily obsessive.

Recently, I was at a seminar at the Portage Annual Conference, led by Judy Denziloe from Action For Leisure. Portage is a programme that enables parents of young children with disabilities to work in a focused way with their child, guided by professionals. The seminar was entitled Developing Inclusive Play and Early-years Services, and to provoke debate, Judy asked us to prioritise this list of potentially inclusive practices:

Resources which show positive images of disabled people
Disability equality work with the parents of non-disabled children
Disability equality training for workers
More workers
Wheelchair accessible toilet and ramps to doors
Disability equality work with non-disabled children
Special equipment
Staff who are expert in working with disabled children
'Integration' worker

We were to create a diamond, reflecting our priorities. At the head of the diamond we were to put the most important; below that, the next two most important, then the next three most important, then the next two, and finally the least important.

We were placed in groups and as soon as the exercise started there was a bustle of activity from the Portage workers and other professionals around us. A slightly awkward silence descended on our group, and then one of us muttered, 'Well, I think they're all just as important, actually. You know, I'd like them all to be happening,' and instantly everybody in the group was nodding in agreement. It turned out that we were a group entirely composed of parents.

As a teacher I could look at Judy's headings and come up with a prioritised list. As a parent I feel that I want everything that is on offer, and then some more . . . please.

Who is Robbie?

Of course, wanting everything for your child is commonplace but not necessarily rational. Our starting point must be who Robbie is and what his specific needs are. But this in itself raises many questions and poses difficulties.

'He doesn't look very Down's', 'At least he's not a bad one', 'He's doing so well', 'Their daughter's got a friend whose sister's Down's and she's doing brilliantly at school.' Comments from professionals, friends, family, (the first two have been made by medical staff), show how much Robbie is marked out by this syndrome. It is what people see. It is where they begin their thought process; and how quickly and how far they move beyond that depends on their experiences and consequent perspective.

In many ways Robbie has been presented to us, and will be presented to the educational establishment, as a syndrome. He is a tick-list child. As soon as he was born the tests began. Signs were searched for, chromosomes counted; and then they could get on with checking the heart, the bowel, the thyroid . . .

As well intentioned as people may be when working with our child, they are going through lists of micro and macro stages. As parents it is a challenge not to fall into the same trap. The medical model is all-pervasive, particularly in the early stages. Is it any wonder if as parents we focus on symptoms or on exemplars that rebut those symptoms? And is it any wonder if sooner or later we come to resent those boxes and the questions behind them?

So how do we understand who Robbie actually is and define his personal needs based on that understanding? What's right for Robbie?

The temptation is to fall back on those lists; to concentrate on achieving defined goals and not to let him just get on with it. If we do just let him get on with it, then we might be failing to maximise what he can do. And then we would have failed him. We would have allowed his identifiable weaknesses to overcome his strengths.

This is the conundrum we face. Until Robbie can develop a reliable voice of his own, we must interpret for him, and our interpretation is constantly drip-fed by the deficit model. This carries real dangers. For example, we can easily lower our expectations. Evidence suggests that, from the earliest stages, mothers talk to their children with Down syndrome in a different way from the way they talk to their other children. Hardly surprisingly, then, this different way of talking may affect a child's rate of conceptual development and vocabulary acquisition.

There is the danger that we read the textbook and fulfil the prophecy. But equally there is the risk that we miss something that in hindsight should have been patently obvious. For example, atlantoaxial instability: 20 per cent of people with Down syndrome have instability in the upper two vertebrae of the neck. No scans are carried out for this condition. When stress is exerted in this region during physical activity dislocation is a particular risk for the 20 per cent. Contact sports such as rugby, or twisting activities such as trampolining, are potentially very dangerous. But it also means that horseplay with other kids is riskier, as is falling off a climbing frame or tripping over in the playground.

Does this mean that Robbie should be restricted in all physical activities, that he should only carry them out in closely supervised situations or that we must insist that there should be new equipment bought or adaptations to the school and local environment? Does it mean that his peers should be told about the risks to Robbie? Or should we accept that the chances of any damage are slight even if he is one of the 20 per cent and just avoid the most obviously dangerous situations?

To think the issue through, we must know about the medical characteristics of Down syndrome. But, even though we are so often asked or asking, directly or indirectly, how he fits that medical/deficit model, we do not want that model to pre-empt our treatment of him, nor to unduly direct his development. We do not want it to stop him being himself.

Listening to Robbie

Thankfully, and hardly surprisingly, Robbie's voice is already coming through loud and clear. Emotional communication has been going on since the earliest days, and by 19 months, conceptual communication has become established too. We must build on this communication – it will give him the best chance to rise above the disabling practices of individuals, communities and their institutions.

Believing in him will also empower us. We too suffer disabling practices. Our experiences wear us down. We have to fight education, social and health systems to make sure that our son is included in the way they claim he will be. We have to listen to other parents who tell us that their non-disabled experiences are the same as ours and who equate their search for educational toys with our concerns about the deficit model. But, if we know that our battles are based on what he wants and what he believes is right for him, then we are more likely to have the patience and determination to put up with the disabling practices we face. We will feel we are doing the right thing, and we will be better able to help him overcome the disabling practices that he faces. We will have shared goals, and be more likely to achieve them.

Robbie in school

We want Robbie's school to be aware of the deficit model, the characteristics of his syndrome, but never to use them as a guideline for expectation. We want them to search for his voice, and to listen to his wishes without letting them be an excuse. We want them to believe that he is always capable of doing more than he did yesterday and to want to find the means to support him in consolidating and moving on.

We do not want them to merely itemise Robbie's needs and then try to meet them. We want them to believe he has the right to be educated, to be part of the community, to be a fulfilled and fully active participant in the life of the school, and to believe that by doing just this they will make that establishment stronger.

So how do we see these hopes for his schooling actually coming about? (I notice I have slipped into using we . . . this will need to be discussed with Robbie's mum.) Robbie will probably have a Statement of Special Educational Needs that will define the level of support that he should receive, the nature of that support and its frequency. Targets will be set and his progress towards those targets will be assessed.

Robbie may turn out to be learning disabled. His intellectual development may be so restricted as to cause a long-term adverse effect on his day-to-day life. He may develop physically in ways that could have a long-term impact on the way he learns. The severity of these disabilities, however, will depend on the effectiveness of the provision he receives through the education system, and how well he can access the curriculum.

It is very likely that Robbie will have learning difficulties, but this is not a foregone conclusion. In some areas, or in many areas, he may achieve the standards of many other students.

No one can honestly predict what is achievable. Many of the developmental characteristics of people with Down syndrome, upon which predictions are based, have been defined using individuals denied the opportunity to develop as they could. My sister, for example, had no real education until she was in her late teens. Many of her generation were even denied talk as a baby, since it was deemed unnecessary. Versions of this attitude are still prevalent today, and will for many people be immensely disabling. How can we know what is actually possible, therefore?

Against this backdrop, however, the local authority, schools and outside agencies will identify Robbie's 'special educational needs' in the areas of:

Communication and interaction
Cognition and learning
Behaviour, emotional and social development
Sensory or physical

As parents we too will be involved in this process, and as Robbie grows, his involvement will become increasingly significant. The main concerns outlined in this statement will then be translated into individual education plans that will direct classroom activities.

I understand the need for such an approach. I appreciate that we are looking for specific assistance in a world with limited resources, and that criteria seem a sensible way to govern selection. I know that the organisation of the contemporary classroom requires close planning and measurable and justifiable targets. But I do not believe that this will necessarily achieve the best results for my son.

Difficulty in learning arises in context. It is of the moment. If Robbie does not understand why someone in a story does something then his ability to interact and learn from that story will be greatly reduced. He needs to understand at that moment. I do not want individual education plans that focus attention on specific aspects of the curricula at the expense of these other micro-learning contexts. I want Robbie's schools to demonstrate flexibility in assessing his moment-to-moment needs, rather than sticking dogmatically to agreed plans.

I also wish for flexibility in ways of working from those allocated to Robbie through the statement. The Velcro model of support fills me with dread. I do not wish Robbie to have support staff who will work solely and permanently with him to the exclusion of those around him. However good the intention, the outcome is a powerful image of isolation. It will drive other students away. I want Robbie's academic needs to be understood in relation to the setting of the classroom. He is part of the whole, not someone whose learning is merely taking place alongside the others. And like everyone else he must be challenged in as many ways as possible.

I hope that in the classroom there will be a broad range of groupings that allow everyone to interact. I hope that support staff, teaching assistants and classroom teachers will operate in a spirit of teamwork. I hope they will all be taking turns to work with all students, changing tack and altering plans as and when individual students' academic, personal and socio-cultural needs require them to. I hope too that preparation work, planning and assessment can occur in an informed and cooperative spirit, even when time restraints make this difficult. I know that it is possible to achieve such classrooms and such a learning environment, but it requires the will of all involved.

The staff and students in the class can achieve, on their own, the supportive culture described above, but it is far more likely to happen if they are supported by management at all levels of the school and local authority. I want the cooperation imposed by legislation on those in positions of authority to be absorbed in spirit too.

I am concerned, though, with the focus the system is currently giving to targets and statistics. I don't want Robbie to be left behind because the rest are being driven forward to the next mark in the sand. I don't want these notional targets to be striven for at the expense of my children's and their community's quality of life.

Implicit in nearly all I have just written is the idea that Robbie will attend a mainstream school rather than a special school. We want this to happen. We believe it is a simple right that he be educated in the community in which he lives. If he needs to go to a special school then it is an admission of the system's failure and an example of disabling practice. This is not to say that any special school he should attend is lesser, nor should operate with a culture other than that described above. For many who attend these schools it is the community in which they are allowed to express themselves best, and are enabled to develop best.

We live in a small village, where the children go to the village primary school and then generally move to the comprehensive in the nearest town. If Robbie is to develop within the community of a special school then his school friends will never come from his neighbours nor his village. So why might we consider Robbie attending a special school? There seem only two possible motivations: the standard of his academic development, or the school's failure to make him part of the school community. It may be that the local schools don't deliver the appropriate quality education for our son. They may not have the facilities or ability or will to include him. As far as I am concerned this would be unjustifiable failure, and it would be against the spirit of the recent legislation if not the letter of the law. We would fight for improvements, but ultimately we must not sacrifice Robbie's best interests for our beliefs. He must not be a guinea-pig for a failing system. If he wishes to go elsewhere or if the system is so inadequate as to be denying him access to any community, then we would have to move him.

I hope therefore that Robbie will be going to our local primary school and then the local comprehensive, and then on to further and higher education if he so wishes. I hope that the establishments he becomes part of share our beliefs in allowing Robbie to achieve as much as he can within a supportive community.

Nothing out of the ordinary?

Robbie is going to need access to all mainstream school activities, as well as a few additional ones, to support his development. This will require pupils, staff and parents who understand and share a supportive school ethos, and are capable and willing to see this carried through in the classroom. However, as far as I am aware, Robbie is the first child with Down syndrome who will have attended our local primary school. Will they therefore need to prepare in some way for his arrival? Ideally they would not. Ideally, the systems they have in place for all the other children with additional needs who have passed through the school or are currently attending should be more than adequate. And yet . . .

Here comes the medical model, shouting inside my head . . .

How much do we want and need them to know about the syndrome?

There are dozens of factors that potentially will have a significant impact on Robbie's ability to communicate, participate, and comprehend. Can I expect the school, and those who work with Robbie, to be aware of all of those factors and to bear them in mind? Can I expect them to do the same for every syndrome and condition that causes people to be disabled? And don't I want them to treat everyone as an individual anyway? The teacher inside me sees the parent wanting to have his cake and eat it.

But as a parent that is exactly what I do want. The school will not have every syndrome and condition to cope with. They will have a few. It will not be a deluge of learning that needs to take place. It is an open state of mind. It is about being a learning organisation. It is about taking a multi/interdisciplinary approach. The

Special Educational Needs Coordinator and outside bodies will hopefully step in to help supply the appropriate information that can be passed on in the classroom. As a parent I believe I should also take some responsibility for this and should pass on to the school my understanding of Robbie. But I should do so in the same manner in which I expect the school to conduct themselves. I hope to work with the school in partnership. It must not be about confrontation or dogma, but should be a flexible and open relationship, with Robbie as the focus. It should not be any different from the way that other students are treated. It is just that at times communication will need to be more intensive to achieve similar goals.

I feel it is important, too, for the school to consider the positive contributions that Robbie will make to the classroom and to the school. I am not merely referring to the inherent lesson that diverse people in a diverse community have diverse needs, but to the specific experiences he has. For example, Robbie will have a second language. He will use both sign language and English on a constant basis. This presents an opportunity for the school and for its pupils for which I hope staff will train.

Robbie is used to learning through seeing, hearing and doing. Knowing this should encourage staff to use various materials and teaching approaches. It should encourage teachers to question their normal ways of interacting, and question their expectations of all. This in turn will benefit all students and their different learning styles. Similarly, it is likely that Robbie will need tasks to be delivered in short, clearly-defined segments, with clear links to what has come before and to what will follow. He will need review and repetition. None of this is exactly revolutionary. It is widely seen as good practice, but it is useful to be reminded of the need to carry it through, and Robbie will serve as such a reminder. If it is not being done properly then he will likely be the first to fall behind.

I hope therefore that Robbie will be in a classroom where such good practice is standard, rather than being applied as an add-on just for him. I hope for effective teamwork at all levels and in all areas of school. I hope for a culture where people care to include my son because they believe it is the best thing to do. I hope for a culture that attempts to disable barriers that discriminate against any individual within the school. I hope for a system that is flexible in defining what a child's personal and academic needs are and avoids squeezing him into a box. I hope that my son will be given the freedom to voice his ideas, and develop his own beliefs, without being encouraged to simply tag along with the majority. I hope for a school that encourages close ties between individuals but not at the expense of a communal awareness.

At the present moment I have hopes that the local primary school may be the sort of school I have described above, but I cannot be absolutely certain. Ironically, my first inclusion issue involved Robbie's sister. Isabel joined the reception class part-time from September. Four days a week she went to the local playgroup in the morning, then had lunch and then in the afternoon was taken down to her school by her mum. Unfortunately, this transfer cut right across Robbie's morning sleep. He had previously slept from 11.30am to 1.30pm, but now he had to be awake between 12.30 and 1.15 while Isabel was taken down to school. Within one week of Isabel starting her new routine it was clear that the changes to his day meant he was not getting enough sleep in the morning or sleeping so late in the afternoon that he did not sleep at night. He was constantly over-tired. None of the activities that we carry out with him were happening as they should. In our heads a statistic began to blare. Nearly 50 per cent of children with Down syndrome suffer sleep deprivation leading to behavioural and learning complications. Armed with the papers that explored this deficit model evidence, we approached the school to ask if Isabel could join them from the start of the day. The answer was a categoric refusal. The school followed local authority guidance, applying it as a rule. The head teacher could only be flexible if we got a directive from the local authority, something that would never be achievable in time. He reminded us too that it was not their pupil being affected but the sibling. We pointed out that the sibling would be their pupil soon, but that nonetheless our concern was with our daughter. We explained our only other option was to arrange for various different parents to bring her down on our behalf. Not only could we not expect such a consistent commitment from relative strangers over four months, but Isabel would be the only child being moved in such a way. Why should she be clearly marked out because of her brother? Was this not a genuine inclusion issue?

The head teacher said he wanted to do something to help. He visited the playgroup and arranged for the playgroup organisers to oversee Isabel's transfer to school. His consistent application of the rule was intact, Robbie got his sleep, and other parents were not unduly troubled. Whether Isabel feels she is being marked down as different in some way . . .? Well, as a fellow sibling of a person with Down syndrome, I am sure she does.

Of course, we are not talking long-term psychological damage here and the head teacher had demonstrated a real desire to help us out. We are pleased that he wished to assist us, in many ways it was admirable . . . but his need to be seen to apply rules consistently is still ringing a few alarm bells.

So – I wish for a school where rules are guidelines and where pupils, staff and parents understand that different responses are needed in different circumstances. This doesn't mean I don't want the school to have formal disciplinary procedures. I believe they are necessary. Often they will be a useful tool in helping Robbie and his peers develop their own self-discipline. Individuals need to learn that society reckons some activities are unacceptable. But society's systems must also examine themselves. They must consider how they encourage individuals to act unacceptably, or how they make it inevitable that an individual's natural actions will be deemed unacceptable.

I want Robbie and his peers to feel motivated, to be involved, to enjoy their education, and to have tasks with a challenge at their core. As they move through the system I want them to have a feeling of achievement and a growing sense of who they are. It is not just self-discipline that I wish for, but also self-understanding, self-identity, and an awareness of others and their impact upon them.

In line with the spirit of current legislation, I wish our schools to help all students to develop intellectually, emotionally, socially, culturally, physically, academically and personally within a genuine cross-section of the community in which they are growing up. In addition, I want my children to be given the chance to learn in the way that suits them best and to see others learning likewise. This way they will come to understand something never taught to me during my schooldays, that doing something differently does not mean being different.

A couple of weeks ago I was talking to Steve, the father of Leo, a young boy the same age as Robbie. Leo has Down syndrome, a hole in his heart, and a twin brother who shares neither of these conditions. Before the twins were even born the parents had been told by a leading consultant that there was nothing he could do to help them if they chose not to abort Leo.

Leo's parents understand all too clearly that the society into which he was born has very different expectations of him and his twin brother. They understand too that in all likelihood Leo will not live beyond his twenties. When Steve told me this, it initially felt like such a different set of concerns from mine. My bottom line is what will happen to Robbie when I am dead and buried.

Steve then told me about a friend of his, who was talking to him just before the twins' birth. The friend had said that all lives have a beginning, middle and end. The important thing is getting the middle bit right. Steve told me how this had made so much sense to him. It's all about getting the middle bit for Leo right. It's all about his quality of life. However long Leo is alive, his father wants him to have the best possible life that he can.

This is all most of us want for anyone. Where's the difference?

So here is my wish. I wish for my son to have the best possible life that he can. Will he?

When I look at Robbie, I am no more fearful that he will die before me than I am about my daughter dying before me. In either case, the pain would be horrendous. But, rational or not, my fear about them surviving me is different. I feel that the chances are that Isabel, like her mother and father before her, will find it relatively simple to make a place for herself in this community, but for Robbie I do not have that same certainty.

Will he be enabled or will we disable him?

I have seen how my sister was treated. I have also visited appalling, dehumanising places of care in this country and beyond. I do not feel that humans have changed as much as legislation and good practice may lead us to believe. My son is a very few steps from cruelty, from being teased and demeaned and isolated.

Robbie's best hope for a good quality of life must happen in a way that makes me irrelevant. He must have the support of his friends and colleagues in his community. He must be included in that community as early as everyone else. He needs to have grown within his society, to have a strong self-identity and a clear place that reflects that identity. And the great thing is, if he has those things, then when I'm not around it will seem like nothing out of the ordinary.

One of the recurring themes of this volume is the need to listen to the many different voices offering their experience of inclusion and exclusion. Jonathan Rix, struggling to make sense of the many, often competing, voices that offer perspectives on Robbie, his young son, shows us that listening can be a challenging process. But, as earlier chapters have shown, it is even more important to ensure that Robbie's own voice is heard.

CHAPTER 9

Changing the discourse on 'race' and special educational needs

Fernando Almeida Diniz and Khushi Usmani

In this article Fernando Almeida Diniz and Khushi Usmani make clear the lack of consideration given in Scotland, and in the UK more widely, to issues of race, particularly in relation to Special Educational Needs. They deliver a wake-up call to local and national institutions, and also to individuals, to detail and examine their own practices and to listen to those most affected by years of denial, the minority ethnic children and their families.

This article is an account of our attempts to influence the current discourse on special educational needs (SEN) in Scotland, from an antiracist perspective. After mapping the national context, issues and changing circumstances following Scottish devolution, we summarise some of the evidence that we [with Sophie Pilgrim] presented to the Scottish Parliament's Inquiry into SEN and assess the extent to which this is reflected in the final Report. More recently, we [with Vijay Patel] were invited to make a presentation to the National SEN Advisory Forum, chaired by the Deputy Minister for Education. Finally, we briefly mention a number of research and development projects that are being undertaken to promote practical change in service provision for children and families in Scotland.

It is sometimes suggested that Special Education is the very area in which discrimination, such as racism, does not happen and that where problems arise, these are just glitches in a well-resourced, well-meaning and equitable sector. Yet, we know that disabled children experience high levels of social control in schooling (Allan 2000; Watson *et al.* 2000) and that 'race' is a compounding factor (Ahmed *et al.* 1998). We also know that the construct of 'SEN' is itself enmeshed in competing arguments about social, political and economic forces that impinge on marginalised groups of children who match particular constructions of 'disability' or 'special needs'. The field remains deeply contested, even without introducing controversial issues like 'race'.

As in other countries, SEN has had more than its share of consultation exercises and national reports in the last decade. What is striking in all of these initiatives, as in educational research, is the continuing neglect of the issue of 'race'. Thus, the racialisation of policy and service provision has meant that the interests of black minority ethnic disabled children and their families have largely remained invisible in Scotland (Netto *et al*. 2001; Stalker 2000).

Immediately after it was established, the Scottish Parliament announced that its Committee for Education was to hold an Inquiry into SEN. Could this offer an opportunity for change or would it be yet another 'colour-blind' exercise? Would the spirit of 'devolution' make a difference? As we later said, when invited to meet with the Committee: *We are quite skilled at submitting written evidence; we are even more skilled at looking at documents that appear thereafter to see whether there is any glimmer of evidence of anything having been taken note of* (SP 2001: 124).

Adopting an antiracist perspective

Our involvement in this area stems from our personal histories of racial oppression as black people living in Scotland, as well as our professional experiences. There is a systemic under-representation of minority ethnic people in all sectors of public life, including the new Parliament. As two highly visible black professionals in education, we have witnessed the absence of fundamental progress in tackling racial discrimination in mainstream statutory and voluntary sector institutions. Recruitment patterns for professional training courses are a prime example of this; we are aware that there have been no bilingual educational psychologists admitted to Scottish University courses in the last ten years. This is hardly surprising, given that universities are only recently beginning to acknowledge the existence of discriminatory practices in employment and institutional life (Carter *et al*. 1999). The same applies to the training of teachers, social workers and allied professionals (CERES 2001). Meanwhile, the past decade has seen the rapid growth of a vibrant Scottish black minority voluntary sector, staffed by black professionals who have often left the statutory services; this is an issue that is rarely acknowledged as problematic. We are both active 'volunteers' in MELDI [Minority Ethnic Learning Disability Initiative], an organisation that was established to provide advocacy support to black minority ethnic disabled persons and their families because of the levels of institutional barriers that they encounter in their daily lives. It is perhaps interesting to note that we gained access to meet the Inquiry as members of MELDI, rather than as representatives of our respective employing institutions. The issue is one faced by other marginalised groups, i.e., one of overcoming institutional barriers within mainstream organisations to ensure that their 'voices' can be heard.

Key points in our evidence

Recognising the unique opportunity that we had to influence national policy, we were clear about the task ahead. Our overall strategic message to the Committee was that: *The discourses on special educational needs and inclusive education are themselves exclusive.*

They have failed to recognise issues of race and racism. . . . MELDI exists because mainstream services are failing to give due regard to racial, ethnic and cultural diversity in service provision . . . our success in removing the barriers for individual families . . . is also our failure (SP 2001: 120).

In essence, we were not there to argue for the 'special needs' of an 'Other' group of children, but to convey the substantive theme of the reality of systemic racism that had to be acknowledged before strategic change in developing racially inclusive provision for all in Scotland could be effected. A recent audit of Scottish research commissioned by the Scottish Executive (Netto *et al.* 2001) looked at the results of studies in housing, education, social care, health, criminal justice, employment and rural affairs. The report noted a number of common themes that ran through all the work:

- the invisibility of race in statistical data, policy documents, practice
- institutional and structural barriers to access
- racial harassment and multiple discrimination (including gender and disability)
- differentiated models of provision were needed
- cultural insensitivity in multi-agency working practices.

Strategic institutional change aimed at tackling discrimination on this scale, rather than the 'quick fixes' for single-issue problems, meant that we were proposing a rethink of the underlying conceptual framework that would determine aims and objectives for future initiatives. The framework we developed is presented below.

Conceptual framework: social justice

Almeida Diniz (1999) has argued that discussions of the interconnections between 'race' and SEN polices have been hampered by competing discourses that have often been conducted by different interest groups, in separate 'fora'. For instance, arguments about the educational performance of black pupils have centred on notions of 'underachievement', 'school exclusions' or 'bilingualism' and been conducted within discourses about 'antiracist education' or 'bilingual education'; rarely have links been made with discourses on SEN. Currently, the sole reference to issues of ethnic diversity is a clause in the legislation on SEN that states that learning difficulties that arise from the child's home language should not be equated with the legal definition of 'learning difficulties'. In our view, this approach is outdated and has spawned a spurious labelling of South Asian and Chinese pupils (rarely African-Caribbean or Turkish) as 'bilingual'. The effect of this form of thinking is that it has tended to trap black and minority ethnic communities in a permanent category of 'otherness', of fixed ethnicities and identities. Emphases on 'their' languages and cultures may also have deflected attention from the reality of racial discriminatory practices that have led to the misdiagnosis of the genuine barriers that some pupils experience in learning (Almeida Diniz and Reed 2001; Usmani 1999).

Given these disputes and the issues surrounding the murders of Stephen Lawrence, and of Imran Khan and Surjit Singh Chokkar in Scotland, we explicitly chose to advocate an approach that acknowledges 'racial oppression' as a force in Scottish society and the injustices experienced by black minority ethnic communities. We argued that the racialisation of social policy and practice meant that traditional notions of 'access' and 'participation' evident in mainstream 'social inclusion' and 'inclusive education' discourses were unlikely to command the confidence of black minority ethnic communities. Our framework for change was one underpinned by the notion of Social Justice and Human Rights.

Analysis and key messages

We pointed to the accumulating research evidence that demonstrated that Scottish social research, policy and public life had remained largely 'colour-blind' (see the other articles in this journal):

- educational research, including the vast investment in SEN studies has, this far, failed to acknowledge ethnic and racial diversity
- there is no national policy, ethnic monitoring or research data on the assessment, placement and performance of black minority ethnic pupils in SEN provision, despite the recommendations of the CRE report (1996)
- other systemic barriers in the delivery of statutory and voluntary sector services include the severe shortage of black minority ethnic and linguistically diverse professionals in the workforce, all of which have resulted in the marginalisation of families in accessing support services
- parents of disabled children were severely under-represented in making decisions about their children, had little knowledge of 'Records of Needs' and complained that professionals had low expectations of them (Almeida Diniz 1997; Chamba *et al.* 1999).

We suggested that in order to develop racially inclusive service provision, policy makers and agencies would need to develop mechanisms to ensure that:

- black minority ethnic communities are explicitly acknowledged and valued, their dignity and aspirations recognised and they play an active part in policy formulation
- services are designed to give due regard to factors of racial, ethnic, cultural, linguistic and religious diversity
- ethnic monitoring is implemented to assure equitable provision
- all professionals are committed and culturally competent to support diverse communities in Scotland.

Promoting strategic institutional change

Our purpose here was to offer some ways of promoting positive institutional change in practice. It was obvious to us that the agenda for change requires a long-term strategy but we wished to ensure that what was done was underpinned by clear principles. Rather than produce a shopping list of wants, we took the view that the Inquiry had to decide if and how it was committed to social justice in its thinking and the extent to which black minority ethnic communities, including disabled persons, were included in the Scottish education system and society

We concluded our presentation by stressing our view that, whereas much had to be done to change institutional structures and cultures, there was an onus on each of us to work towards achieving social justice: *Once the philosophy of inclusive education is entrenched in the education system, it will remove some of the barriers of racism. The difficulty is in people letting go of prejudice that gives them social advantage. We need to create a way of making people feel more confident in themselves, so that they do not need the social advantage and therefore the prejudice. Racism exists because it gives advantages to some people* (SP 2001: 129).

The report of the Scottish Parliament's inquiry (2001)

As this inquiry was one of the first to be undertaken by the new Scottish Parliament, the open manner in which the Committee conducted itself in seeking to deal with a deeply contested field of social policy is a significant change from previous encounters. We have welcomed the Inquiry's approach and have been heartened by its willingness to listen. In terms of the specific concerns that we raised, this is what the Report has achieved.

- It has not been hidebound by the terms of reference that appeared restricted to issues of the practice of 'integration'. It highlights the weakness of current policy in which there is a *'tendency to emphasise a discrete population defined as having special educational needs, with separate decisions about their educational provision'* (SP 2001: 2). Instead it makes a clear distinction between the latter view and its expressed preference for the concept of 'inclusive education', which it defines as: *Maximising the participation of all children in mainstream schools and removing environmental, structural and attitudinal barriers to their participation* (SP 2001: para.7). In our view, this represents a conceptual shift in emphasis from constructions of SEN and disability that resonate in alternative understandings of 'inclusive education'. Were the Scottish Parliament to accept the Report's recommendation, it would be a significant move and one within which issues of 'race' and 'ethnicity' would coherently fit.

- It acknowledges the existence of 'institutionalised racism' as a feature in special education, citing our statement about the exclusive nature of current mainstream discourses (SP 2001: para. 17), and states: *Racial equality issues are not given sufficient consideration and black and minority ethnic families are disadvantaged by insufficient information and an inequitable distribution of resources. There is a shortage of bilingual Educational Psychologists and evidence from MELDI indicates that schools are generally not inclusive of children's culture, background and experiences, or that of their parents* (SP 2001: para. 41). It recommends that: *The Scottish Executive should undertake systematic ethnic monitoring and ensure that this informs strategy* (para. 7, xix). Such an explicit acknowledgement is rare in SEN policy discourses in the UK, but it is in keeping with Macpherson's recommendation that: *There must be an unequivocal acceptance of institutional racism and its nature before it can be addressed, as it needs to be, in full partnership with members of minority ethnic communities* (Macpherson Report 1999: 6.48).

Both these features make for encouraging changes in the national approach, though we are conscious that achieving systemic change to meet the ideals advocated is a more challenging goal. Much more important is the fact that the Race Relations Act (Amendment Bill) 2000 now make such understandings of 'inclusion' a requirement. There are major changes taking place to promote social justice and inclusion across all sectors of Scottish society. But there are contradictions, one of which stems from the fact that the National SEN Forum has been charged to develop a strategic plan for future policy and provision. If 'inclusion' is a goal for all of Scotland's communities, shouldn't the development of an inclusive education system be the responsibility of the whole community? This is a development that will be watched with interest by all who are committed to developing a socially just society in Scotland.

In order to achieve an improvement in SEN provision for black minority ethnic children we have an urgent need for:

- data on the assessment, placement and performance of black minority ethnic pupils with SEN provision
- clear national policy and a strategic plan in relation to recent 'race' and disability legislation
- action to address the lack of black and bilingual professionals in schools and support services
- professional development for all involved.

We are now engaging with the Forum to continue the development of education policy and practice. MELDI is also undertaking research, development and consultancy work and has a number of Projects related to this topic.

Current MELDI R and D projects

Like other voluntary organisations, the work of MELDI is funded by grants from a range of funding bodies. Scottish Executive's 'SEN Innovation Grants' scheme has supported three projects that MELDI is developing in partnership with the University of Edinburgh, the City of Glasgow and other agencies. All the initiatives are designed to foster institutional change in SEN practice, within an antiracist perspective.

Project 1: Empowering Black Minority Ethnic Families of Disabled Children

The aim is to produce a multimedia training programme and resources that can be used by agencies to support families to access services for their children, within an antiracist family-centred perspective.

Project 2: Promoting Institutional Change in multi-agency work

The aim is to produce a self-evaluation 'protocol' to sensitise statutory and voluntary agencies to consider how their services give due regard, without discrimination, to racial equality.

Project 3: Promoting Professional Practice

The aim is to produce a training pack to sensitise individual professionals to the main implications of recent legislative changes in relation to services for minority ethnic disabled persons and their families.

Concluding thoughts

Two years ago, Almeida Diniz (1999) published an article in the *British Journal of Special Education*, calling for an open debate on the problematic issues surrounding the assessment and placement of black minority ethnic children in special education across the UK. In the intervening period, concerns about asylum seekers, refugees and racism have reached crisis proportions. Yet, little has been heard from leading academics, policymakers and practitioners in this field in response to the Macpherson Report or the Race Relations Act 2000. Our recent experience in Scotland gives some cause for optimism that things can change.

References

Ahmed, W., Darr, A., Jones, L. and Nasir, G. (1998) *Deafness and Ethnicity: Services, policy and politics*. Bristol: The Polity Press.

Allan, J. (2000) *Actively Seeking Inclusion: Pupils with special educational needs in mainstream schools*. London: Falmer Press.

Almeida Diniz, F. (1997) Working with families in a multi-ethnic European context. In Carpenter, B. (ed.) *Families in Context: Emerging trends in family support*. London: David Fulton.

Almeida Diniz, F. (1999) Race and special educational needs in the 1990s. *British Journal of Special Education*, **26**(4), 213–17.

Almeida Diniz, F. and Reed, S. (2001) Inclusion: the issues. In Peer, L. and Reid, G. *Successful Inclusion in Secondary Schools*. London: David Fulton.

CERES (2001) *A year on from the Lawrence Inquiry Report: lessons for Scottish education*. Conference report. Edinburgh: Centre of Education for Racial Equality.

Chamba, R. *et al.* (1999) Minority ethnic families caring for a severely disabled child. *Findings* (Ref 539). York: Joseph Rowntree Foundation.

CRE (1996) *Special Educational Need Assessment in Strathclyde Region*. London: CRE.

Macpherson of Cluny (1999) *The Stephen Lawrence Inquiry* (Macpherson Report). London: HMSO.

Netto G. *et al.* (2001) *Audit of Research on Minority Ethnic Issues in Scotland from a 'Race' Perspective*. Edinburgh: Scottish Executive Central Research Unit.

Scottish Parliament (2001) *Report on Inquiry into Special Educational Needs*: Education, Culture and Sports Committee, 3rd report. Edinburgh: Stationery Office.

Stalker, K. (2000) Supporting disabled children and their families in Scotland: A review of policy and research. *Foundations N90*. York: Joseph Rowntree Foundation.

Usmani, K. (1999) The influence of racism and cultural bias in the assessment of bilingual children. *Educational and Child Psychology*, **16**(3), 44–54.

Watson, N. *et al.* (2000) *Life as a Disabled Child*. www.esrc.ac.uk

Fernando Almeida Diniz and Khushi Usmani force us to question our assumptions about our attitudes, practices and policies. We are reminded that we must take time and step back so as to examine the assumptions underlying all that we do as individuals and within organisations.

CHAPTER 10

Has classroom teaching served its day?

Donald McIntyre

This is an abridged version of a chapter by Donald McIntyre. Given the importance of pedagogy in developing inclusive education we have selected McIntyre's discussion of how classroom teaching practices, developed over two centuries, are reaching the limits of their effectiveness. He highlights areas where change is essential and proposes a way forward.

Introduction: what is teaching?

Teaching is a relatively easy concept to define: teaching is acting so as deliberately and directly to facilitate learning. While *what* is done to achieve the purpose of teaching may be almost infinitely diverse, it is the purpose of these activities, not the activities themselves, which is definitive. Similarly, teaching of important kinds is undertaken in many different contexts and by many people in diverse roles. The concept of teaching has no implications for *where* or *by whom* teaching is done. It is only the purpose of the activity, that of facilitating learning, that is crucial to the definition.

This definition of teaching is of course a crude one, which might properly be the subject of various elaborations and qualifications. Yet the central truth that it offers is of much more than semantic importance, since it emphasises the point that, in a world where the importance of learning is beyond debate, nothing can be taken for granted about the importance of any kind of teaching, except its purpose of facilitating learning. Answers to the question of what kind of teaching is needed or is useful must always be contingent on answers to other questions, primarily about what will best facilitate the kinds of learning that we most want.

We have become accustomed to having various institutions designed for the facilitation of learning, and it is a matter of judgement as to whether it will be helpful to go back to first principles to question the value of any of these institutions. Two such institutions which each have a history of at least two or three millennia are those of *professional teaching* and *schools*. Arguments have certainly been offered, some decades ago, for questioning the usefulness of these institutions for the twenty-first century (Illich 1976. Reimer 1971). Yet the scale of the learning in which everyone needs to engage for twenty-first century living makes the idea of doing without schools look increasingly like a romantic dream. For the purposes of this essay it will be assumed that schooling is necessary, and that professional teaching is necessary to make it work. But it will not be assumed that schooling needs to be organised as it was in the twentieth century. On the contrary, this essay argues that a more significant issue concerns the dominant way in which professional teaching in schools has been structured during the last century or two, and it asks how well suited that way of structuring professional teaching is for the contentious and problematic tasks which schoolteachers currently, face. That dominant way of structuring professional teaching in schools is taken to be classroom teaching.

In raising this issue, the essay seeks quite explicitly to challenge current suggestions that the central issues facing schooling are to be construed primarily in terms of *teachers'* skills:

> Expectations of politicians, parents and employers of what schools should accomplish in terms of student achievement, broadly conceived, have been rising for over twenty years. And they will continue to accelerate as we take further steps into the information age or the knowledge society. [...] It is plain that if teachers do not acquire and display the capacity to redefine their skills for the task of teaching, and if they do not model in their own conduct the very qualities – flexibility, networking, creativity – that are now key outcomes for students, then the challenge of schooling in the next millennium will not be met.
>
> (Hargreaves 1999: 122–3)

While David Hargreaves' above diagnosis of the situation must be very largely correct, the argument here is that he, together with the British government, its Teacher Training Agency and many others, is wrong to suggest that the solution can be found simply through the further development of teachers' expertise. The general thesis of this essay is instead that, however hard teachers work, however sensitive they are to what is needed, however skilled they become, there are limits to what is possible through the classroom teaching system that we have inherited. Furthermore, we may be approaching these limits now, at a time when much more is being expected of schools; and so it is unlikely that expectations can be met except by going beyond the classroom teaching system.

The system of classroom teaching

During the last two centuries, and therefore during the entire history of public systems of schooling in most countries, classroom teaching has been the dominant form of schoolteaching. The most fundamental characteristics of classroom teaching are that a teacher is located in one enclosed room with a group – a class – of pupils for whose teaching he or she is directly responsible. Schools, on this model, are little more than organised collections of classrooms, with virtually all the organised teaching and learning being classroom based. Gradually, during the history of classroom teaching, there has been a trend towards classroom specialisation, with differentiation according to the subjects being taught in them: gymnasia, laboratories, art and music rooms, technical workshops of various kinds and latterly computer rooms. In general, however, these specialist spaces have been types of classroom, with the fundamental characteristics identified above, rather than alternative ways of organising teaching and learning. Libraries, and sometimes resource centres of a broader character, have tended to be the only places in schools other than classrooms designed for learning, but even these have rarely been designed for alternative ways of organising teaching.

Classroom teaching became the dominant pattern of schoolteaching in England after a long period of competition, in the first half of the nineteenth century, with the monitorial system, in which one teacher was responsible for the teaching of all pupils in the school, but only indirectly for most of them. Only the senior pupils were taught by the teacher, and they in turn were responsible for teaching their juniors. [. . .]

The dominance of classroom teaching has been such that, throughout the twentieth century, it was very widely taken for granted as the 'natural' way of organising teaching and schooling. It clearly has very considerable merits as a way of organising schooling, from both managerial and pedagogical perspectives. Managerially, it makes the individual teacher unambiguously responsible for the teaching and learning in his or her classroom; it allows pupils to be categorised tidily and allocated to teachers according to whatever variables are deemed appropriate: age, prior attainments, general or subject-specific ability, and/or course, and it allows teachers and/or classes to be matched with appropriate rooms.

Pedagogically, Hamilton (1986) informs us, it was attractive to early advocates of classroom teaching such as Adam Smith because it allowed direct two-way communication between the teacher and the pupils (currently known as whole-class interactive teaching) and because it allowed pupils to observe each other's performances easily and so encouraged emulation of the most successful. In some respects, it has also proved to offer a highly flexible framework for teaching, adaptable to group and individualised working, and to various kinds of practical as well as language-based activities.

Perhaps the key feature of classroom teaching as a system for schooling is that all responsibility for facilitating pupils' learning is concentrated on the individual teacher. Whatever has been decided or demanded by government, parents, headteacher, head of department or others has to be 'delivered' by the classroom teacher, who is unambiguously accountable for everything that happens in the classroom. This simple truth is, furthermore, not lost on the other inhabitants of the classroom: the pupils too learn quickly that it is the teacher who has total authority over their classroom activities and is responsible for facilitating their learning, which militates strongly against the development of learning activities not planned by the teacher (cf Holt 1969, 1971). As school effectiveness scholars are gradually coming to understand, the effectiveness of schooling under this system depends overwhelmingly on what the individual teacher, alone in the classroom with his or her pupils, is able to do.

Having been developed and adapted over two centuries, unquestioned as the appropriate way of delivering schooling on a mass scale, classroom teaching must be assumed to be the pattern for schooling in the future unless there are very persuasive arguments to the contrary. Here I shall aim first to understand something of what classroom teaching involves from the perspective of teachers themselves. Next, I shall consider some of the demands for development which schools are currently being asked to meet; and I shall explore the relationship of these demands to the nature of teachers' classroom expertise. We can then consider some of the possible implications for the future.

Life in classrooms

The above subheading is borrowed from the title of a book by Philip Jackson, published in 1968. It was one of the first and most influential of the many studies which, in the last 30 years, have sought very usefully to stand back from the question 'What ought teachers to be doing?' to ask the prior question 'How can we best understand what teachers do?'

One of the features of classrooms that Jackson noted was that they are busy and crowded places, which led to 'four unpublicised features of school life: delay, denial, interruption, and social distraction' (Jackson 1968: 17) and imposed severe constraints upon how teachers and pupils could work. Later investigators have picked up this theme of the complexity of classroom life. [. . .]

For example, the tension between 'covering' a set curriculum and preparing pupils for external assessments on one hand, and trying to teach for understanding or the development of autonomy on the other, can be a major complicating factor in teachers' work. Similarly, trying to ensure thorough learning while at the same time trying to 'sell' the subject can add to the complexity. And the ever-widening range of responsibilities given to teachers, for example for identifying pupils' special needs or possible symptoms of child abuse, or checking immediately on unexplained absences, makes classroom teaching an extraordinarily complex job.

How do teachers cope with this complexity?

It seems that, very rationally, teachers prioritise and develop sophisticated skills for dealing with priority aspects of their task. [. . .] Teachers must, to survive with any degree of satisfaction, be able to deal with the unpredictable, immediate, public, simultaneous, multidimensional demands of classroom life in ways that win and maintain some respect from their pupils, their colleagues, their managers and themselves. What precisely that means will vary according to the particular context, including for example the age of the pupils and whether they have come willingly to school. [. . .]

The sophisticated skills that teachers develop for dealing with classroom life are far from adequately understood. This is partly due to the inherent isolation of traditional classroom life: the teacher, alone in the classroom, has to make things happen and has to deal with what happens. Unlike the doctor, the lawyer, the engineer or the architect, the teacher cannot discuss with colleagues most of the priority decisions that need to be made before making them; and, to judge from teachers' practice, there seems little point in discussing them afterwards. Since there is no apparent point in talking about their classroom expertise, the inherently tacit nature of that expertise is compounded by the lack of need to articulate it. Many commentators have remarked on teachers' lack of any specialist language for discussing their work. Jackson, for example, noted that 'when teachers talk together, almost any reasonably intelligent adult can listen in and comprehend what is being said' (Jackson 1968: 143). It is only in recent years, therefore, that researchers have begun to find out, through purposeful investigation, something of the nature of teachers' expertise. [. . .]

Expert teaching seems then to involve the use of complex schemata of diverse kinds, developed through experience, through which teachers intuitively recognise typical situations or pupils and relate these to what they themselves want to achieve and to the ways they have learned to achieve these goals. They are able, from the vast amount of information constantly available, both to filter out irrelevant information and to use the relevant information in highly efficient ways. It is not of course simply a matter of teaching various *types* of lessons to different *types* of pupils, using appropriate *types* of activities and making appropriate *types* of reaction to whatever *types* of situation arise: each lesson, each pupil, each activity, each situation and each reaction is unique. Part of the importance of thinking intuitively seems to be that instead of recognising examples of formally defined categories and then responding to 'the type', experienced teachers generally appear to recognise situations or pupils as being 'like' others that they have encountered in the past. They seem to be guided by their past experience both in being able to tune in to the general nature of the situation and also in knowing which distinctive features of the unique new situation need to be taken into account.

Studies of teachers' thinking while engaged in interactive teaching (e.g. Brown and McIntyre 1993; Cooper and McIntyre 1996) consistently suggest that teachers take account of a very large number of situational and pupil factors in making classroom choices about how to go about achieving their purposes, and also in judging what standards are appropriate in assessing how well things go. For each of the many 'decisions' that teachers appear to make almost instantaneously in the course of most lessons, there are likely to be several factors involved. Many of these factors are elements of teachers' knowledge about their pupils, both individually and as groups: for example, how able, attentive, confident, tenacious or mature they are. Other factors relate to the current state of pupils, as observed by the teacher: for example, whether they are excited, tired, bored, bewildered or enthusiastic. In addition, there are a wide variety of other conditions of which teachers take account, including their own stable or temporary characteristics (e.g. expertise, tiredness), the availability of accommodation, equipment, materials and time, characteristics of the content of the lesson, the weather, and other things going on. [. . .]

Teachers are not, of course, engaged in interactive teaching all the time. They also spend a good deal of time planning for their teaching, making and recording assessments of students' work, and preparing materials. One might expect their thinking to be very different in these quite different circumstances, when they are away from their pupils. That does indeed seem to be the case, but experienced teachers' planning does not contrast with the intuitive nature of their classroom decision-making to the extent that it approximates to the widely prescribed 'rational planning model'. Far from focusing first on desired outcomes and then planning how to attain them, experienced (and novice) teachers' planning seems generally to focus first and most on teaching content and on pupil activities, to involve a cyclical process through which initial ideas are gradually developed, and to be heavily dependent on visualisation of the intended teaching activity in the specific context of their own classrooms (Clark and Peterson 1986): a feel for the situation is apparently very important in preactive teacher thinking also. Significant too is the consistent research finding that, among the many kinds of planning in which teachers regularly engage, 'lesson planning is rarely claimed as an important part of the repertoire of experienced teachers' (*Ibid.*, 262). Presumably, given that one has a general idea of how the lesson will fit into longer-term plans, the unpredictability of classroom life makes dependence on one's interactive skills a more fruitful and flexible way of dealing with detailed aspects of a lesson than planning in advance; this is another way of prioritising what is important. [. . .]

The argument in summary

Research on the nature of expert classroom teaching suggests that expert classroom teachers are highly impressive in the complexity of the information that they constructively take into account in order to achieve their purposes. Their expertise seems exceptionally well tuned to the realities of classroom teaching. It involves:

(1) very sophisticated, experience-based schemata;
(2) highly intuitive judgements and decision-making;
(3) largely tacit, individual and quite private expert knowledge;
(4) prioritisation and simplification geared to teaching purposes, for example, through
   ● short-term perspectives
   ● working within classroom walls
   ● simplification of differences among pupils
   ● practicality.

Some limitations of current classroom teaching

Having developed as a very distinctive type of expertise over the last two centuries, classroom teaching is at its best very good at doing certain kinds of things, less good at others. Of course, not all good classroom teaching is the same: most strikingly, classrooms for different age-groups tend to be very different. The early years classroom, in which the teacher is not only with the same class throughout the school day, but also aspires to the multifaceted development of each 'whole child', is very different from the narrowly focused A-level classroom in which the teacher's expertise may be directed solely towards examination success. But these are, it is claimed, variations on a central theme: classroom teaching, with one adult figure responsible for the learning of a substantial number of young people within one large room for substantial periods of time, has its distinctive strengths and limitations.

Its strengths, as already argued, are reflected in its total and virtually unchallenged dominance of schooling throughout the twentieth century. It has allowed mass schooling on an unprecedented scale not only to be possible but also to achieve enormous success: it has kept millions of young people of ever-increasing ages off the labour market and generally peaceful and law-abiding; and it has enabled most of them to be literate, numerate and to acquire diverse qualifications and knowledge which have allowed them more or less to thrive in societies that have been changing at an accelerating rate.

None the less, it is the limitations of this classroom teaching system which are most frequently commented upon. [...] Many of the complaints made about the inadequacies of schoolteaching in recent years can best be understood as complaints about teachers' failure to take account in their teaching of various kinds of information or evidence. These complaints are therefore seen as fundamental challenges to the sophisticated kind of classroom expertise upon which teachers have learned to depend, with its emphasis on the intuitive and the tacit, on prioritisation and on simplification. It is not suggested that it is impossible for classroom teachers to respond to any such demands: there is plenty of evidence that classroom teaching is, within limits, quite flexible, and that classroom teachers can, when motivated by strong convictions or pressures, adapt their teaching to take account of new kinds of information. It is suggested, however, that classroom teaching is not at all well suited as a system to meeting the demand that all these multiple kinds of information should be used by teachers. It is further suggested, therefore, that it is this unsuitability of classroom teaching as a system that has led teachers to be generally unresponsive to these demands and complaints, even though the use of each of these kinds of information can plausibly be argued to contribute to increased teaching effectiveness.

Four ways have already been discussed in which classroom teachers characteristically make their task more manageable by prioritising, and simplifying, the information available to them. Each of these has brought with it complaints and demands for change from critics who believe that pupils' learning could be more effectively facilitated if such prioritisation and simplification were avoided. On the other hand, informed observers might reasonably argue that, unfortunate as it is that teachers do not make fuller use of the wider range of information potentially available to them, neglect of that information is a reasonable price to pay for the benefits of skilled classroom teaching. However, if it is the case that mounting complaints of diverse kinds are all to be understood as consequences of the complexity of classroom life and of teachers' best efforts to cope with it, then it might seem that the balance of the argument has swung against the classroom system, and that the costs to be paid for continuing to rely upon it are too great. The focus of the essay now turns to five major areas of concern:

(1) differentiation;
(2) formative assessment;
(3) home-school partnership;
(4) students' own perspectives;
(5) teaching as an evidence-based profession.

These will be examined in turn below.

Differentiation

Teachers widely depend on notions of 'general ability' in their classroom teaching. They do so in varying the materials they use, the tasks they set, the questions they ask, the explanations they offer and the standards they set, according to the perceived needs of pupils of differing abilities. Although strongly opposed by many commentators because of its oversimplifying dependence on 'general ability' (e.g. Hart 1996, 1998), such differentiation tends to be officially encouraged in the UK, both by politicians and by Her Majesty's Inspectorate, as a realistic way of taking account of differences among pupils. Alongside such encouragement, however, come repeated complaints that teachers do not differentiate adequately among their pupils.

Both inspectors and researchers have sought to judge the adequacy with which teachers vary tasks to take account of differences in ability (HMI 1978; Bennett *et al.* 1984; Simpson 1989), and have with some consistency concluded that, both for more able and for less able pupils, tasks are often poorly matched to student needs. Teachers, it appears from these studies, tend in practice to overestimate the capabilities of children whom they see as 'less able' and to underestimate the capabilities of pupils whom they see as 'more able'.

Why does this happen? The researcher who was conducting one of these studies (Simpson 1989) fed her findings back to the primary school teachers involved and asked them to comment. The teachers agreed that the tasks they set probably, did over- and underestimate pupils' capabilities as the research report suggested, and commented as follows.

(1) There were limits to the number of different groups or distinctive individuals with which they could cope at any one time.

(2) Having a wide spread of ability in their classes was greatly preferable for both teachers and children to grouping children into classes according to ability.

(3) Whereas the study had been concerned only with children's 'academic' needs, it was also important to cater for their diverse social and emotional needs.

(4) They deliberately gave special attention and extra resources to the lower ability pupils, because their need for teaching help was greater.

(5) More able children in the classroom were a valuable resource in that they offered models of effective learning and problem-solving which could help the learning of the other children.

(6) It was more useful for children's education to be broadened than for them to 'shoot ahead' of their peers; however, the provision of breadth depended on the availability of appropriate resources and time.

(7) While the research had concentrated on number and language tasks, it was necessary to provide a wide curriculum.

(8) If able children appeared to be over-practising, it was almost certainly related to the teachers' concern to ensure that the basic skills had been thoroughly mastered; the teachers had to be mindful of the prerequisites for the children's learning with the next teacher, the next stage of the curriculum, or the next school to which they were going.

The problem, these teachers suggest, is not with teachers' knowledge of the different learning needs of different children, nor even with finding ways of catering for these needs. The problem is that the careful professional prioritisation which is necessary in dealing with the complexity of classroom teaching involves the simplification or neglect of much available information, with the inevitable consequence that interested parties whose priorities are different from those of the teachers will, to some extent, be disappointed. We must recognise, they are telling us, the limits of what is possible through classroom teaching.

Formative assessment

In the last few years, the concept of differentiation seems to some extent to have been replaced as a solution to the problems of classroom teaching, as offered for example in inspection reports, by that of formative assessment. Here the focus is less on stable differences among children and more on the use of information about their current individual achievements and problems, as discovered through their teachers' assessments, to guide their future learning. Unlike assessment for other purposes, for this purpose 'the aspiration is that assessment should become fully integrated with teaching and learning, and therefore part of the educational process rather than a "bolt-on" activity' (James 1998: 172).

Formative assessment is a much less contentious idea than differentiation by ability, and indeed it is difficult to find any cases of people arguing against it. It is such an obviously sensible idea that academic commentators have been queuing up for around 30 years to commend it to teachers (e.g. McIntyre 1970; Scriven 1967). It has recently been given new impetus and importance by an authoritative review of research in the field by Black and Wiliam (1998), whose main conclusion is 'The research reported here shows conclusively that formative assessment does improve learning. The gains in achievement appear to be quite considerable . . . among the largest ever reported for educational interventions.' They also report, however, that there is 'extensive evidence to show that present levels of practice in this aspect of teaching are low' (*Ibid.*).

Why is it that, despite 30 years of propaganda, teachers appear to make little use of formative assessment in their classroom practice? Is it, as Black and Wiliam suggest, because there has not been sufficient external encouragement and support for such good practice? A more plausible hypothesis might be that regular effective formative assessment so adds to the complexity of classroom teaching as to make it an impracticable option for teachers. [. . .] Torrance and Pryor (1998: 151) conclude that the impact of formative assessment is 'complex, multifaceted, and is not necessarily always as positive as might be intended by teachers and as some advocates of formative assessment would have us believe'. They describe two ideal types of classroom assessment. *Convergent assessment*, which is 'routinely accomplished', is characterised by 'analysis of the interaction of the child and the curriculum from the point of view of the curriculum' and is close to what is done in much current classroom assessment practice. *Divergent assessment*, which 'emphasises the learner's understanding rather than the agenda of the assessor', is 'aimed at prompting pupils to reflect on their own thinking (or) focusing on . . . aspects of learners' work which yield insights into their current understanding' and 'accepts the complexity of formative assessment'. Developed instances of divergent assessment were found to be rare, to derive from 'ideological commitments to a "child-centred approach" and [to be] not necessarily as well structured as they could and (we would argue) should be'. While Torrance and Pryor consider that both types of classroom assessment have their place, they suggest that 'divergent assessment is the more interesting approach, and the one that seems to offer more scope for positively affecting children's learning' (*Ibid.*, 154); and they go on to make more detailed suggestions about how the quality of formative assessment may be improved.

Increasingly, then, researchers seem to be able to provide teachers with detailed guidance – about how they can use formative assessment in ways that will contribute significantly to their students' effective learning. There is, however, a problem: all the advice offered by Black and Wiliam and by Torrance and Pryor to teachers seems to involve sustained, high quality, non-routine interaction – either orally or in writing – between the teacher and either individual students or small groups. How far does this advice take account of the complexity of classroom life, and of the sophisticated ways in which expert teachers have learned to work effectively in classrooms through rigorous prioritisation, simplification and intuitive decision-making? We can have a good deal of confidence in the validity of these researchers' conclusions that it is feedback from, and interaction with, teachers of the kinds they suggest which can best facilitate pupils' learning. What may well be doubted is that the current lack of frequency of such practices in classrooms is a consequence of teachers' ignorance or lack of understanding of what would be valuable, or the lack of external encouragement. On the contrary, it would seem much more likely that, sensing that effective formative assessment depends on such unrealistic, high-quality engagement with individual pupils, teachers do not attempt widely to build such assessment into their classroom teaching. Current efforts to encourage and support teachers in the fuller and more effective use of formative assessment may prove this wrong, and show instead that the researchers' insights into good classroom practice are far ahead of the insights of most teachers. However, a more plausible expectation would be that the researchers' guidance will founder on their failure to take account of the real constraints imposed by classroom teaching as a system.

The point of the argument is not, of course, that we must resign ourselves to the present levels of effectiveness achieved by classroom teaching. It is instead that, if our schooling system is to become substantially more effective, through for example taking account of new insights into the effective use of formative assessment, this improvement may depend on a questioning of the system of classroom teaching which we have learned to take for granted. It would be wrong to leave this section without noting that James, Black and Wiliam, and Torrance and Pryor offer some seeds of ideas about what such questioning might lead to, ideas to which I shall return.

Home–school partnership

British traditions of schooling have involved very limited levels of collaboration between the school and the home. Throughout the twentieth century, however, there has been a sustained critique of these traditions from progressive educational thinkers, including increasing numbers of teachers, especially in primary schools. They argue that 'meaningful' education of 'the whole child' depends, among other things, on children's experience of continuity across the home–school divide. The most important assault on the separation of schooling from home life came in the 1960s when successive studies, culminating in the Plowden Report (1967), demonstrated very clearly that children's progress and success throughout schooling were closely related to the nature of their home background. Although initially these research findings were often interpreted rather naively as showing a simple causal relationship between home characteristics and educational success, even this led to calls for closer home–school relationships aimed at encouraging parents to take greater interest in their children's school learning and to become more involved in the work of the school. Subsequent thinking, much influenced by the powerful theoretical contributions of Bourdieu (especially Bourdieu and Passeron 1977) and of Bernstein (1970, 1975) and by research such as that of Tizard and Hughes (1984), has increasingly construed the problem not in terms of the deficiencies of working-class homes but as resulting from the gap between the home lives of many children and their school experiences. Accordingly it has emphasised the need for schools to work in partnership with parents, the primary educators of their children, in order to bridge that gap.

What is most needed, it has been argued, most forcibly by Atkins and Bastiani (1988), is for teachers to listen to parents. Teachers' classroom practice, it is suggested, can be made much more effective if they have the benefit of parents' authoritative insights into their children's lives away from school: their interests, their talents, their achievements, their aspirations and their learning needs. The argument is surely persuasive, since parents have much more opportunity, and generally more motivation, to understand their own children than teachers can have, especially secondary school teachers who are weekly teaching over a hundred students. Yet there is very little evidence of teachers being motivated to listen to such valuable information. The opportunities created for such sharing of information tend, again especially in secondary schools, to be rare and brief, and most of the talking seems generally to be done by the teachers. On the whole, parents do not complain. They have for the most part accepted the ideology of professionalism and are ready to accept that teachers know best; and so they learn not to offer their insights about their children to a system that clearly does not want to hear them.

It is very tempting to be critical of teachers because of their apparent unwillingness to work in genuine partnership with parents, and especially because of their lack of readiness to take advantage of the information that parents could provide. But classroom teachers have to select and to use the information that they find most conducive to the management of many pupils' learning activities in a classroom. The information that parents can provide, based as it is on a completely different perspective, may not be easily usable by teachers. Randell (1998), in a study of different perspectives on students' progress in their first year at secondary school, found that teachers talked about the individual students in a largely judgemental way – the two dimensions of ability and hard work/good behaviour suggested earlier – whereas parents talked predominantly about their needs. Teachers, it seemed, found it difficult, and also perhaps of questionable value, to adapt their classroom practice to take account of the distinctive needs that parents perceived their children to have.

It may thus be the case that the information which parents think they call usefully offer teachers to facilitate their children's learning cannot generally be effectively used to inform classroom teaching. The problem remains that the progress made by school systems in recent decades in serving the more socially and economically disadvantaged half of the population has been very slow; and it seems highly improbable that better progress can be made in future unless schools develop more genuine and effective ways of working in partnership with disadvantaged communities and families. It is probably unreasonable and unproductive to continue to place the major responsibility for engaging effectively in such partnerships on individual teachers working within the constraining framework of classroom teaching.

Students' own perspectives

While teachers are for the most part supportive, stimulating and selfless in the hours they put in to help young people, the *conditions of learning* that are common across secondary schools do not adequately take account of the social maturity of young people, nor of the tensions and pressures they feel as they struggle to reconcile the demands of their social and personal lives with the development of their identity as learners.

(Rudduck *et al.* 1996: 1)

That is how Rudduck and her colleagues summarise what they learned from secondary school pupils in their extensive study of pupils' own perspectives on their schooling. In introducing their book, they also quote Silberman and agree with his dictum that 'we should affirm the right of students to negotiate our purposes and demands so that the activities we undertake with them have greatest possible meaning to all' (Silberman 1971: 364). Teachers are under increasing pressure not only to take responsibility for students' attainment of learning targets but also to listen to students' voices and to take fuller account of their perspectives on their schooling. This seems to be partly in response to a view that students' rights need to be more widely respected in schools, but perhaps even more because of a recognition that improved school effectiveness will depend in large measure on the creation of conditions of learning which take fuller account of what students feel and think.

One of the major themes in the research reports from Rudduck and her colleagues concerns the significance of pupils' sense of having some control over their own learning:

It was noticeable that when pupils spoke about work that they had designed themselves and that they felt was very much their own – whether project work in technology or work in art – they had a strong sense of purpose, strategy and goal. [. . .] Clearly, the meaningfulness of particular tasks is greater when pupils have a degree of control over the planning and execution of the work: they have a greater sense of ownership.

(Rudduck *et al.* 1996: 48)

However, pupils did not *expect* to have control over their learning. [. . .] The researchers describe too 'pupils who *wanted* to learn but felt that they had little control over their own learning' (*ibid.*, 46). Sometimes blame was attached to teachers, sometimes to their own past behaviour or absences, sometimes to other (disruptive) pupils, but rarely did the pupils feel that they themselves were in a position to overcome any learning problems they had.

In classroom teaching, it is the teacher who has responsibility for determining the activities to be engaged in and the learning tasks to be undertaken. The teacher can, of course, share this responsibility with pupils or take account of pupils' interests and felt needs in deciding what to do. Cooper and McIntyre (1996) found that the teachers whom they studied always took some account of their pupils' perspectives. They characterised the teaching they observed as varying from *interactive* teaching, in which pupils' contributions would be taken into account within the framework of teachers' predetermined plans, to *reactive* teaching, in which teachers were willing to take more fundamental account of pupils' concerns in deciding what to do. They found reactive teaching less common, and apparently more complex, since the teacher's plans depended on finding out and using information about the different perspectives of the pupils in a class as well as about the set curriculum.

Arguments that secondary school students are not sufficiently treated as partners in their own learning are highly persuasive, both in terms of their rights to have their perspectives taken into account and also instrumentally in terms of their commitment to learning. The lack of control which students generally have over their own lives in institutions that would claim to be serving their interests can indeed be seen as quite remarkable. Within the context of classroom teaching, however, the task for the teacher of treating students as partners while continuing to take responsibility for classroom activities and outcomes cannot but be seen as adding to the complexity of the teacher's task.

Teaching as an evidence-based profession

There has been vigorous debate over recent years about the usefulness of educational research. Although the obvious target of most of the criticism has been educational researchers, a much more fundamental challenge implicit in this debate has been in relation to classroom teachers. The aspiration of the powerful groups who have been promoting this debate – that teaching should be directly informed by research evidence about the relative effectiveness of different practices – gives research an importance hitherto undreamed of, but asks teachers to transform their ways of working. It asks that teachers should somehow integrate into their subtle, complex, tacit and intuitive decision-making the very different propositional kind of knowledge offered by research results. Teaching would therefore become a less idiosyncratic craft, and instead one informed by a standard but constantly developing set of validated generalisations about the consequences of using clearly specified practices in specified types of context. The Teacher Training Agency outlines this conception of teaching and research:

Good teachers relish the opportunity to draw upon the most up to date knowledge. They continually challenge their own practice in order to do the best for their pupils. They want to be able to examine what they do in the light of important new knowledge, scientific investigation and evaluation, disciplined enquiry and rigorous comparison of practice in this country and in others – provided such resources are relevant to their field and accessible. Many of the resources they need to do this are, or ought to be, precisely those provided by good research.

(Teacher Training Agency 1996: 2)

As yet there is a relatively modest corpus of such knowledge, especially in relation to the British context. However – and this is the complaint against educational researchers – this can in very large measure be explained by the neglect over the last 20 years by British researchers of the kinds of research which could have generated such knowledge. [. . .] There is no reason to believe that a useful body of such knowledge could not be generated. [. . .] Much more problematic, however, is the idea that such knowledge, if available, would be used by classroom teachers. The authors of the review of educational research commissioned in England by the Department for Education and Employment had some sense, on the basis of their assessment of current practice, that this could not be taken for granted:

Whatever the relevance and the quality of the research and the user-friendliness of the output, its eventual impact will depend on the willingness and the capacity of policy-makers and practitioners to take research into account in their decision-making and their actions. This relies on a commitment to the principle, an understanding of what research can offer, and the practical capacity to interpret research.

(Hillage *et al.* 1998: 53)

It depends on all that, but in relation to classroom teaching it depends much more on how such research-based knowledge can be integrated into the kind of classroom expertise on which teachers currently rely: the two kinds of knowledge are so different that this seems highly problematic. [. . .]

Summary of the argument

Having first sought to outline the nature of the expertise which teachers have successfully developed for the distinctive task of classroom teaching, with its considerable strengths but also with some limitations, my aim in this section has been to exemplify the mounting pressure on the classroom teaching system. I have outlined five major kinds of information to which teachers are increasingly being urged to become more responsive, but there is as yet little sign of this happening. In each case, I have argued that it is not realistic to ask teachers to take account of the additional information while maintaining the kind of expertise which has made classroom teaching a viable and indeed very successful system. I have emphasised that classroom teaching has been quite flexible as a system, and that classroom teachers have shown themselves to be highly adaptable; so it may be quite possible for highly motivated teachers to incorporate any one of these five demands into their classroom expertise, or to go a little way towards absorbing all of them. None the less, I am persuaded that the classroom teaching system is near to its limits, and that it will not be able to respond adequately to the accelerating 'expectations . . . of what schools should accomplish' (Hargreaves 1999: 122).

The argument here has been focused on the classroom teacher's position as solely responsible for what happens in his or her classroom, on the complexity of classroom life, on the teacher's need to find special ways of handling very large amounts and diverse kinds of information, and finally on the lack of realism in asking teachers to attend carefully to an accumulation of new kinds of information traditionally neglected. That is one kind of argument for believing that classroom teaching may have served its day. But we should note briefly that there are other very good arguments which could lead us to the same conclusion. One of these is that classroom teaching seems peculiarly ill-suited to most of the more exciting possibilities for using information technology to enhance the quality of learning in schools, as seems to be reflected in the very limited impact it has had on schooling in the last quarter century. Another might be that the very strong boundary which we have noted between classroom learning and learning in other contexts has been accepted for long enough, and that schools must, to enhance their effectiveness and usefulness, find ways of organising learning activities so that these *normally*, not just exceptionally, relate to pupils' learning in other contexts. More pragmatic arguments might emphasise the escalating costs of provision for 'lifelong learning' and consequent pressures for greater efficiency in schooling, or the likelihood that the shortage of well-qualified subject teachers in secondary schools will be endemic. The pressures on the viability of the classroom teaching system are of many kinds.

The way ahead

To offer a clear vision of how schooling might be more effectively organised than on the classroom teaching system would be as foolhardy as it is unnecessary. There seems little doubt that change via a new system will come, but – we must hope and seek to ensure – only gradually over the next 20 years. New approaches will need to be developed, tested, modified and perfected, preferably with the help of careful research. A major constraint will be the architecture of schools, very obviously designed for classroom teaching and very badly designed for anything else. So, as new approaches are tried and found useful, they will be built into the architecture of new schools and then, one hopes, found even more useful. The change should properly be piecemeal, but it may come about in relatively efficient, rational and well-researched ways under the control of professional educators, or chaotically and through a series of reluctant and unhappy compromises to cope with external economic and political pressures. If we are clear about why change is necessary and about the principles by which the changes should be guided, the benefits can be maximised and the pain of change minimised.

What should we be seeking in a new system? Some elements of what is needed are obvious and are already apparent on a small scale in changing patterns of teachers' work. The problems of the classroom teaching system may properly be viewed as resulting from an over-dependence on certain elements which in themselves have considerable merits. The aim must be not to abandon these valuable elements, but to achieve a new balance in which dependence on their strengths does not automatically lead to problems because of their limitations. There are at least four ways in which a proper balance will require radical change:

- *Especially in secondary schools, a very different balance must be achieved between students and teachers in terms of responsibilities for generating and using information about students' achievements and needs in making decisions about their learning objectives and activities.* The research on formative assessment strongly suggests that the improved learning which can come from formative assessment is most likely through students themselves gaining a thorough understanding of the criteria for effective learning, through them assessing themselves, individually and as peers, and through them having opportunities, encouragement and responsibilities for using the information from such assessment in order to improve their understanding and skills. Students, of course, have to learn how to do these things and how to take these responsibilities, and facilitating that learning must be an important task for schools; but while this move towards greater student responsibility is no doubt possible to some degree in classrooms, it seems much more likely to happen where the social settings more obviously reflect this shift in responsibilities.

- *A very different balance must be achieved between reliance on intuitive, tacit and private decision-making and on collaborative, explicit and evidence-based decision-making.* In all complex professional activities, as Dreyfus and Dreyfus (1986) and Schon (1983), for example, have argued, there is necessarily a heavy dependence on tacit and intuitive understanding and decision-making, just as in teaching. Classroom teaching is distinctive, however, in the scale of its dependence on such decision-making, with very little use being made traditionally of attempts to evaluate and synthesise available evidence, explicitly or rationally or collaboratively, as a basis for decision-making. The astonishingly wide acceptance of Schon's idea of reflective practice as an ideal for classroom teaching might reasonably be interpreted as a recognition of the rarity and

111

difficulty of such explicit consideration of the evidence and of the choices to be made for important classroom decisions. The need for a change springs both from the inherent merits of rational thinking and use of evidence for the most important decisions, and also from the current state of affairs where – as has been demonstrated – even expert, intuitive, classroom decision-making cannot take account of much of the evidence which could be highly relevant for facilitating learning. Already in recent years, a greater proportion of the time and professional energy of teachers has been spent on gathering information, explicitly analysing it, sharing it and discussing its implications with colleagues, and planning collaboratively for pupils' learning. The work of schoolteachers should move increasingly in this direction, with more and more decision-making being explicit, rationally justified and corporate, and with such decision-making being a larger part of teachers' work, while face-to-face teaching, though still important, will occupy less of teachers' time. As in other professions, teachers' capacities for expert intuitive decision-making must continue to be of great importance, but it should cease to be all-important. How it can best be used to complement more explicit decision-making is a matter that will require extensive research and learning from experience.

- *A very different balance must be achieved between exclusive decision-making by professional schoolteachers and shared decision-making with adults who are not professional teachers.* Schoolteachers have, and will continue to have, a crucial and distinctive kind of expertise for facilitating learning. However, partly because they have been fully occupied with classroom teaching, and partly in order to simplify their classroom teaching work, teachers have denied themselves a great deal of valuable information and insights, and have failed to develop vital shared understandings with others. A slightly greater proportion of teachers' time and professional energies seems currently to be being spent on collaborative planning with other adults who are not fellow-teachers. The work of schoolteachers should move much more in this direction, with increased consultation and joint decision-making with learning support staff, with parents, with community members, with employers and with other specialist professional workers: again, this will be possible only in so far as less time is spent in face-to-face teaching.

- *A very different balance must be achieved between the amount of pupils' learning done in classroom teaching groups and the amount done in other kinds of social groups and settings.* Individual work in resource centres, on work experience and other contexts has increased and should increase further, as should small-group work on joint projects and investigations in different contexts. Much of this work in contexts other than classrooms is likely to be related to diverse uses of computers and other modern technology. Teachers should spend much more of their time in planning and evaluating and in negotiating, with other teachers, with students and with others. However, they should continue to spend much of their time in face-to-face contact with students, individually and with groups of different sizes. Teaching – deliberately and directly facilitating learning – must continue to be their overriding responsibility.

The problem inevitably seems a good deal clearer than the solution. This essay has aspired only to offer a tentative formulation of the problem and some very preliminary ideas towards a solution. It seems likely that the changes needed will be of different kinds and different degrees in different contexts and for different groups of pupils, for example perhaps being much more fundamental at secondary school level than at primary. Much of the school-based research and development work of the next 20 years should be directed towards formulating and investigating possible solutions.

References

Atkins, J. and Bastiani, J. (1988) *Listening to Parents: An approach to the improvement of home–school relations*. London: Croom Helm.

Bennett, N., Desforges, C., Cockburn, A. and Wilkinson, B. (1984) *The Quality of Pupil Learning Experiences*. London: Lawrence Erlbaum Associates.

Bernstein, B. (1970) Education cannot compensate for society. In D. Rubinstein and C. Stoneman (eds) *Education for Democracy*. Harmondsworth: Penguin, 104–16.

Bernstein, B. (1975) *Class, Codes and Control, vol. 3*. London: Routledge & Kegan Paul.

Black, P. and Wiliam, D. (1998) Assessment and classroom learning, *Assessment in Education*, 5 (1).

Bourdieu, P. and Passeron, J. C. (1977) *Reproduction in Education, Society and Culture*. London and Beverly Hills: Sage.

Brown, S. and McIntyre, D. (1993) *Making Sense of Teaching*. Buckingham: Open University Press.

Clark, C. M. and Peterson, P. L. (1986) Teachers' thought processes. In M. C. Wittrock (ed.) *Handbook of Research on Teaching, 3rd edn*. New York: Macmillan, 255–96.

Cooper, P. and McIntyre, D. (1996) *Effective Teaching and Learning: Teachers' and pupils' perspectives*. Buckingham: Open University Press.

Dreyfus, H. L. and Dreyfus, S. E. (1986) *Mind over Machine: The power of human intuition and expertise in the era of the computer*. New York: Macmillan.

Hamilton, D. (1986) Adam Smith and the moral economy of the classroom system. In P. H. Taylor (ed.) *Recent Developments in Curriculum Studies*. Windsor: NFER-Nelson, 84–111.

Hargreaves, D. H. (1999) The knowlege-creating school, *British Journal of Educational Studies*, 47 (2), 122–44.

Hart, S. (ed.) (1996) *Differentiation and the Secondary Curriculum: Debates and dilemmas*. London: Routledge.

Hart, S. (1998) A sorry tale: ability, pedagogy and educational reform. In *British Journal of Educational Studies*, 46 (2), 153–68.

Hillage, J., Pearson, R., Anderson, A. and Tamkin, P. (1998) *Excellence in Research on Schools*. Research Report RR74. London: Department for Education and Employment.

HMI (Her Majesty's Inspectorate) (1978) *Mixed Ability Work in Comprehensive Schools*. London: HMSO.

Holt, J. (1969) *How Children Fail*. Harmondsworth: Penguin.

Holt, J. (1971) *The Underachieving School*. Harmondsworth: Penguin.

Illich, I. (1976) *Deschooling Society*. Harmondsworth: Penguin.

Jackson, P. W. (1968) *Life in Classrooms*. New York: Holt, Rinehart & Winston.

James, M. (1998) *Using Asessment for School Improvement*. Oxford: Heinemann.

Lortie, D. C. (1975) *Schoolteacher*. Chicago: University of Chicago Press.

McIntyre, D. (1970) Assessment for teaching. In D. Rubinstein and C. Stoneman (eds) *Education for Democracy*. Harmondsworth: Penguin, 164–71.

Plowden Report (1967) *Children and Their Primary Schools*. London: HMSO.

Randell, S. (1998) Parents, teachers, pupils: Different contributions to understanding pupils' needs? Unpublished D. Phil diss., University of Oxford.

Reimer, E. (1971) *School Is Dead*. Harmondsworth: Penguin.

Rudduck, J., Chaplain, R. and Wallace, G. (eds) (1996) *School Improvement: What can pupils tell us?* London: David Fulton.

Schon, D. A. (1983) *The Reflective Practitioner*. London: Temple Smith.

Scriven, M. (1967) *The Methodology of Evaluation*. American Educational Research Association.

Silberman, M. L. (1971) Discussion. In M. L. Silberman *The Experience of Schooling*. New York: Holt, Rinehart & Winston.

Simpson, M. (1989) *A Study of Differentiation and Learning in Schools*. Aberdeen: Northern College.

Teacher Training Agency (1996) *Teaching as a Research-based Profession*. London: Teacher Training Agency.

Tizard, B. and Hughes, M. (1984) *Young Children Learning: Talking and thinking at home and at school*. London: Fontana.

Torrance, H. and Pryor, J. (1998) *Investigating Formative Assessment*. Buckingham: Open University Press.

McIntyre hopes that change will be a gradual and thoughtful process but the outcomes he envisages are still radical ones. Students will need to become more reflective and knowledgeable about their own learning and educational performance. Teachers working with such students will do so across a wide range of situations and activities. This requires a new social context, in which there is much greater collaboration with other members of the school community. The resulting organisation, should it evolve, would be much more inclusive and one in which the voices of students are more influential.

CHAPTER 11

New technology and inclusion: the world (wide web) is not enough

Kieron Sheehy

Kieron Sheehy examines the value of Information and Communication Technology (ICT) to the development of inclusive education. He considers uses of the technology at the start of the 21st century and its potential for the future. He highlights the danger of new technology being used to recreate old exclusionary practices, underlining why we must evaluate every change in relation to the inclusion of all.

Those striving for inclusive education are working towards a situation of equal access and participation, within the educational system, for all children and young people. This vision is based on a human rights perspective in which students are

> Learning together in ordinary pre-school provision, schools, colleges and universities with appropriate networks of support. Inclusion means enabling all students to participate fully in the life and work of mainstream settings, whatever their needs. There are many different ways of achieving this and an inclusive timetable might look different for each student.
>
> (CSIE 2002)

Being 'digitally connected' is becoming a critical aspect of our educational and social experiences. Equal access to and participation in such learning experiences is consequently now part of inclusive approaches to education.

The relationship between inclusion and technology can be explored in many different ways. In this chapter we shall consider three interdependent aspects: the possession and usage of technology, the social inclusion that using technology might facilitate, and the learning opportunities and personal agency that were previously denied or are only afforded through new technologies.

The possession and usage of technology

The development of the internet and the arrival of the 'Information Age' have led to concerns that information poverty may become a new form of social exclusion. Consequently it has been argued that access to the internet should be seen as a basic right (Pavely 2002). Those unable to use and access new technologies will be placed outside key economic and social activities and there is evidence that information poverty will follow existing patterns of economic inequality in society (Webster 1995; Schiller 1996; Loader 1998, cited in Facer and Furlong 2001). In line with this trend disabled people have reported that the greatest barriers to their internet access are financial ones (Sinks and King 1998, cited in Seale 2001). There is a large overlap between social and educational inclusion.

> I think that computers are good and help you with school, but we are poor and cannot afford one. If I had one I could catch up with everyone, but it will never happen (Boy, aged 13, Rural Town Secondary).
>
> (Facer and Furlong 2001: 455)

Within schools computer ownership can become entwined with constructions of ability rather than being seen as reflecting material and cultural backgrounds that confer advantages.

> It's all the brainy ones … they're all on the highest table who have them [computers] anyway (Girl, aged 10/11, Rural Market Town).
>
> People who have the computers know everything – the ones who have got them at home. Sometimes they're boys and sometimes they're girls, but it's all the brainy ones (Boy, aged 11, Rural Market Town).
>
> (Facer and Furlong 2001: 458)

The way in which technology is used, and how it affects inclusion, cannot be disembedded from the culture which is using it. This is seen in comparisons of the different ICT practices found across different countries (Süss *et al.* 2001) and also the ways individual families exploit the same technology for different social and cultural purposes (Valentine and Holloway 2001). These influences have led to the advantages of 'the Internet revolution' as being seen largely as a middle-class phenomenon (Burrows 1999) and suggests that giving all young people access to cyberspace will not necessarily be a panacea for the inequalities of the material world. A simplistic notion of access equating with equality may, in fact, reinforce existing inequalities (Facer *et al.* 2001).

Thoughtful strategies, developed to promote social inclusion in relation to ICT and employment, take a broader view than access alone. For example, Brown *et al.* (2002) give the example of a 'social firm'. This not only designs materials that are accessible and relevant for potentially excluded groups, but also employs people at risk of exclusion, and distributes the learning materials freely, on and off-line.

The social implications of the internet

The Internet is transforming the way many people interact, allowing communication with people who would otherwise be unreachable, and dealing with situations that 'cannot be managed face to face' (Lefort 2000).

'Homepage culture' enables people to present and develop their own identities within an on-line community. A study of the homepages of adults with Down's syndrome showed that they were used to expressing multi-identities – 'identities that are the same and different as other people with Down syndrome' (Seale 2001: 352). The homepage authors had control over the social groups they wished to be identified with and how this membership was constructed. Such groups are based on interest rather than geography with people becoming producers and distributors of their own 'cultural products' (Kenway 2001), speaking for themselves rather than being spoken for.

This illustrates how new opportunities for communication and self-presentation might act positively. However, the nature of such benefits is not always clear-cut. In a project called 'Creating a Shared Learning Space' (Peck 1998), geographically segregated students with physical and developmental disabilities 'met', socially interacted with, and completed curricular tasks with students in a 'typical public school'. All their interactions occurred in cyberspace and the communication systems that the children used ranged from

> Typical 11 and 12-year old verbal and written language to symbolic picture communication systems. All students were able to work together by using the 'least common communicator', a system of symbolic pictures. This allowed students to engage with 'common curriculum units at levels appropriate to their . . . abilities'.
>
> (Peck 1998: 1)

The technology enabled a diverse range of pupils to work together for the first time and new avenues of communication were opened up, to the benefit of all concerned. However, the disabled students remained within a private special educational school, physically separated from their peers. One needs to ask whether such examples are moving towards inclusion or are simply novel experiences that allow segregation to continue. How this is judged depends to a large extent on the values one sees as underpinning technological development. For some, the internet is simply 'layering new inequalities over old' (Kenway 2001: 151), largely due to the role of market forces.

> There are massive efforts on the part of the internet's corporate owners to try to direct it to become a technique of marginalisation and control. [. . .] Pre-95 it was mostly referred to as an 'information superhighway': post-95 it was 'free shopping'. The effort is to direct people towards commerce or diversions such as pornography.
>
> (Chomsky 2002)

Yet, even against this backdrop the internet is capable of delivering opportunities for social contact between previously isolated people, and, through this contact, providing empowerment.

Sally Pavely (1999) posted the question 'What does empowerment mean to you?' to 'Usupport', a mailing list for self-advocates and supporters of people with learning difficulties. Nancy Pellegerino's reply indicates the power of ICT in relation to advocacy.

> I'm a Self-Advocate of People First of Massachusetts. Working with computers is a lot of fun and we can all learn from our own mistakes, we can all learn from computers, it's so easy to use it. I talk to people all over the world and learn from them as well. When I get upset I have people on line to make me feel good. We have people all over the world to talk to and it's great.
>
> (Pavely 1999: 38)

The replies Pavely received indicated that empowerment was about feeling in control of one's life, and getting support from others when needed, but in a way that allowed that control to be maintained. ICT could, and did, facilitate this process.

Disabled university students have reported positively on the use of computer-mediated conferencing (CMC):

> It allows me to communicate even when my face is very painful, and I can type at the speed that is most comfortable with as much rest as I need. Voice input is also available through the programme.

> The benefit of being able to contact such empathetic fellow-students by CMC is inestimable: it is possible to say things over this medium which would seem too trivial for either a telephone call or a letter, but I certainly feel better for saying them.

> . . . without CMC I would have given up my studies.
>
> (Debenham 2002)

For students with limited communication skills, technology can help to develop their skills while supporting independence and increased interpersonal contact in the 'real world'.

> Jacob is using different messages on his communication aid to interact with peers and staff. He is using a simple communication aid which allows him to take part in class language activities and to interact with his helpers to ask for things to meet his personal needs. His communication aid is set with relevant messages for different activities and situations. He uses it for turn-taking, joining in with simple language games and simple interactions requesting and responding. He is learning how to take part in basic social activities.
>
> (Walter 1999: 64)

The above examples suggest that ICT can facilitate social change at different levels, from cultural change, to empowerment and advocacy for groups, to supporting the beginnings of interpersonal skills for individuals. It is therefore important to explore the ways in which we can best develop these new opportunities for learning.

Opportunities for learning

The production of a skilled industrial workforce has been a significant factor in the history of educational development. It is no coincidence that the design of the school and classroom reflected the design of the factory. Children can be presented with pre-ordained chunks of information in a systematic way and passed along the 'educational conveyor belt' in 'age batches'. However, it is not difficult to imagine that this might change. Seymour Papert (1993) envisaged a future in which 'Knowledge machines' offered children a richer way of finding out about the world, one that is based on their own experiences and interests and presented through virtual reality. Virtual reality is a computer-generated environment. It produces a three-dimensional experience and the user is 'immersed' in it (Standen *et al.* 2001).

> A child who has grown up with the freedom to explore provided by such machines will not sit quietly through the standard curriculum dished out in most schools today. Already, children are made increasingly restive by the contrast between the slowness of School and the more exciting pace they experience in videogames and television. But the restiveness is only a pale precursor to what will come when they can freely enter virtual realities of animals in Africa or wars in ancient Greece . . . reading will no longer be the unique primary access road to knowledge and learning, and it should therefore no longer be the dominant consideration in the design of School.
>
> (Papert 1993)

Broadly speaking there are three 'levels' reflecting the ways in which new technology might influence educational practices (McCormick and Scrimshaw 2001; Twining 2002), and each has a different outcome in terms of inclusion. ICT can

- be used to make existing practices more efficient;
- move teaching 'beyond efficiency';
- transform conceptions of a subject.

Knowledge of these levels can usefully inform decisions about how we might best develop education with ICT.

1 ICT can be used to make existing practices more efficient

The production of assessed course work in secondary schools is an example of increasing efficiency. Course work needs to be of a high presentational quality and can be produced using a specified template and then automatically spellchecked.

Students can access a wider range of material, resources and people through ICT. This supports opportunities for all to engage with the curriculum. For example, through the use of simplified text versions of onscreen information, clear and consistent layouts and voice read options (Paveley 2002).

Students can control computer-based activities and programs via a variety of different 'input devices'. There exists a wide range of adapted keyboards, screens, mice or control buttons and voice-activated controls. Touch screens are particularly helpful when younger children are being taught (Dobbins and Bickel 1982, cited by Sands and Bucholz 1997).

Learners can also receive feedback on what they have done. This might be through a simple spellchecker or speech feedback. A speech feedback facility enables a computer to read out words on the monitor screen and has become established as a means of improving reading performance (Reinking and Bridwell-Bowles 1991). Optional speech feedback – where the spoken form of a word is available on request – is as effective for 7-year-olds beginning reading as traditional teacher-guided reading (Reitsma 1988, cited by Singleton and Simmons 2001). Programmes that combine speech feedback with a game format are enjoyable and motivating for children who have previously experienced failure in developing literacy (Singleton and Simmons 2001).

> [the programme] is easier to jump in and out of to support your class . . . Children can clearly see where they are going. It has action games to grab their attention . . . [the programme] has built in motivation.
> (A teacher describing a computer-based reading programme in McGee *et al.* 2000)

Such programmes essentially transfer existing pedagogical practice into a new format and use technology to provide immediate feedback, enjoyable activities and a degree of pupil control.

The Talking Computer Project (Miles and Clifford 1994) used 'talking computers' to read typed input produced by the children themselves. This more interactive approach appears to be highly successful in developing reading skills. In another study, 14 adolescents spent approximately ten hours working with their computers and eight of them recorded average gains of 13 months on a standardised reading test (Clifford 1999). Miles' and Clifford's (1993) studies have also shown that younger children with specific reading difficulties can make significant progress with this form of computer feedback.

Taking this interactivity a stage further are speech recognition programmes that enable all computer functions, such as opening email and word processing applications, to be controlled by speaking into a microphone. When word processing, the user's speech is recorded and written onto the screen for the child. Such programmes are readily available and increasingly affordable. Speech recognition systems have been found useful by people with a wide variety of physical impairments (Call Centre 1999). Voice recognition can also have beneficial effects in improving reading and spelling for students with specific and persistent literacy difficulties (Miles et al. 1998), and has been associated with improvements in self-esteem, and the use of more sophisticated language and vocabulary (Call Centre 1999).

New technology often acts in a prosthetic way by helping someone to complete a particular, existing task, rather than being an educational tool in itself. VICAID (Vocational Integration through Computer Assistance for Intellectually Disabled people) is a prosthetic system designed for people with severe learning disabilities. Furniss et al. (2001) explain that it is similar to a radically simplified palmtop computer, offering users pictorial symbols to help complete tasks, in supported employment settings. Its advantages are that it is responsive to the behaviour of the learner/worker and easily portable. One is able to access instructions at an appropriate pace and to obtain instructional prompts at a time and in a manner appropriate to the task and the user. Such 'prosthetic devices' have the potential to allow active participation in activities when people have yet to develop the skills to do so independently.

2 ICT can move teaching 'beyond efficiency'

ICT can significantly extend the horizons and value of an activity. An example of this is 'The Spike Net Story' (Ware 2002). Spike is a teddy bear who travels to schools in other countries. He keeps a record of his visits and logs them through photographs and on-line diary entries. This activity arose from a school's email work and has led to pupils contacting others around the world. Rather than using ICT to recreate an existing practice in cyberspace or simply to access traditional material electronically, the potential of communication technology is used to promote learning in more meaningful and interesting ways. It gives students an increased opportunity for involvement with their own learning and their world. Such activities do not necessarily always use ICT (Twining 2002), but ICT makes it possible for a more diverse range of children to engage with a greater diversity of approaches, as seen in the Shared Learning Space example mentioned previously.

3 Transforming conceptions of the subject with ICT

Some subject areas are defined largely by the technology that they use and hence technological change can have a profound effect upon them. McCormick and Scrimshaw (2001) cite the following quotation to illustrate this.

> Our current definitions of literacy are quite narrow: text read and text written, with some critical awareness of others' work, covers much of it. Multimedia, however, offers us many corridors to support communication, many corridors for success: music, speech, aural ambience, text, video, animation, graphics and symbols, a second language or more, synchronous or asynchronous time and more. It allows us this portfolio of communication possibilities individually, collaboratively, in private, in public, in the same place or in different locations. The problem this brings is of a need for a much broader definition of literacy, clearly now encompassing oracy and graphicacy for example . . . The problem for our curriculum is to decide which subsets of these multiple media we will encourage or how small a set we are prepared to tolerate and at which ages. Again it is because the rapid advances in technology have made so much possible that we are now faced with the unenviable task of deciding what is essential . . . Rather than striving for an increasingly elusive common agreement, perhaps we should simply recognize that multimedia has guaranteed diversity . . . A text-based curriculum built around individual endeavour would arguably produce dysfunctional learners in a technological world, which is a highly controversial conclusion to emerge from the promise of multimedia technology.
> (Heppell 1998: 8–9, cited by McCormick and Scrimshaw 2001: 48)

By transforming the nature of 'what counts' within a subject area and as subject knowledge, a diversity of experiences, methods of communicating and learning become constructed and accepted. This has the potential to produce situations in which teachers and students work together in new ways and can accommodate a diverse range of learners and ways of learning.

As we have seen, technological practices cannot be easily disembedded from the society in which they arise. By using technology to carry out traditional 'Industrial Age' practices more efficiently it is easy for us to recreate non-inclusive pedagogical practices. Inclusive pedagogy is not about giving people access to situations that recreate inequalities. Rather, inclusive pedagogy should build upon a different model of learning and knowledge. I suggest that inclusion is best served through constructivist pedagogy and that ICT offers a way forward in developing this. The Centre of Applied Special Technology (1998, cited in Blamires 1999) proposes three principles of a 'universal design for learning' to support inclusion:

- representing curriculum content in different modalities (textual, auditory, visual)
- giving learners many ways of expressing and controlling their outputs (for example, digital image manipulation or multimedia projects)
- multiple options for engagement and motivation (including personally relevant feedback and appropriate scaffolding).

Again, these seem to arise more easily from a constructivist view of learning.

Currently, the potential of ICT is unlikely to be realised within schools. The rhetoric of inclusion, with its emphasis on celebrating difference and embracing diversity, clashes with the rhetoric of 'high' standards in narrow prescriptive curricular areas. The latter produces a particular version of ability, curriculum, learning and teaching that contradicts movement towards inclusion (Hall et al. 2002) Using ICT to increase the efficiency of this process will not develop an inclusive pedagogy.

> The process of transforming education for equity requires that teachers . . . understand and challenge the contradictions that underpin the notion of purporting to provide educational excellence through a vehicle (the current provision of schooling) which is inaccessible, founded on notions of competition, organized and resourced according to market forces, geared towards eliminating difference through standardised practices and assessment and informed by a view of education as narrow academic achievement . . . schooling, itself [becomes] a vehicle for perpetuating discrimination and inequality . . .
>
> (Lloyd 2000: 147)

This view contrasts with political voices that promote the internet, and ICT in general, as 'a means through which we can participate and contribute to a society in which learning is increasingly accessible and adapted to individual needs' (Blair 2001, cited by Pavely 2002: 44) but do not address the underlying assumptions concerning learning. We know that students have differing interests, learn in different ways and at differing rates, so why do we cling to a classroom design and curriculum that denies this? The need to bring students together, into the same physical space, for periods of time that are defined by administrative rather than educational needs will be increasingly challenged. If we are to develop inclusion through the use of ICT then a paradigm shift is needed, not simply in training and access but in our models of the curriculum and how children learn (Phelan 2002). We should use it to power completely new tasks rather than performing old jobs better.

Personal agency and virtual reality

In Virtual Reality (VR) the user is able to act in real time and get rich sensory feedback. In this sense it has the possibility to create an alternative reality. There are several features that make VR environments particularly useful for people with learning disabilities and physical impairments and that have benefits for all users (Standen *et al.* 2001).

(1) People are often denied real world experiences because their carers are scared of the consequences. In VR one can learn by making mistakes without suffering dangerous consequences.

(2) Access to real world environments may be limited or hard to arrange. For example the virtual courtroom provides an innovative solution to courtroom access and practice (Cooke *et al.* 2002).

(3) In virtual environments, rules and abstract concepts can be made comprehensible through additional language and symbol support. The key features needed to understand an environment can be highlighted.

These positive features might also be construed as reflecting real world goals and rights often denied to particular groups. We have a long way to move in developing these sufficiently in the real world and it will be interesting to see the extent to which the development of 'inclusive VR environments' influences real world design and access.

Skills developed in VR have been found to transfer to and improve subsequent real world abilities, for example in finding one's way around particular locations (Cromby *et al.* 1996). But while the use of VR to produce changes in 'real life performance' is an important and useful goal for some, to see it as its sole purpose will limit its potential and its possible value to users.

In terms of identifying the usefulness of VR environments for disabled people Rizzo (2002) writes:

> It should likely be assumed that success in addressing the goals for specific clinical group needs will be a 'never-ending' empirical process governed by a healthy mix of theory, psychometrics, philosophy and, for better or worse, economics!

(Rizzo 2002: 568)

In the past the discourses and practices indicated in this quote have often contributed to the segregation and exclusion of disabled people. There is, however, a growing awareness of the dangers of transferring old practices into VR environments (Cromby *et al.* 1996) and some evidence that teachers are feeling encouraged to use VR to facilitate scaffolded, student-centred, activities. Whether VR will act to promote, recreate or hinder inclusion remains to be seen.

Conclusion: We have the technology...

Over 20 years ago Cegelka and Lewis (1983) identified several challenges arising from the post-industrial age. These remain important questions for inclusion in the twenty-first century.

- How can we best reduce the dissonance between cognitive disability and the high-technology society?
- How can we provide a supportive environment to offset the effects of disability (*sic*) without denying the individual control over his or her destiny?
- How do we deal with the ethical issues of determining to whom to deploy limited fiscal resources?
- How can we ensure equity in access to technology and other advances to all members of the population, including those at the lower ends of the economic continuum?

(Cegelka and Lewis 1983: 71–2)

This chapter has indicated ways in which ICT is addressing the first two of these questions. The third and fourth concern social and political issues, from which a more complex view emerges. To be included in society will increasingly involve access to, and participation in, the practices and benefits derived from technology. We cannot reliably predict where the interaction of technology, inclusive ideals and our social context will lead us. However, if we are to develop an education system that benefits all of us on this journey then a paradigm shift, in how we think about learning, is necessary.

References

Blamires, M. (ed.) (1999) *Enabling Technology for Inclusion*. London: Paul Chapman Publishing.

Brown, D. J., Powell, H. M. and Battersby, S. (2002) Design guidelines for interactive multimedia learning environments to promote social inclusion. *Disability and Rehabilitation*, **24**, (11–12), 587–97.

Burrows, R. (1999) Reflexive modernization, wired self-help and the virtual middle classes. Paper presented at *Inclusion or Exclusion: Access to the Internet and Public Participation*. Virtual Society? 10th November 1999. School of Geography, University of Leeds, England.

Call Centre (1999) *Teaching Literacy Using Technology*. http://callcentre.education.ed.ac.uk/downloads/swbook/swbook11.pdf#11.3 (Accessed 24.01.03).

Cegelka, P. T. and Lewis, R. B. (1983) The once and future world: portents for the handicapped. *The Journal for Special Educators*, **19** (4), 61–73.

Chomsky, N. (2002) Interviewed by Hamish Mackintosh. *Guardian*, Thursday October 17: http://www.guardian.co.uk/online/story/0,3605,812886,00.html (Accessed 24.01.03).

Clifford, V. (1999) Using ICT to support children's literacy acquisition. Research seminar. Department of Psychology, Queens University Belfast. 9th December.

Cooke, P., Laczny, A., Brown, D. J. and Francik, J. (2002) The virtual courtroom: a view of justice. Project to prepare witnesses or victims with learning disabilities to give evidence. *Disability and Rehabilitation*, **24** (11), 634–42.

Cromby, J. J., Standen , P. J. and Brown, D. J. (1996) The potentials of virtual environments in the education and training of people with learning disabilities. *Journal of Intellectual Disability Research*, **40** (6), 489–501.

CSIE (2002) http://inclusion.uwe.ac.uk/csie/studnts02.htm#DefiningInclusion (Accessed 15.10.02).

Debenham, M. (2002) Computer-mediated communication (CMC) and disability support. *Addressing Barriers to Study*. York: TechDis. www.techdis.ac.uk/resources/cmc01.html (Accessed 24.01.03).

Facer, K. and Furlong, R. (2001) Beyond the myth of the 'Cyberkid': young people at the margins of the information revolution. *Journal of Youth Studies*, **4** (4), 451–69.

Facer, K., Furlong, J., Furlong, R. and Sutherland, R. (2001) Home is where the hardware is: young people, the domestic environment, and 'access' to new technologies. In I. Hutchby and J. Moran-Ellis (eds) *Children, Technology and Culture: the impacts of technologies in children's everyday lives*. London: Routledge Falmer, 13–27.

Furniss, F., Lancioni, G., Rocha, N., Cunha, B., Seedhouse, P., Morato, P. and O'Reilly, M.F. (2001) VICAID: development and evaluation of a palmtop-based job aid for workers with severe developmental disabilities. *British Journal of Educational Technology*, **32** (3), 277–87.

Hall, K., Collins, J., Nind, M., Sheehy, K. and Benjamin, S. (2002) *Assessment and inclusion/exclusion: SATurated models of pupildom*. Paper presented at British Educational Research Association Conference, University of Exeter, September.

Kenway, J. (2001) The information superhighway and postmodernity: the social promise and the social price. In Paechter, C., Preedy, M., Scott, D. and Soler, J. (eds) *Knowledge, Power and Learning. Learning Matters: Challenges of the Information Age*. London: Paul Chapman Publishing, 149–66.

Lefort, R. (2000) Internet to the rescue of democracy. *The UNESCO Courier*, (June). http://www.unesco.org/courier/2000_06/uk/connex.htm (Accessed 8.02.03).

Lloyd, C. (2000) Excellence for all children–false promises! The failure of current policy for inclusive education and implications for schooling in the 21st century. *International Journal of Inclusive Education*, **4** (2), 133–51.

McCormick, R. and Scrimshaw, P. (2001) Information and communications technology, knowledge and pedagogy. *Education, Communication and Information*, **1** (1), 37–57.

McGee, P., Day, T. and Sheehy, K. (2000) *Evaluation of 'Units of Sound'*. Commissioned research report submitted to Department of Education and Science. Dublin: DES.

Miles, M. and Clifford, V. (1993) Talk Back. *Special Children*, **68** (September), 38–41.

Miles, M. and Clifford, V. (1994) cited in Call Centre (1999) *Teaching Literacy Using Technology*. http://callcentre.education.ed.ac.uk/downloads/swbook/swbook11.pdf#11.3 (Accessed 24.01.03).

Miles, M., Martin, D. and Owen, J. (1998) *A Pilot Study into the Effects of Using Voice Dictation Software with Secondary Dyslexic Pupils*. Devon Education Authority. (Unpublished).

Papert, S. (1993) *Obsolete Skill Set: the 3 Rs*. [www document] http://www.wired.com/wired/archive/1.02/1.2_papert.html (Accessed 28.01.02).

Paveley, S. (1999) Advocacy and self-advocacy. In M. Blamires (ed.) *Enabling Technology for Inclusion*. London: Sage, 37–52.

Paveley, S. (2002) Inclusion and the Web: strategies for improving access. In Abbott, C. (ed.) *Special Educational Needs and the Internet: issues for the inclusive classroom*. London: Routledge Falmer, 44–52.

Peck, A. F. (1998) *Using Shared Cyberspace for Inclusion of Students with Intensive Disabilities*. [www document] http://www.jsrd.or.jp/dinf_us/csun_98/csun98_173.htm (Accessed 29.01.02).

Phelan, A. (2002) Inclusion through ICT: the wider view. In Abbott, C. (ed.) *Special Educational Needs and the Internet: issues for the inclusive classroom*. London: Routledge Falmer, 146–63.

Reinking, D. and Bridwell-Bowles, L. (1991) Computers in reading and writing. In Barr, R., Kamil, M.L., Mosenthal, P.B. and Pearson, P.D. (eds) *Handbook of Reading Research 2*. New York: Longman, 310–40.

Rizzo, A. (2002) Editorial: Virtual reality and disability: emergence and challenge. *Disability and Rehabilitation*, **24** (11–12), 567–9.

Sands, S. and Buchholz, E. S. (1997) The underutilization of computers to assist in the remediation of dyslexia. *International Journal of Instructional Media*, **24** (2), 153–75.

Seale, J. K. (2001) The same but different: the use of personal Home Page by adults with Down syndrome as a tool for self-presentation. *British Journal of Educational Technology*, **32** (3), 343–52.

Singleton, C. and Simmons, F. (2001) An evaluation of Wordshark in the classroom. *British Journal of Educational Technology*, **32** (3), 317–30.

Standen. P. J., Brown, D. J. and Cromby, J. J. (2001) The effective use of virtual environments in the education and rehabilitation of students with intellectual disabilities. *British Journal of Educational Technology*, **32** (3), 289–99.

Süss, D., Suoninen, A., Garitaonandia, C., Juaristi, P., Koikkalainen, R. and Oleaga, J. (2001) Media and childhood in three European countries. In Hutchby, I. and Moran-Ellis, J. (eds) *Children, Technology and Culture: the impacts of technologies in children's everyday lives*. London: Routledge Falmer, 28–41.

Twining, P. (2002) Conceptualising computer use in education: introducing the Computer Practice Framework (CPF). *British Educational Research Journal*, **28** (1), 95–110.

Valentine, G. and Holloway, S. (2001) 'Technophobia': parents' and children's fears about information and communication technologies and the transformation of culture and society. In Hutchby, I. and Moran-Ellis, J. (eds) *Children, Technology and Culture: the impacts of technologies in children's everyday lives*. London: Routledge Falmer, 58–78.

Walter, R. (1999) Developing social communication. In M. Blamires (ed.) *Enabling Technology for Inclusion*. London: Sage Publications, 61–72.

Ware, D. (2002) Spike the bear and an on-line special school. In Abbott, C. (ed.) *Special Educational Needs and the Internet: issues for the inclusive classroom*. London: Routledge Falmer, 65–72.

Kieron Sheehy helps us to understand the potential of Information and Communication Technology for the communication of ideas and the development of community and individual identity. But he reminds us that, regardless of the tool we use, our ways of doing things must always be underpinned by a genuine commitment to be inclusive. If this is not the case then exclusionary pressures soon build up upon one group or another.

Part 3

Looking from within: perspectives of learners and disabled people

CHAPTER 12

Social model or unsociable muddle?

Richard Light

This chapter is take from the Disability Awareness in Action website and provides a useful overview of the origins and evolutions of the social model of disability. It also highlights some of the tensions and controversies.

It is becoming increasingly clear that one of the key issues in disability activisim – the social model of disability – is subject to repeated attacks, particularly within the academic community. What is equally clear is that much of the 'bad press' has been prompted by interpretations of the social model that many of us would find particularly strange. As you might expect, academic discussion is often marked by both completely incomprehensible language and a startling lack of humility – each writer seems to assume that their contribution offers an invaluable new insight and that anyone who does not accept it must be hopelessly stupid or badly informed.

This article seeks to describe, in straightforward terms, what the social model means to a great many disabled activists, including those of us at DAA [Disability Awareness in Action]. We believe that it is time for disabled activists to remind academics that the social model originated with *us*, and that *we* still have use for it! Despite our concerns about harmful criticism of the social model, we wholeheartedly endorse attempts to offer a more comprehensive or inclusive social *theory* of disability. This article is not intended to condemn efforts to theorise disability and what it means, but it is a heartfelt plea for theorists to understand the damage that is done by sweeping claims as to the social model's shortcomings, without proposing alternatives that are acceptable to the disability community. We are in no doubt that repeated attacks on the social model, particularly where no acceptable alternative is proposed, cause harm. We hope that this article makes it clear why so much is at stake.

The origins of the social model

The origins of what would later be called the 'social model' can be traced to an essay by a disabled Briton: *A Critical Condition*, written by Paul Hunt and published in 1966. In this paper, Hunt argued that because people with impairments are viewed as 'unfortunate, useless, different, oppressed and sick' they pose a direct challenge to commonly held Western values. According to Hunt, people with impairments were viewed as:

- 'unfortunate' because they are unable to 'enjoy' material and social benefits of modern society
- 'useless' because they are considered unable to contribute to 'economic good of the community', and
- marked as 'minority group' members because, like black people and homosexuals, they are perceived as 'abnormal' and 'different'.

This analysis led Hunt to the view that disabled people encounter 'prejudice which expresses itself in discrimination and oppression.' The relationship between economics and cultural attitudes toward disabled people is a vital part of Hunt's understanding of the experience of impairment and disability in Western society.

The UPIAS definition

Ten years later, the Union of the Physically Impaired Against Segregation (UPIAS) developed Paul Hunt's work further, leading to the UPIAS assertion, in 1976, that disability was:

> the disadvantage or restriction of activity caused by a contemporary social organisation which takes little or no account of people who have physical impairments and thus excludes them from participation in the mainstream of social activities.

It must be acknowledged that the UPIAS definition of 'disability' only refers to *people who have physical impairments*, and the failure to include any other types of impairment has led some people to claim that the social model only applies to wheelchair users.

We would make two responses to such criticism: firstly, that the group 'people who have physical impairments' includes many people who are not wheelchair users. Secondly, and far more importantly, the statement was made by an organisation whose membership was made up of people with physical impairments – *how could UPIAS speak for any other group of disabled people*? The vital feature of the UPIAS statement and, indeed, Paul Hunt's 1966 essay, is that for the first time disability was described in terms of restrictions *imposed* on disabled people by *social* organisation.

The social model is born

It was not until 1983 that the disabled academic, Mike Oliver, described the ideas that lay behind the UPIAS definition as the 'social model of disability'. The 'social model' was extended and developed by academics like Vic Finkelstein, Mike Oliver and Colin Barries in the UK and Gerben DeJong in the USA (amongst others), and extended by Disabled Peoples' International to include *all* disabled people. So, while the original formulation of the social model may have been developed by people with physical impairments, the insight that it offered was quickly seen as having value to all disabled people. To suggest that the social model amounts to a conspiracy by one group of disabled people against the remainder is, therefore, either incorrect or mischievous.

The social model – an evolving idea

It is an inevitable aspect of human development that new ways of interpreting the world around us are introduced by an individual or, more often, a small group of people. It is simply the support and agreement of a wider group that transforms these interpretations into a social movement – precisely what happened with the African-American civil rights movement and feminism. As more and more people are introduced to these new interpretations, so the original ideas are questioned, argued over, developed and refined – precisely what happened to the social model of disability.

For those of us at DAA, the evolving nature of the social model, made possible by the interest it has generated throughout the disabled community, is a positive and necessary thing. Knowledge is always partial – the best that we can achieve at a particular time and place – but subsequent debate has ensured that the social model remains relevant to our lives, primarily because it still has the power to change dramatically the way disabled people think about themselves and their place in the world. What can be more liberating than the discovery that being disabled does not have to be viewed negatively – as some failure or weakness in us – and that there are people all over the world who feel a sense of community because of disability?

The social model and different impairments

DAA's work is driven by an *inclusive* view of the disabled community – defined quite simply as those people who choose to identify themselves as 'disabled'. We are aware that not all groups of disabled people adopt such an inclusive approach, sometimes using both formal rules and informal sanctions to discourage people who are not seen as belonging to 'their' group, but such difficulties are caused by the individuals involved, not the social model! The construction of the social model which DAA adopts defines 'disability' quite simply as: 'the *social* consequences of having an impairment.' It is unquestionably the case that using 'disability' to describe such a huge and very different group of people is difficult, not least because the label is artificial and because too much is usually taken for granted when the wider community talk about 'the disabled'.

It is also the case that all members of the disabled community have not had the same opportunity to have their opinions heard. Self-advocacy ultimately depends on individuals being prepared to advocate for themselves. Demanding the right to advocate for ourselves is a dynamic process, it is not something that others can give to, or provide for us (although the space and opportunity to be heard may). No matter how much disability advocates might want to be joined by under-represented groups within the disability community, this requires those groups to want to be part of the wider community. Blaming the social model for the undoubted shortcomings of the disability movement is, quite simply, unreasonable!

While the academic community may view it differently, for the disability movement the social model provides a way of thinking about disability that accords with our experience of being disabled people – that disability is caused by the attitudinal, physical and communication barriers imposed on us, rather than the effects of our impairments. Despite the artificial nature of the label 'disabled', this shared experience of external barriers allows disabled people, irrespective of their different impairments, to feel a sense of shared identity. Having a shared identity as 'disabled people' need not and, in our opinion, should not, interfere with our identities as people with specific impairments, nor should they cause some impairment-specific needs to be promoted at the expense of others. The disability movement can only remain strong and effective when we each respect the enormous diversity within the movement.

After years of campaigning and persuasion, the social model has offered a valuable and effective tool for helping people, disabled and non-disabled alike, to view disability in a way that does not put the 'blame' for disability on the disabled person. Disability equality trainers, activists and academics have used the insight provided by the social model to make a real difference in all areas of social, political and economic life. It is also true that the changes won by disabled campaigners are unpopular with those who see their authority, power and, in some cases, wealth, being eroded by social model ideals.

Theorising disability is important, but it's time that some of those who do theorise adopt a little more humility and understanding before making public attacks on the social model.

While Richard Light is not attempting to contribute directly to the debates on inclusion, his honest appraisal here is relevant to inclusion. When we theorise about inclusive education we should not shy away from forming and articulating our own ideas, but we will do this more effectively if we also listen to, and learn from, each other, recognising achievements and debates in other domains. This author writes from the multiple perspective of being a disabled person and someone with a long history in policy formation at (inter)national and regional levels. He reminds us that academic theorising can and does have an impact on real world struggles.

CHAPTER 13

Including all of our lives: renewing the social model of disability

Liz Crow

In this chapter Liz Crow, a disabled feminist active in the disabled people's movement, gives one of the clearest explanations of the social model of disability we have found. Her narrative is rich with discussion of the complexities involved as disabled people take charge of the debates about their experiences. The chapter had its origins in an article written for *Coalition*, one of the journals of the British disabled people's movement, before appearing as an extended chapter in Jenny Morris' edited collection *Encounters with Strangers: Feminism and Disability*.

My life has two phases: before the social model of disability, and after it. Discovering this way of thinking about my experiences was the proverbial raft in stormy seas. It gave me an understanding of my life, shared with thousands, even millions, of other people around the world, and I clung to it.

This was the explanation I had sought for years. Suddenly what I had always known, deep down, was confirmed. It wasn't my body that was responsible for all my difficulties, it was external factors, the barriers constructed by the society in which I live. I was being dis-abled – my capabilities and opportunities were being restricted – by prejudice, discrimination, inaccessible environments and inadequate support. Even more important, if all the problems had been created by society, then surely society could un-create them. Revolutionary!

For years now this social model of disability has enabled me to confront, survive and even surmount countless situations of exclusion and discrimination. It has been my mainstay, as it has been for the wider disabled people's movement. It has enabled a vision of ourselves free from the constraints of disability (oppression) and provided a direction for our commitment to social change. It has played a central role in promoting disabled people's individual self-worth, collective identity and political organisation. I don't think it is an exaggeration to say that the social model has saved lives. Gradually, very gradually, its sphere is extending beyond our movement to influence policy and practice in the mainstream. The contribution of the social model of disability, now and in the future, to achieving equal rights for disabled people is incalculable.

So how is it that, suddenly to me, for all its strengths and relevance, the social model doesn't seem so water-tight anymore? It is with trepidation that I criticise it. However, when personal experience no longer matches current explanations, then it is time to question afresh.

Disability is 'all'?

The social model of disability has been our key to dismantling the traditional conception of impairment[1] as 'personal tragedy' and the oppression that this creates.

Mainstream explanations have centred on impairment as 'all' – impairment as the cause of our experiences and disadvantage, and impairment as the focus of intervention. The World Health Organisation defines impairment and related concepts as follows:

> *Impairment*: Any loss or abnormality of psychological, physiological, or anatomical structure or function. *Disability*: Any restriction or lack (resulting from impairment) of ability to perform an activity in the manner or within the range considered normal for a human being. *Handicap*: A disadvantage for a given individual, resulting from an impairment or disability, that limits or prevents fulfilment of a role that is normal, depending on age, sex, social or cultural factors for that individual.
>
> (United Nations Division for Economic and Social Information 1983: 3)

Within this framework, which is often called the medical model of disability, a person's functional limitations (impairments) are the root cause of any disadvantages experienced and these disadvantages can therefore only be rectified by treatment or cure.

The social model, in contrast, shifts the focus from impairment onto disability, using this term to refer to disabling social, environmental and attitudinal barriers rather than lack of ability. Thus, while impairment is the functional limitation(s) which affects a person's body, disability is the loss or limitation of opportunities resulting from direct and indirect discrimination. Social change – the removal of disabling barriers – is the solution to the disadvantages we experience.

This way of seeing things opens up opportunities for the eradication of prejudice and discrimination. In contrast, the medical model makes the removal of disadvantage contingent upon the removal or 'overcoming' of impairment – full participation in society is only to be found through cure or fortitude. Small wonder, therefore, that we have focused so strongly on the importance of disabling barriers and struggled to dismantle them.

In doing so, however, we have tended to centre on disability as 'all'. Sometimes it feels as if this focus is so absolute that we are in danger of assuming that impairment has no part at all in determining our experiences. Instead of tackling the contradictions and complexities of our experiences head on, we have chosen in our campaigns to present impairment as irrelevant, neutral and, sometimes, positive, but never, ever as the quandary it really is.

Why has impairment been so excluded from our analysis? Do we believe that admitting there could be a difficult side to impairment will undermine the strong, positive (SuperCrip?) images of our campaigns? Or that showing every single problem cannot be solved by social change will inhibit or excuse non-disabled people from tackling anything at all? Or that we may make the issues so complex that people feel constructive change is outside their grasp? Or even that admitting it can sometimes be awful to have impairments may fuel the belief that our lives are not worth living?

Bring back impairment!

The experience of impairment is not always irrelevant, neutral or positive. How can it be when it is the very reason used to justify the oppression we are battling against? How can it be when pain, fatigue, depression and chronic illness are constant facts of life for many of us?

We align ourselves with other civil rights movements and we have learnt much from those campaigns. But we have one fundamental difference from other movements, which we cannot afford to ignore. There is nothing inherently unpleasant or difficult about other groups' embodiment: sexuality, sex and skin colour are neutral facts. In contrast, impairment means our experience of our bodies *can* be unpleasant or difficult. This does not mean our campaigns against disability are any less vital than those against heterosexism, sexism or racism; it does mean that for many disabled people personal struggle related to impairment will remain even when disabling barriers no longer exist.

Yet our insistence that disadvantage and exclusion are the result of discrimination and prejudice, and our criticisms of the medical model of disability, have made us wary of acknowledging our experiences of impairment. Impairment is safer not mentioned at all.

This silence prevents us from dealing effectively with the difficult aspects of impairment. Many of us remain frustrated and disheartened by pain, fatigue, depression and chronic illness, including the way they prevent us from realising our potential or railing fully against disability (our experience of exclusion and discrimination); many of us fear for our futures with progressive or additional impairments; we mourn past activities that are no longer possible for us; we are afraid we may die early or that suicide may seem our only option; we desperately seek some effective medical intervention; we feel ambivalent about the possibilities of our children having impairments; and we are motivated to work for the prevention of impairments. Yet our silence about impairment has made many of these things taboo and created a whole new series of constraints on our self-expression.

Of course, the suppression of concerns related to impairment does not mean they cease to exist or suddenly become more bearable. Instead this silencing undermines individuals' ability to 'cope' and, ultimately, the whole disabled people's movement. As individuals, most of us simply cannot pretend with any conviction that our impairments are irrelevant because they influence so much of our lives. External disabling barriers may create social and economic disadvantage but our subjective experience of our bodies is also an integral part of our everyday reality. What we need is to find a way to integrate impairment into our whole experience and sense of our selves for the sake of our own physical and emotional well-being, and, subsequently, for our individual and collective capacity to work against disability.

As a movement, we need to be informed about disability *and* impairment in all their diversity if our campaigns are to be open to all disabled people. Many people find that it is their experience of their bodies – and not only disabling barriers such as inaccessible public transport – which make political involvement difficult. For example, an individual's capacity to attend meetings and events might be restricted because of limited energy. If these circumstances remain unacknowledged, then alternative ways of contributing are unlikely to be sought. If our structures and strategies (i.e. *how* we organise and offer support in our debates, consultation and demonstrations) cannot involve all disabled people, then our campaigns lose the contributions of many people. If our movement excludes many disabled people or refuses to discuss certain issues then our understanding is partial: our collective ability to conceive of, and achieve, a world which does not disable is diminished. What we risk is a world which includes an 'elite' of people with impairments, but which for many more of us contains no real promise of civil rights, equality or belonging. How can we expect anyone to take seriously a 'radical' movement which replicates some of the worst exclusionary aspects of the society it purports to change?

Our current approach to the social model is the ultimate irony: in tackling only one side of our situation we disable ourselves.

Redefining impairment

Our fears about acknowledging the implications of impairment are quite justified. Dominant perceptions of impairment as personal tragedy are regularly used to undermine the work of the disabled people's movement and they rarely coincide with disabled people's understandings of their circumstances. They are individualistic interpretations: our experiences are entirely explained by each individual's psychological or biological characteristics. Any problems we encounter are explained by personal inadequacy or functional limitation, to the exclusion of social influences.

These interpretations impose narrow assumptions about the varying experiences of impairment and isolate experience from its disabling context. They also segregate us from each other and from people without impairments. Interpreting impairment as personal tragedy creates fear of impairment and an emphasis on medical intervention. Such an interpretation is a key part of the attitudes and actions that disable us.

However, the perception of impairment as personal tragedy is merely a social construction; it is not an inevitable way of thinking about impairment. Recognising the importance of impairment for us does not mean that we have to take on the non-disabled world's ways of interpreting our experience of our bodies. In fact, impairment, at its most basic level, is a purely objective concept which carries no intrinsic meaning. Impairment simply means that aspects of a person's body do not function or they function with difficulty. Frequently this is taken a stage further to imply that the person's body, and ultimately the person, is inferior. However, the first is fact; the second is interpretation. If these interpretations are socially created then they are not fixed or inevitable and it is possible to replace them with alternative interpretations based on our own experience of impairment rather than what our impairments mean to non-disabled people.

We need a new approach which acknowledges that people apply their own meanings to their own experiences of impairment. This self-interpretation adds a whole new layer of personal, subjective meanings to the objective concept of impairment. The personal interpretation incorporates any meaning that impairment holds for an individual (ie, any effects it has on their activities), the feelings it produces (eg, pain) and any concerns the individual might have (eg, how their impairment might progress). Individuals might regard their impairment as positive, neutral or negative, and this might differ according to time and changing circumstances.

With this approach the experiences and history of our impairments become a part of our autobiography. They join our experience of disability and other aspects of our lives to form a complete sense of ourselves.

Acknowledging the relevance of impairment is essential to ensuring that people are knowledgeable about their own circumstances. An individual's familiarity with how their body works allows them to identify their specific needs. This is a precursor to meeting those needs by accessing existing information and resources. Self-knowledge is the first stage of empowerment and gives a strong base for individuals to work collectively to confront disability and its impact upon people with impairments.

We need to think about impairment in three related ways:

- First, there is the objective concept of *impairment*. This was agreed in 1976 by the Union of Physically Impaired Against Segregation (UPIAS 1976) and has since been developed by Disabled People's International (DPI) to include people with a range of non-physical impairments:

    Impairment: lacking all or part of a limb, or having a defective limb, organism or mechanism of the body.

- Second, there is the individual interpretation of the *subjective experience of impairment* in which an individual binds their own meanings to the concept of impairment to convey their personal circumstances.
- Finally, there is the impact of the wider *social context* upon impairment, in which misrepresentation, social exclusion and discrimination combine to disable people with impairments.

It is this third aspect to impairment which is not inevitable and its removal is the primary focus of the disabled people's movement. However, all three layers are currently essential to an understanding of our personal and social experiences.

Responses to impairment

We need to reclaim and acknowledge our personal experiences of impairment in order to develop our key debates, to incorporate this experience into the wider social context and target any action more precisely. One critical area of concern is the different responses to impairment, for ultimately these determine our exclusion or inclusion.

Currently, the main responses to impairment divide into four broad categories:

- *avoidance/'escape'*, through abortion, sterilisation, withholding treatment from disabled babies, infanticide and euthanasia (medically assisted suicide) or suicide
- *management*, in which any difficult effects of impairment are minimised and incorporated into our individual lives, without any significant change in the impairment
- *cure* through medical intervention
- *prevention* including vaccination, health education and improved social conditions.

The specific treatments that emerge from these responses differ markedly according to whether they are based on the medical or social model. Currently, the treatment available is dominated by the medical model's individualistic interpretation of impairment as tragic and problematic and the sole cause of disadvantage and difficulty. This leads policy-makers and professionals to seek a 'solution' through the removal of impairment. Each of the above responses is considered, at different times and in different contexts, to be valuable in bringing about the perceived desired outcome of reducing the number of people with impairments. The result is often a fundamental undermining of our civil and human rights.

For example, although not currently legal in Britain, euthanasia and infanticide are widely advocated where the 'quality of life' of someone with an impairment is deemed unacceptably low. An increasing number of infanticide and euthanasia cases have reached the courts in recent years, with judgments and public responses implying increasing approval. Infanticide is justified on grounds that 'killing a defective infant is not morally equivalent to killing a person. Very often it is not wrong at all.'[2] Suicide amongst people with impairments is frequently considered far more rational than in people without, as though impairment renders it the obvious, even the only, route to take. Ruth Bailey's chapter has illustrated how assumptions of the inevitable poor quality of life with an impairment dominate the development of prenatal screening and abortion. These approaches have created a huge research industry, and foetal screening and abortion are now major users of impairment-related resources.

Prevention of impairment through public health measures receives only minimal consideration and resourcing. The isolation of impairment from its social context means the social and economic causes of impairment often go unrecognised. The definitions of prevention are also questionable, in that foetal screening and subsequent abortion are categorised by mainstream approaches as preventative, whereas in reality such action is about the elimination of impairment.

Where removal of impairment is not possible, mainstream approaches extend to the management of impairment, although this remains one of the most under-resourced areas of the health service. However, much of the work in this area, rather than increasing an individual's access to and control over the help that they might need, is more about disguising or concealing impairment. Huge amounts of energy and resources are spent by medical and rehabilitation services to achieve this. For example, many individuals are prescribed cosmetic surgery and prostheses which have no practical function and may actually inhibit an individual's use of their body. Others are taught to struggle for hours to dress themselves when the provision of personal assistance would be more effective.

There are a number of critical flaws in mainstream interpretations of impairment and associated responses. First, little distinction is made between different people's experience of impairment or different aspects of a single impairment – or indeed, whether there may be positive aspects to some impairments. Instead, resources are applied in a generalised way to end impairment, regardless of the actual experience and interpretations of the individuals concerned. With the development of genetic screening, intervention aims to eliminate people with specific types of impairment altogether. Rarely is consideration given to the positive attributes of impairment, for example, the cystic fibrosis gene confers resistance to cholera which is an important benefit in some parts of the world. Associations are being identified between some impairments and creative or intellectual talent, while impairment in itself requires the development of more cooperative and communitarian ways of working and living – an advantage in a society with so much conflict to resolve.

Second, impairment is presented as the full explanation, with no recognition of disability. Massive resources are directed into impairment-related research and interventions. In contrast, scant resources are channelled into social change for the inclusion of people with impairments. For example, research will strive to 'cure' an individual of their walking difficulty, whilst ignoring the social factors which make not walking into a problem. There is little public questioning of the distribution of funds between these two approaches. Additionally, such assumptions inhibit many disabled people from recognising the true causes of their circumstances and initiating appropriate responses.

A third criticism is that, while these responses to impairment are seen as representing the interests of disabled people, they are made largely by people with no direct experience of impairment, yet are presented as authoritative. Disabled people's knowledge, in contrast, is frequently derided as emotional and therefore lacking validity.[3] Although mainstream interventions are presented as being for the benefit of disabled people, in fact they are made for a non-disabled society. Ingrained assumptions and official directives make it clear that there is an implicit, and sometimes explicit, intention of population control. Abortion, euthanasia and cure are presented as 'quality of life' issues, but are also justified in terms of economic savings or 'improvement' to populations.[4]

It is counteracting these and related concerns which motivates the disabled people's movement. The social model of disability rejects the notion of impairment as problematic, focusing instead on discrimination as the key obstacle to a disabled person's quality of life. The logical extension of this approach is to seek a solution through the removal of disability and this is what the disabled people's movement works towards.

As a result, the overriding emphasis of the movement is on social change to end discrimination against people with impairments. There is a strong resistance to considering impairment as relevant to our political analysis. When impairment is discussed at all within the disabled people's movement it tends to be in the context of criticising mainstream responses. We have, for example, clearly stated that foetal screening for abortion and the implicit acceptance of infanticide for babies with significant impairments are based on assumptions that our lives are not worth living. Our intervention in public debates in recent years about medically assisted suicide (euthanasia) has exposed the same assumption. In contrast, we have asserted the value of our lives and the importance of external disabling barriers, rather than impairment in itself, in determining quality of life. The same perspective informs our criticisms of the resources spent on attempting to 'cure' people of their impairments.

It is this rejection of impairment as problematic, however, that is the social model's flaw. Although social factors *do* generally dominate in determining experience and quality of life – for example requests for euthanasia are more likely to be motivated by lack of appropriate assistance than pain (Seale and Addington-Hall 1994) – impairment *is* relevant. For fear of appearing to endorse mainstream responses, we are in danger of failing to acknowledge that for some individuals impairment – as well as disability – causes disadvantage.

Not acknowledging impairment also lays the disabled people's movement open to misappropriation and misinterpretation. For example, disabled people's concerns about genetic screening and euthanasia have been used by 'pro-life' groups to strengthen their arguments. Equally, the movement's rejection of medical and rehabilitation professionals' approaches to treatment and cure has not been accompanied by an exploration of what forms of intervention *would* be useful. Our message tends to come across as rejecting all forms of intervention when it is clear that some interventions, such as the alleviation of pain, in fact require more attention and resources. In both cases, the reluctance of the disabled people's movement to address the full implications of impairment leaves its stance ambiguous and open to misuse.

It is also clear that, by refusing to discuss impairment, we are failing to acknowledge the subjective reality of many disabled people's daily lives. Impairment *is* problematic for people who experience pain, illness, shortened lifespan or other factors. As a result, they may seek treatment to minimise these consequences and, in extreme circumstances, may no longer wish to live. It is vital not to assume that they are experiencing a kind of 'false consciousness' – that if all the external disabling barriers were removed they would no longer feel like this. We need to ensure the availability of all the support and resources that an individual might need, whilst acknowledging that impairment *can* still be intolerable.

This does not imply that *all* impairment is intolerable, or that impairment causes *all* related disadvantage; nor does it negate the urgency with which disability must be confronted and removed. It simply allows us, alongside wider social and political change, to recognise people's experiences of their bodies. Without incorporating a renewed approach to impairment we cannot achieve this.

A renewed social model of disability

We need to take a fresh look at the social model of disability and learn to integrate all its complexities. It is critical that we recognise the ways in which disability and impairment work together. The social model has never suggested that disability represents the total explanation or that impairment doesn't count – that has simply been the impression we have given by keeping our experiences of impairment private and failing to incorporate them into our public political analysis.

We need to focus on disability *and* impairment: on the external and internal constituents they bring to our experiences. Impairment is about our bodies' ways of working and any implications these hold for our lives. Disability is about the reaction and impact of the outside world on our particular bodies. One cannot be fully understood without attention to the other, because whilst they can exist independently of each other, there are also circumstances where they interact. And whilst there are common strands to the way they operate, the balance between disability and impairment, their impact and the explanations of their cause and effect will vary according to each individual's situation and from time to time.

We need a renewed social model of disability. This model would operate on two levels: a more complete understanding of disability and impairment as social concepts; and a recognition of an individual's experiences of their body over time and in variable circumstances. This social model of disability is thus a means to encapsulating the total experience of both disability and impairment.

Our current approach is based primarily on the idea that once the struggle against disability is complete, only the impairment will remain for the individual and there will be no disadvantage associated with this. In other words, when disability comes to an end there will be no socially-created barriers to transport, housing, education and so on for people with impairments. Impairment will not then be used as a pretext for excluding people from society. People with impairments will be able to participate in and contribute to society on a par with people who do not have impairments.

In this non-disabling society, however, impairment may well be unaltered and some individuals will find that disadvantages remain. Removal of disability does not necessarily mean the removal of restricted opportunities. For example, limitations to an individual's health and energy levels or their experience of pain may constrain their participation in activities. Impairment *in itself* can be a negative, painful experience.

Moreover, whilst an end to disability means people with impairments will no longer be discriminated against, they may remain disadvantaged in their social and economic opportunities by the long-term effects of earlier discrimination. Although affirmative action is an important factor in alleviating this, it is unlikely to be able to undo the full scale of discrimination for everyone.

Our current interpretation of the social model also tends to assume that if *impairment* ceases, then the individual will no longer experience disability. In practice, however, they may continue to be disabled, albeit to a lesser degree than previously. Future employment opportunities, for example, are likely to be affected by past discrimination in education even when impairment no longer exists.

In addition, an end to impairment may trigger a massive upheaval to those aspects of an individual's self-identity and image formed in response to disability and impairment. It can also signal the loss of what may be an individual's primary community. These personal and collective identities are formed in response to disability. That further changes may be required in changing circumstances is a sign of the continuing legacy of disability.

Our current approach also misses the fact that people can be disabled even when they have no impairment. Genetic and viral testing is now widely used to predict the probability of an individual subsequently acquiring a particular impairment. Fear has been expressed that predisposition to impairment will be used as a basis for discrimination, particularly in financial and medical services.[5]

There are also circumstances in which disability and impairment exist independently, and change in one is not necessarily linked to change in the other. For example, disability can dramatically ease or worsen with changes to an individual's environment or activities even when their particular impairment is static. Leaving a purpose-built home to go on holiday, for example, may give rise to a range of access restrictions not usually encountered, even though an individual's impairment remains the same. Equally, an employee with an impairment may find their capacity to succeed at work is confounded within one organisation but fully possible in another simply because of differences in the organisations' equality practices.

Where level of impairment increases, disability does not necessarily follow suit if adequate and appropriate resources are readily available to meet changes in need. A new impairment, a condition which fluctuates or a progressive impairment may mean that an individual needs additional or changing levels of personal assistance, but disability will remain constant if that resource is easily accessed, appropriate and flexible.

Perhaps most importantly, however, disability and impairment *interact*. Impairment must be present in the first instance for disability to be triggered: disability is the form of discrimination that acts specifically against people with (or who have had) impairments. This does not mean that impairment causes disability, but that it is a precondition for that particular oppression.

However, the difficulties associated with a particular impairment can influence the degree to which disability causes disadvantage. For example, an individual with a chronic illness may have periods in which their contact with the social world is curtailed to such an extent that external restrictions become irrelevant. At times of improved health the balance between impairment and disability may shift, with opportunities lost through discrimination being paramount.

Impairment can also be caused or compounded by disability. An excessively steep ramp, for example, might cause new impairment or exacerbate pain. An inaccessible health centre can restrict the availability of health screening that would otherwise prevent certain impairments, whilst inadequate resourcing can mean that pain reduction or management techniques are not available to many of the people who need them. Medical treatments – including those used primarily for cosmetic purposes – can cause impairment; for example, it has now emerged that a 'side effect' of growth hormone treatment is the fatal Creutzfeldt-Jakob disease.

Discrimination in general can also cause major emotional stress and place mental health at risk. Our reluctance to discuss impairment obscures this aspect of disability. If we present impairment as irrelevant then, even where impairment is caused by disability, it is, by implication, not a problem. This limits our ability to tackle social causes of impairment and so diminishes our campaigns.

Like disability, other experiences of inequality can also create or increase impairment. For example, abuse associated with racism or heterosexism, sexist pressure to modify physical appearance and lack of basic provision because of poverty can all lead to impairment. A significant proportion of people become active in the disabled people's movement as a result of such experiences, or through a recognition of these (and other) links that exist between oppressions.

Different social groups can also experience diverse patterns of impairment for a variety of social and biological reasons. Impairment for women, for example, is more likely to be associated with chronic pain, illness and old age (Morris 1994: 210–12). Excluding the implications of impairment risks reducing the relevance of the social model of disability to certain social groups. For example, the most common cause of impairment amongst women is a chronic condition, arthritis, where the major manifestation of impairment is pain. Unless the social model of disability incorporates a recognition of the patterns of impairment experienced by different social groups, there will be a failure to develop appropriate services.

Impairment can also be influenced by other external factors, not necessarily discriminatory, which may be physical, psychological or behavioural. Differences in cultural and individual approaches to pain and illness, for example, can significantly affect the way a person feels, perceives and reacts to pain. The study of pain control has revealed that pain can be significantly reduced by a range of measures, including by assisting individuals to control their own treatment programmes and through altered mental states associated with meditation or concentration on activity. Yet the limited availability of such measures to many people who could benefit extends this to the sphere of disability.

Social factors can, at the most fundamental level, define what is perceived as impairment. Perceptions of norms and differences vary culturally and historically. As mainstream perceptions change, people are defined in and out of impairment. Many people labelled 'mentally ill', for example, simply do not conform to contemporary social norms of behaviour. Other inequalities may contribute to the identification of impairment. For example, racist classifications in the school psychological service have led to a disproportionately high number of black compared to white children in segregated units for 'the emotionally and behaviourally disturbed', whilst it is relatively recently that the sexuality of lesbians and gay men has ceased to be officially defined as 'mental illness'.

Mainstream perceptions tend to increase the boundaries of impairment. The logical outcome of a successful disabled people's movement is a reduction in who is perceived as having an impairment. An absence of disability includes the widespread acceptance of individuality, through the development of a new norm which carries an expectation that there will be a wide range of attributes within a population. With an end to disability, many people currently defined as having an impairment will be within that norm. Impairment will only need definition as such if *in itself* it results in disadvantages such as pain, illness or reduced options.

Conclusion

I share the concerns expressed by some disabled people that some of the arguments I have put forward here could be used out of context to support the medical model of disability, to support the view that the experience of impairment is nothing but personal tragedy. However, suppression of our subjective experiences of impairment is not the answer to dealing with these risks; engaging with the debates and probing deeper for greater clarity might well be.

I am arguing for a recognition of the implications of impairment. I am not supporting traditional perspectives on disability and impairment, nor am I advocating any lessening of the energies we devote to eliminating disability. Acknowledging our personal experiences of impairment does not in any way disregard the tremendous weight of oppression, nor does it undermine our alignment with other civil rights movements. Certainly, it should not weaken our resolve for change. Disability remains our primary concern, *and* impairment exists alongside.

Integrating those key factors into our use of the social model is vital if we are to understand fully the ways that disability and impairment operate. What this renewed social model of disability does is broaden and strengthen the current social model, taking it beyond grand theory and into real life, because it allows us to incorporate a holistic understanding of our experiences and potential for change. This understanding needs to influence the structure of our movement – how we organise and campaign, how we include and support each other. A renewed approach to the social model is vital, both individually and collectively, if we are to develop truly effective strategies to manage our impairments and to confront disability. It is our learning and support within our own self-advocacy and political groups, peer counselling, training and arts that enable us to confront the difficulties we face, from both disability and impairment. It is this that allows us to continue working in the most effective way towards the basic principle of equality that underpins the disabled people's movement.

It is this confronting of disability and aspects of impairment that underpins the notion of disability pride which has become so central to our movement. Our pride comes not from 'being disabled' or 'having an impairment' but out of our response to that. We are proud of the way we have developed an understanding of the oppression we experience, of our work against discrimination and prejudice, of the way we live with our impairments.

A renewed approach to the social model is also relevant in our work with non-disabled people, particularly in disability equality training. Most of us who run such courses have avoided acknowledging impairment in our work, concerned that it confirms stereotypes of the 'tragedy' of impairment or makes the issues too complicated to convey. Denying the relevance of impairment, however, simply does not ring true to many non-disabled people: if pain, by definition, hurts then how can it be disregarded? We need to be honest about the experiences of impairment, without underplaying the overwhelming scale of disability. This does not mean portraying impairment as a total explanation, presenting participants with medical information or asking them to fantasise impairment through 'experiential' exercises. Instead, it allows a clear distinction to be made between disability and impairment, with an emphasis on tackling disabling barriers.

The assertion of the disabled people's movement that our civil and human rights must be protected and promoted by the removal of the disabling barriers of discrimination and prejudice has gained significant public support in recent years. It is this social model of disability which underpins the civil rights legislation for which we have campaigned, and civil rights will remain the centre of our political attention.

At a time when so many people – disabled and non-disabled – are meeting these ideas afresh, we need to be absolutely clear about the distinction between disability and impairment. The onus will remain upon disabled people to prove discrimination and there will still be attempts to refute our claims by using traditional perceptions of impairment. To strengthen our arguments we must peel away the layers and understand the complexities of the way disability and impairment work so that our allegations of discrimination are watertight. This is necessary now in our campaigning for full civil rights and will remain necessary when we claim justice under the legislation which will inevitably follow that campaign.

At this crossroads in disabled people's history, it is time for this renewed approach to the social model and the way we apply it. Disability is still socially created, still unacceptable, and still there to be changed; but by bringing impairment into our total understanding, by fully recognising our subjective experiences, we will achieve the best route to that change, the only route to a future which includes us all.

Notes

1 Along with many disabled people I feel some discomfort at the word impairment because it has become so imbued with offensive interpretation. Perhaps we need to replace impairment with an alternative term.

2 Professor Peter Singer, Director of the Centre for Human Bioethics, Monash University, Australia: quoted in Erika Feyerabend, 'Euthanasia in the Age of Genetic Engineering', *Reproductive and Genetic Engineering*, Vol. 2, No. 3, pp. 247–9, no date given.

3 For example, a medical law committee drawing up recommendations for withdrawing treatment from newborn babies with impairments, specifically excluded disabled adults or the parents of disabled children from the committee because 'the emotional discussion, which might have been likely, would have been very unhelpful and even counterproductive to the matter on hand', Prof Dr med. H.D. Hiersche in his introductory speech to the German Association of Medical Law on 'Limits on the Obligation to Treat Severely Handicapped Newborns', 27–29 June 1986.

4 A new screening test for Down's syndrome is recommended for all pregnant women on the grounds that the £88 test will reduce the cost per 'case' discovered (and, presumbly, aborted) from the current £43,000 to £29,500. See *Pulse*, 25 May 1991.

In an unpublished paper, a philosopher at Saarbrucken University in Germany used economic decision theory to quantify the value of life, including measuring which people should be subjected to involuntary euthanasia ('euthanasees'). Reported by Wilma Kobusch in a press statement; in *Gelenkirchen*, 5 November, 1991.

5 'Further Examples of Threats to Life', *Newsletter 13*; Disability Awareness in Action, January 1994.

References

Morris, J. (1994) Gender and Disability. In French, S. (ed.) *On Equal Terms: working with disabled people*. Oxford: Butterworth Heinemann.

Seale, C. and Addington-Hall, J. (1994) Euthanasia: why people want to die earlier. *Social Science and Medicine*, **39** (5), 647–54.

Union of the Physically Impaired Against Segregation (1976) *Fundamental Principles of Disability*. UPIAS.

United Nations Division for Economic and Social Information (1983) *World Programme of Action Concerning Disabled Persons*. United Nations.

Liz Crow has, in this chapter, provided a powerful illustration of a recurring theme in this volume and the Learning from Each Other course – that of each of us having complex social identities. Our attempts to understand diversity and to theorise about experiences of marginalisation and oppression are more meaningful when they address the reality of our being more than any single aspect of our difference.

CHAPTER 14

Towards an affirmation model of disability

John Swain and Sally French

In this chapter John Swain and Sally French argue that a new model of disability is emerging within the literature by disabled people and within disability culture, expressed most clearly by the Disability Arts Movement. They call this the affirmation model; it is in direct opposition to the personal tragedy model and builds on the social model. The chapter and the model are positive affirmations of identity and of the life experience of being impaired and disabled.

'Proud, angry and strong'

The aim of this paper is to explore and trace the emergence of a model of disability which arises out of disability culture. For the purposes of the paper we call it *the affirmative model*. It is essentially a non-tragic view of disability and impairment which encompasses positive social identities, both individual and collective, for disabled people grounded in the benefits of life style and life experience of being impaired and disabled. This is succinctly expressed by the title of Johnny Crescendo's song, which is well known within British disability culture and has been often performed at disability arts events: *proud, angry and strong*. As argued here, this model is significant in theoretical terms, addressing the meaning of 'disability', but also more directly to disabled people themselves, in validating themselves and their experiences. It is significant, too, in understanding the 'disability divide', that is the divide between being disabled and being non-disabled. [. . .]

Across the divide: existing models

The divide we are discussing here is not in the categorisation of people as disabled and non-disabled. Despite the evident personal, social and political reality of this conception of a divide, we believe it is problematic in a number of ways, two of which are particularly pertinent to this paper. Firstly, a division cannot be made on the grounds of impairment. The divide between disabled and non-disabled people is not that one group has impairments while the other does not. Indeed, many non-disabled people have impairments, such as short and long sight, and impairment cannot be equated with disability. Secondly, the divide between two groups cannot be sustained on the basis that one is oppressed while the other is not. Non-disabled people can be oppressed through poverty, racism, sexism and sexual preference, as indeed are many disabled people. Furthermore, oppressed people can also be oppressors. Disabled people, for instance, can be racist. Whatever definition of oppression is taken, it will apply to some non-disabled, as well as disabled, people.

The divide we are addressing is in perceptions of disability, in terms of the meaning it has in people's lives and social identity. Perceptions and the experiences on which they are founded vary considerably, not least as many people become disabled in later life having constructed understandings and lifestyles as non-disabled people. Nevertheless, there is a divide in perceptions which is most clearly related to a divide in experiences, being disabled or non-disabled.

The first question, then, is one of conceiving this divide in different models of disability. The opposition of the social model to an individual, particularly medical, model of disability is well established (Oliver 1996; Priestley 1999) and is clearly crucial to understanding the disability divide. The social model was born out of the experiences of disabled people, challenging the dominant individual models espoused by non-disabled people (French & Swain 1997). Nevertheless, it is our experience that many non-disabled people readily accept the social model, albeit superficially and at a basic conceptual level. Non-disabled people can generally accept that a wheelchair-user cannot enter a building because of steps (i.e. the person is disabled by barriers in an environment built for non-disabled people). Non-disabled people are much more threatened and challenged by the notion that a wheelchair-user could be pleased and proud to be the person he or she is.

The rejection of a tragic view and establishment of an affirmative model is far more problematic and not centrally addressed by the social model of disability. Essentially, the social model redefines 'the problem'. Disability is not caused by impairment or a function of the individual, but the oppression of people with impairments in a disabling society. The non-tragic view of disability, however, is not about 'the problem', but about disability as a positive personal and collective identity, and disabled people leading fulfilled and satisfying lives. Whilst the social model is certainly totally incompatible with the view that disability is a personal tragedy, it can be argued that the social model has not, in itself, underpinned a non-tragedy view. First, to be a member of an oppressed group within society does not necessarily engender a non-tragedy view. There is, for instance, nothing inherently non-tragic about being denied access to buildings. Secondly, the social model disassociates impairment from disability. It, thus, leaves the possibility that even in an ideal world of full civil rights and participative citizenship for disabled people, an impairment could be seen to be a personal tragedy. There is, for instance, nothing inherently non-tragic about having legs that cannot walk or feel.

In recent years a number of disabled people, particularly women, have sought to extend the social model of disability. Their major criticism has been the neglect of impairment

(Morris 1991; Crow 1992; French 1993; Keith 1994; Abberley 1996; Crow 1996; Pinter 1996; Wendell 1996; Garland Thomson 1997; Hughes and Paterson 1997; Shakespeare and Watson 1997; Wendell 1997). However, it can be argued that any concentration on impairment will be counterproductive for disabled people. Shakespeare states:

> The achievement of the disability movement has been to break the link between our bodies and our social situation and to focus on the real cause of disability i.e. discrimination and prejudice. To mention biology, to admit pain, to confront our impairments has been to risk the oppressive seizing of evidence that disability is 'really' about physical limitations after all.
>
> (1992: 40)

Likewise, Oliver warns:

> There is a danger in emphasising the personal at the expense of the political because most of the world still thinks of disability as an individual, intensely personal problem. And many of those who once made a good living espousing this view would be only too glad to come out of the woodwork and say that they were right all along.
>
> (1996: 5)

Crow, in this volume, however, points out that 'an impairment such as pain or chronic illness may curtail an individual's activities so much that the restriction of the outside world becomes irrelevant' and that '. . . for many disabled people personal struggles relating to impairment will remain even when disabling barriers no longer exist'. The argument is basically, then, one of admitting that there may be a negative side to impairment and accounting for this by extending the social model.

It seems to us that this debate is limited in two major respects. First, it is notable that 'pain and chronic illness' are the recurring examples of impairments not addressed by the social model. This has distorted the debate. Pain and chronic illness are neither impairments nor restricted to the experiences of disabled people. Non-disabled people experience both pain and chronic illness. Indeed, in the pursuit of physical fitness, pain can be actively pursued by non-disabled people: 'no gain without pain'. Secondly, within this debate, impairment is regularly equated with personal tragedy. It is our contention that an affirmative model is developing out of individual and collective experiences of disabled people which directly confronts the personal tragedy model not only of disability but also of impairment.

Better dead than disabled?

The tragedy model is so dominant, so prevalent and so infused throughout media representations, language, cultural beliefs, research, policy and professional practice that we can only hope to cover a few illustrative examples. In terms of media representations, disabled characters (played by non-disabled actors) were featured in two major family films televised during the 1998 Christmas period when we were planning this paper.

The first was *A Christmas Carol*, which included two disabled characters. The best known is, of course, the pitiable and pathetic Tiny Tim whose tragedy of using a crutch is miraculously overcome at the end of the picture when he runs to meet the enlightened Scrooge. The other is a blind man, with both a dog and a white stick, who appears as a beggar. In the final scene, the humanised Scrooge can donate money in the proffered hat, for which the tragic figure of the cap-in-hand (handicapped) blind man is clearly grateful. The other film, again widely celebrated for the general sentiments it portrays, was *It's a Wonderful Life*. This features just one disabled character, Mr Potter, who is rich, evil, twisted, frustrated and in a wheelchair. No other explanation for his inhumanity, which includes theft, is offered other than his response to a life as a wheelchair user (despite the fact that he is the richest man in the town). It is the tragedy that has twisted him. The only other evil character, a minor character, in the film is the man who pushes the wheelchair. The tragedy, it seems, begets evil even by association.

Research can also clearly demonstrate the tragedy model. In a trial of a newly developed form of insulin, research subjects with diabetes were required to complete a questionnaire about '. . . you and your diabetes . . . the way you feel and how diabetes affects your day to day life.' With each question was a choice of four answers ranging, basically, from 'very much' to 'not at all'. The first question set the scene: 'Do you look forward to the future?', with the implication that the tragedy of diabetes may negate any hope for the future. The 32 questions are peppered with words of tragedy, such as 'fear', 'edgy', 'worry' and 'difficult'. Some questions address psychological responses to the tragedy, such as: 'Do you throw things around if you get upset or lose your temper?,' 'Do you get touchy or moody about diabetes?' and 'Do you hurt yourself or feel like hurting yourself when you get upset?' Two questions invoke the essence of the tragedy model: 'Do you even for a moment wish that you were dead?' and 'Do you wish that you had never been born?' Thus, the ultimate version of the tragedy model is that physical death is better than the social death of disability.

Perhaps the most intrusive, violating and invalidating experiences, for disabled people, emanate from the policies, practices and intervention, which are justified and rationalised by the personal tragedy view of disability and impairment. The tragedy is to be avoided, eradicated or non-disabled (normalised) by all possible means. Such are the negative presumptions held about impairment and disability, that the abortion of impaired foetuses is barely challenged. As Disability Awareness in Action (1997) states, there is considerable and growing pressure on mothers to undergo prenatal screening and to terminate pregnancies in which an impairment has been detected. The use of genetic technology in its different forms in so called 'preventative' measures is, for many disabled people, an expression of the essence of the personal tragedy model, better dead than disabled. The erroneous idea that disabled people cannot be happy, or enjoy an adequate quality of life, lies at the heart of this response. The disabled person's problems are perceived to result from impairment, rather than the failure of society to meet that person's needs in terms of appropriate human help and accessibility. There is an assumption that disabled people want to be 'normal', although this is rarely voiced by disabled people themselves who know that disability is a major part of their identity. Disabled people are subjected to many disabling expectations, for example to be 'independent', 'normal', to 'adjust' and 'accept' their situation. It is these expectations that can cause unhappiness, rather than the impairment itself.

There are a number of different possible explanations of this tragedy view of disability. It is sometimes thought to reflect a deep irrational fear by non-disabled people of their own mortality (Shakespeare 1994). An alternative explanation, however, suggests that the tragedy perspective has a rational, cognitive basis constructed through experiences in disablist social contexts. Fundamental to understanding non-disabled people's tragedy view of disability is the possibility of crossing the divide: 'there but for fortune go you or I'. Unlike the divide between people of different genders or different races, non-disabled people daily experience the possibility of becoming impaired and thus disabled (the causal link being integral to the tragedy model). Thus, so called 'irrational fears' have a rational basis in a disablist society. To become visually impaired, for instance, may be a personal tragedy for a sighted person whose life is based around being sighted, who lacks knowledge of the experiences of people with visual impairments, whose identity is founded on being sighted, and who has been subjected to the personal tragedy model of visual impairment. This can be compounded, for non-disabled parents of disabled children, for instance, by beliefs about the benefits that non-disabled people have in education, work and relationships. Such beliefs speak to dominant social values that have a broader application than the disabled-non-disabled divide, particularly through the association of disability with dependence (Oliver 1993) and abnormality (Morris 1991). Thus, the personal tragedy view of impairment and disability is ingrained in the social identity of non-disabled people. Non-disabled identity, as other identities, has meaning in relation to and constructs the identity of others. To be non-disabled is to be 'not one of those'. The problem for disabled people is that the tragedy model of disability and impairment is not only applied by non-disabled people to themselves, it is extrapolated and applied to disabled people.

From this point of view, too, the adherence to a personal tragedy model by disabled people themselves also has a rational basis. For a non-disabled person whose life is constructed on the basis of being non-disabled, the onset of impairment and disability can be experienced as a tragedy, perhaps amplified if it is associated with the trauma of illness or accident. Even in affirming the social model, Oliver and Sapey state:

Some disabled people do experience the onset of impairment as a personal tragedy which, while not invalidating the argument that they are being excluded from a range of activities by a disabling environment, does mean it would be inappropriate to deny that impairment can be experienced in this way.

(1999: 26)

Furthermore, a personal tragedy view can have a rational basis for people with congenital impairments, living through the daily barrage from non-disabled people, experts, parents, and the media invalidating themselves and their experiences. Indeed, within the disabling context we have outlined here, the expression of an affirmative model by disabled people flies in the face of dominant values and ideologies. It is likely to be denied as unrealistic or a lack of 'acceptance', distorted as an expression of bravery or compensation, or simply ignored. The tragedy model is in itself disabling. It denies disabled people's experiences of a disabling society, their enjoyment of life, and their identity and self-awareness as disabled people.

Towards a positive individual identity

An affirmative model is developing in direct opposition to the personal tragedy view of disability and impairment. The writings and experiences of disabled people demonstrate that, far from being tragic, being impaired and disabled can have benefits. If, for example, a person has sufficient resources, the ability to give up paid employment, and pursue personal interests and hobbies, following an accident, may enhance that person's life. Similarly, disabled people sometimes find that they can escape class oppression, abuse or neglect by virtue of being disabled. We interviewed Martha, a Malaysian woman with a visual impairment. She was separated from a poor and neglectful family and sent to a special school at the age of five. She states:

I got a better education than any of them (brothers and sisters) and much better health care too. We had regular inoculations and regular medical and dental checks.

She subsequently went to university and qualified as a teacher. Similarly, many visually disabled people became physiotherapists, by virtue of having their own 'special' college, at a time when their working class origins would have prevented them entering other physiotherapy colleges. None of this is to deny, of course, that many disabled people who are educated in 'special' institutions receive an inferior education and may, in addition, be neglected and abused (Corker 1996).

A further way in which disability and impairment may be perceived as beneficial to some disabled people is that society's expectations and requirements are more difficult to satisfy and may, therefore, be avoided. A disabled man quoted by Shakespeare *et al.* said, 'I am never going to conform to society's requirements and I am thrilled because I am blissfully released from all that crap. That's the liberation of disfigurement' (1996: 81).

Young people (especially women) are frequently under pressure to form heterosexual relationships, to marry and have children (Bartlett 1994). These expectations are not applied so readily to disabled people who may, indeed, be viewed as asexual. Although this has the potential to cause a great deal of anxiety and pain, some disabled people can see its advantages. Vasey states:

> We are not usually snapped up in the flower of youth for our domestic and child rearing skills, or for our decorative value, so we do not have to spend years disentangling ourselves from wearisome relationships as is the case with many non-disabled women.
>
> (1992: 74)

Though it is more difficult for disabled people to form sexual relationships, because of disabling barriers, when they do any limitations imposed by impairment may, paradoxically, lead to advantages. Shakespeare *et al.*, who interviewed disabled people about their sexuality and sexual relationships, state:

> Because disabled people were not able to make love in a straight forward manner, or in a conventional position, they were impelled to experiment and enjoyed a more interesting sexual life as a result.
>
> (1996: 106)

For some people who become disabled their lives change completely though not necessarily for the worse. A woman quoted by Morris states:

> As a result of becoming paralysed life has changed completely. Before my accident it seemed as if I was set to spend the rest of my life as a religious sister, but I was not solemnly professed so was not accepted back into the order. Instead I am now very happily married with a home of my own.
>
> (1989: 120)

The experience of being impaired may also give disabled people a heightened understanding of the oppressions other people endure. French found that most of the forty five visually disabled physiotherapists she interviewed could find advantages to being visually impaired in their work. An important advantage was their perceived ability to understand and empathise with their patients and clients. One person said:

> The frustrations of disability are much the same inasmuch as it is a physical limitation on your life and you think, 'if only' . . . Having to put up with that for so long, I know ever so well what patients mean when they mention those kinds of difficulties.
>
> (French 1991: 1)

Others believed that their visual disability gave rise to a more balanced and equal relationship with their patients, that patients were less embarrassed (for example, about undressing) and that they enjoyed the extra physical contact the visually disabled physiotherapist was obliged to make. One person said:

> Even as students when we had the Colles fracture class all round in a circle, they used to love us treating them because we had to go round and touch them. They preferred us to the sighted physios. I'm convinced that a lot of people think we are better.

> (French 1991: 4)

As for non-disabled people, the quality of life of disabled people depends on whether they can achieve a lifestyle of their choice. This, in turn, depends on their personal resources, the resources within society and their own unique situation. The central assumption of the tragedy model is that disabled people want to be other than as they are, even though this would mean a rejection of identity and self. Nevertheless, the writings of disabled people demonstrate that being born with an impairment or becoming disabled in later life can give a perspective on life which is both interesting and affirmative and can be used positively. Essentially, impairment which is social death and invalidates disabled people in a non-disabled society, provides a social context for disabled people to transcend the constraints of non-disabled norms, roles and identity and affirm their experiences, values and identity. Phillipe explains:

> I just can't imagine becoming hearing, I'd need a psychiatrist, I'd need a speech therapist, I'd need some new friends, I'd lose all my old friends, I'd lose my job. I wouldn't be here lecturing. It really hits hearing people that a deaf person doesn't want to become hearing. I am what I am!

> (Shakespeare *et al.* 1996: 184)

Watson writes of Phil, a disabled participant in research he is conducting:

> Phil sees his acceptance of his impairment as central to his sense of self and well-being . . .

> (1998: 156)

Towards a positive collective identity

As a member of a poetry group of young disabled people, Georgina Sinclair wrote the following poem:

Coming Out
And with the passing of time
you realise you need to find
people with whom you can share.
There's no need to despair.
Your life can be your own
and there's no reason to condone
what passes for their care.
So, I'm coming out.
I've had enough
of passing and playing their game.
I'll hold my head up high.
I'm done with sighs
and shame.

(Tyneside Disability Arts 1999: 35)

In his introduction to the anthology of poetry in which this poem is published, Colin Cameron writes:

> We are who we are as people with impairments, and might actually feel comfortable with our lives if it wasn't for all those interfering busybodies who feel that it is their responsibility to feel sorry for us, or to find cures for us, or to manage our lives for us, or to harry us in order to make us something we are not, i.e. 'normal'.
>
> (Tyneside Disability Arts 1999: 3)

The affirmation of positive identity is necessarily collective as well as individual. The growth of organisations of disabled people has been an expression not only of the strength of united struggle against oppression and discrimination, but also of group identity. Disabled identity, as non-disabled identity, has meaning in relation to and constructs the identity of others. To be disabled is to be 'not one of those'.

Group identity, through the development of the Disabled People's Movement, has underpinned the development of an affirmative model in a number of ways.

(1) The development of a social model of disability has re-defined 'disability' in terms of the barriers constructed in a disabling society rather than as a personal tragedy. Through group identity the discourse has shifted to the shared experience and understanding of barriers. 'Personal tragedy' has been reconceptualised as frustration and anger in the face of marginalisation and institutionalised discrimination.

(2) Simply being a member of a campaigning group developing a collective identity is, for some disabled people, a benefit of being disabled in its own right. It can feel exciting being part of a social movement which is bringing about tangible change.

(3)   Frustration and anger are being collectively expressed. They are expressed through Disability Arts and campaigns of the Disabled People's Movement, rather than being seen as personal problems to be resolved, say, through counselling. The roots of Disability Arts lie in the politicising of disability issues. As Shakespeare *et al.* state:

> Drama, cabaret, writing and visual arts have been harnessed to challenge negative images, and build a sense of unity.
>
> (1996: 186)

The activities are so diverse it is difficult to talk in general terms. However, Vic Finkelstein, who was one of the founders of the London Disability Arts Forum (LDAF) in 1987, stated in his presentation at the launch that his hopes for the future were: 'disabled people presenting a clear and unashamed self-identity.' He went on to say that it was, 'essential for us to create our own public image, based upon free acceptance of our distinctive group identity' (Campbell and Oliver 1996). This development of identity has indeed been central to Disability Arts, challenging the values that underlie institutional discrimination. Through song lyrics, poetry, writing, drama and so on, disabled people have celebrated difference and rejected the ideology of normality in which disabled people are devalued as 'abnormal'. They are creating images of strength and pride, the antithesis of dependency and helplessness.

(4)   Through group identity it is recognised that just because there are benefits from being excluded from non-disabled society (which is capitalist, paternalistic and alienating) this does not mean that disabled people should be excluded. From this way of thinking, disabled people enjoy the benefits of being 'outsiders', but should not be pushed out, i.e. should have the right to be 'insiders' if they so wish.

(5)   Finally, group identity has been, for some, a vehicle for revolutionary rather than revisionist visions of change, often under the flags of 'civil rights' and 'equal opportunities' (Shakespeare 1996). The inclusion of disabled people into the mainstream of society would involve the construction of a better society, with better workplaces, better physical environments, and better values including the celebration of differences. As Campbell and Oliver conclude in their history of the Disabled People's Movement:

> In building our own unique movement, we may be not only making our own history but also making a contribution to the history of humankind.
>
> (1996: 180)

Disabled people, encouraged by the Disabled People's Movement, including the Disability Arts Movement, are creating positive images of themselves and are demanding the right to be the way they are – to be equal, but different.

Towards an affirmative model of disability

[. . .] An affirmative model is being generated by disabled people through a rejection of the tragedy model, within which their experiences are denied, distorted or re-interpreted, and through building on the social model, within which disability has been redefined. The affirmative model directly challenges presumptions of personal tragedy and the determination of identity through the value-laden presumptions of non-disabled people. It signifies the rejection of presumptions of tragedy, alongside rejections of presumptions of dependency and abnormality. Whereas the social model is generated by disabled people's experiences within a disabling society, the affirmative model is born of disabled people's experiences as valid individuals, as determining their own lifestyles, culture and identity. The social model sites 'the problem' within society: the affirmative model directly challenges the notion that 'the problem' lies within the individual or impairment.

Embracing an affirmative model, disabled individuals assert a positive identity, not only in being disabled, but also being impaired. In affirming a positive identity of being impaired, disabled people are actively repudiating the dominant value of normality. The changes for individuals are not just a transforming of consciousness as to the meaning of 'disability', but an assertion of the value and validity of life as a person with an impairment.

The social model has empowered disabled people in taking control of support and services, the establishment of Centres for Integrated Living and the struggle for direct payment being clear expressions of this empowerment. The development of an affirmative model takes this fight squarely into the arena of medical intervention. Some impairments, such as diabetes, epilepsy and those involving pain, can respond to intervention. Just as the social model signified, for disabled people, ownership of the meaning of disability, so the affirmative model signifies ownership of impairment or, more broadly, the body. The control of intervention is paramount. This is an affirmation by disabled people of the right to control what is done to their bodies. It includes the right to know the basis on which decisions of medical intervention are made, the consequences of taking drugs (including side effects), the consequences of not taking drugs, and the alternatives. Disability Action North East states:

> Our movement should campaign for effective healthcare treatments that are under our control, treatments that are Holistic and see our differences not as Geneticists do (as 'defective traits') but as a *positive* sign of our human diversity.
>
> (1998: 3)

It has been argued that the greatest danger for disabled people in addressing impairment is political, with the possibility that impairment is seen to be 'the problem', as in the tragedy model. The danger is clearly apparent in the following quotation from a book entitled *An Introduction to Disability Studies*. Writing about the social model, Johnstone states:

> As an explanation it must somehow begin to incorporate, rather than stand in opposition to the medical/deficit model of disablement.
>
> (1998: 20)

Yet on the previous page he also recognises that:

> The medical model encourages the simplistic view that disability is a personal tragedy for the individual concerned.
>
> (1998: 19)

Indeed, it is for this reason that the social model cannot 'incorporate' the medical model and for this reason, too, that the affirmative model is emerging to strengthen the opposition of the social model to the personal tragedy model.
Oliver states:

> This denial of the pain of impairment has not, in reality, been a denial at all. Rather it has been a pragmatic attempt to identify and address issues that can be changed through collective action rather than medical or other professional treatment.
>
> (1996: 38)

The affirmative model, however, is not about the 'pain of impairment', but on the contrary the positive experiences and identity of disabled people from being impaired and disabled. The social model is collectively expressed, most obviously, through direct action and campaigns in the struggle of the powerless for power. The affirmative model again builds on this particularly through the development of the Disability Arts Movement within which disabled people collectively affirm their positive identity through visual arts, cabaret, song and, as in the following extract by Colin Cameron, poetry.

Sub Rosa
Fighting to establish self-respect ...
Not the same, but different ...
Not normal, but disabled ...
Who wants to be normal anyway?
Not ashamed, with heads hanging,
Avoiding the constant gaze of those who assume
that sameness is something to be desired ...
Nor victims
of other people's lack of imagination ...
But proud and privileged to be who we are ...
Exactly as we are.

(Tyneside Disability Arts 1998)

Rather than being politically threatening to disabled people, the affirmative model builds on and strengthens the Disabled People's Movement, not least by bringing disabled people, who would not otherwise engage in political action, into the Disability Arts Movement.

Finally, in terms of visions of the future, the affirmative model is building on the social model, through which disabled people envisage full participative citizenship and equal rights. Disabled people not only look towards a society without structural, environmental or attitudinal barriers, but also a society which celebrates difference and values people irrespective of race, sexual preference, gender, age or impairment.

In this paper, we have summarised an affirmative model and the social and historical context in which it is emerging. The broader significance of this view of disability and impairment has yet to be fully realised. We conclude by suggesting two directions for development. First, it is central to the concept of 'inclusion'. Policies, provision and practice, whether in community living or education, can only be inclusive through full recognition of disability culture and the affirmative model generated from the experiences of disabled people (Oliver and Barnes 1998). Secondly, an affirmative model also has a role to play in the development of a theory of disability. In his book on *Social Identity*, Jenkins (1996) writes of resistance as potent affirmation of group identity:

> Struggles for a different allocation of resources and resistance to categorisation are one and the same thing . . . Whether or not there is an explicit call to arms in these terms, something that can be called self-assertion – or 'human spirit' – is at the core of resistance to domination . . . It is as intrinsic, and as necessary, to that social life as the socialising tyranny of categorisation.
>
> (1996: 175)

As is so often the case, however, in relation to sociology generally and feminist theory, for instance, existing theory and concepts are rarely explicit in the validation of the experiences of disabled people and are often explicit in invalidation. Jenkins rarely mentions disability, and when he does the same old questions arise:

> Perhaps the most pertinent questions arise out of perceived, typically bodily, impairments: is the neonate to be acknowledged as acceptably human?
>
> (1996: 55)

Better dead than disabled? Quintessentially, the affirmative model is held by disabled people about disabled people. Its theoretical significance can also only be developed by disabled people who are 'proud, angry and strong' in resisting the tyranny of the personal tragedy model of disability and impairment.

References

Abberley, P. (1996) Work, utopia and impairment. In L. Barton (ed.) *Disability and Society: emerging issues and insights*. London: Longman.

Bartlett, J. (1994) *Will You Be Mother? Women Who Choose to Say No*. London: Virago Press.

Campbell, J. and Oliver, M. (1996) *Disabling Politics: understanding our past, changing our future*. London: Routledge.

Corker, M. (1996) *Deaf Transitions: images and origins of deaf families, deaf communities and deaf identities*. London: Jessica Kingsley.

Crow, L. (1992) Renewing the social model of disability. *Coalition*, July, 5–9.

Crow, L. (1996) Including all our lives: renewing the social model of disability. In J. Morris (ed.) *Encounters with Strangers: feminism and disability*. London: Women's Press.

Disability Action North East (1998) *Fighting Back Against Eugenics and the New Oppressors*. Newcastle-upon-Tyne: Disability Action North East.

Disability Awareness in Action (1997) *Life, Death and Rights: bioethics and disabled people*. Special Supplement. London: Disability Awareness in Action.

French, S. (1991) The advantages of visual impairment: some physiotherapists' views. *New Beacon*, **75** (872), 1–6.

French, S. (1993) Disability, impairment or something in between? In J. Swain, V. Finkelstein, S. French and M. Oliver (eds) *Disabling Barriers – enabling environments*. London: Sage.

French, S. and Swain, J. (1997) It's time to take up the offensive. *Therapy Weekly*, **23** (34), 7.

Garland Thomson, R. (1997) Feminist theory, the body and the disabled figure. In J.L. Davis (ed.) *The Disability Studies Reader*. London: Routledge.

Hughes, B. and Paterson, K. (1997) The social model of disability and the disappearing body: towards a sociology of impairment. *Disability & Society*, **12** (3), 225–40.

Jenkins, R. (1996) *Social Identity*. London: Routledge.

Johnstone, D. (1998) *An Introduction to Disability Studies*. London: David Fulton.

Keith, L. (ed.) (1994) *Mustn't Grumble: writings by disabled women*. London: Women's Press.

Morris, J. (ed.) (1989) *Able Lives: women's experience of paralysis*. London: Women's Press.

Morris, J. (1991) *Pride Against Prejudice: transforming attitudes to disability*. London: Women's Press.

Oliver, M. (1993) Disability and dependency: a creation of industrial societies? In J. Swain, V. Finkelstein, S. French and M. Oliver (eds) *Disabling Barriers – enabling environments*. London: Sage.

Oliver, M. (1996) *Understanding Disability: from theory to practice*. Basingstoke: Macmillan.

Oliver, M. and Barnes, C. (1998) *Disabled People and Social Policy: from exclusion to inclusion*. Harlow: Longman.

Oliver, M. and Sapey, B. (1999) *Social Work with Disabled People*, 2nd edn. Basingstoke: Macmillan.

Pinter, R. (1996) Sick-but-fit or fit-but-sick? Ambiguity and identity at the workplace. In C. Barnes and G. Mercer (eds) *Exploring the Divide: illness and disability*. Leeds: Disability Press.

Priestley, M. (1999) *Disability Politics and Community Care*. London: Jessica Kingsley.

Shakespeare, T.W. (1992) A reply to Liz Crow. *Coalition*, September, 40.

Shakespeare, T.W. (1994) Cultural representation of disabled people: dustbins for disavowal? *Disability & Society*, **9**(3), 283–99.

Shakespeare, T.W. (1996) Disability, identity, difference. In C. Barnes and G. Mercer (eds) *Exploring the Divide: illness and disability*. Leeds: Disability Press.

Shakespeare, T., Gillespie-Sells, K. and Davies, D. (1996) *The Sexual Politics of Disability*. London: Cassell.

Shakespeare, T.W. and Watson, N. (1997) Defending the social model. *Disability & Society*, **12**(2), 293–300.

Tyneside Disability Arts (1998) *Sub Rosa: clandestine voices*. Wallsend: Tyneside Disability Arts.

Tyneside Disability Arts (1999) *Transgressions*. Wallsend: Tyneside Disability Arts.

Vasey, S. (1992) Disability culture: it's a way of life. In R. Rieser and M. Mason (eds) *Disability Equality in the Classroom: a human rights issue*. London: Disability Equality in Education.

Watson, N. (1998) Enabling identity: disability, self and citizenship. In T. Shakespeare (ed.) *The Disability Reader: social science perspectives*. London: Cassell.

Wendell, S. (1996) *The Rejected Body: feminist philosophical reflections on disability*. New York: Routledge.

Wendell, S. (1997) Towards a feminist theory of disability. In J.L. Davis (ed.) *The Disability Studies Reader*. London: Routledge.

Rhetoric about celebrating difference as a feature of inclusive education abounds. Through this discussion of the importance of affirming rather than denying who we are, this chapter may have helped to bring this notion to life. A culture in which we are visible, affirmed and valued is also one in which we are more likely to actively participate and to take the risks involved with being a learner.

CHAPTER 15

Having a say

Jenny Morris

This chapter is taken from a study carried out by Jenny Morris on behalf of Scope, a national charity for people with cerebral palsy. At the heart of the study are the direct experiences of 44 young people with high levels of physical, sensory and/or cognitive impairment. All the young people are at risk of social exclusion. While government policy assumes social inclusion is about having a job, for the young people in this study social inclusion is about having friends, choices and being listened to. This chapter reflects the experiences of several young people, who face a number of barriers before they can 'have a say' in their own lives.

For most non-disabled young people, adolescence is a time when they are able to make more and more decisions for themselves – about what they wear, what they do, who their friends are, what music they listen to, and what values they hold. This was not the experience of most of the young people involved in the research project described in this chapter. There were a number of barriers to having a say in their lives, the most important being other people's reactions to their communication needs.

Recognition of communication

In the case of those who have high levels of communication needs, we found it was very common for the people who knew them well (parents, teachers and support workers) to be unable to provide concrete examples of how they communicated. 'I just know when he's not happy because I know him so well' was a common response. This may be a positive aspect of a close relationship but it means that young people may not have a way of communicating with those who do not know them well. It may also mean that they have limited interaction even with those who do know them well. This vulnerability is not necessarily created by impairment but by a failure to establish a means of communicating, and by a failure to share information about or even recognise ways of communicating.

The following dialogue with Gwen's mother illustrates a number of issues common to the situation of many of the young people we visited.

When was the last time Gwen had an assessment of her communication needs? I would imagine at school, I have a speech therapy report – it says Gwen's communication difficulties are profound, that's all it says. *Does she have a way of communicating yes or no?* Yes. *Are they profound then?* Well they're not. Gwen I think has 95 per cent understanding, so if she has that understanding, if there was a way through . . . For years I've fought this, for years I've said it's not 'profound', but I'm just tired of that now, if that's what they say . . . you can't go on battling. *How does she communicate yes and no?* Yes is a positive look at you and if it's no then she looks away from you. It's eye contact. It's the only thing she has which is really accurate. Her movement isn't accurate. *Do they work with that at school?* Yes but they've been trying to go forward with a more universally acceptable form of communication because not everyone on first meeting Gwen will understand her. So they want her to be tactile [ie they want her to touch switches or pictures as a means of communicating], which is very difficult for Gwen because she's very athetoid, her movements aren't controlled. *So why do they think being tactile might be appropriate?* Well I think they think it's what society would expect. *So how does she communicate with them at school?* I think they just know her now. She really indicates with body language. She really has quite explicit body language. If she wants the loo she does this shuffling, if she's thirsty she tongues, she looks a lot at what she wants, until you get the message. If you don't get the message quickly she'll get agitated and you'll have to ask her and she'll try and eye point, gesture. *What about responding to questions?* If I asked her a question, like do you like music? Yes, she'd smile. *And if I went through a list of different kinds of music?* You mean would she choose, probably, but she likes a lot of music, from classical, to pop to rap. *But if I closed the question, if I said do you like classical music?* Yes, she'd say yes. *If I asked her something more complicated, like do you feel you have a say?* I wonder what her response would be. I think she'd understand but I must say I don't think she has a say, not in what she's going to do in the future. *Why's that do you think?* Because there's so little on offer for her, so what would it matter what she wants to do?

Possibly the most shocking fact here is that Gwen is 19 and was about to leave school. During all her years of education she had not apparently had access to effective assessment of, and response to, her communication needs. Instead, she was labelled as having 'profound communication difficulties' and this undoubtedly contributed to her mother's limited expectations of Gwen's communication abilities. Rather than working with the methods of communication which suited Gwen, the school tried to get her to communicate in a way which was particularly unsuited to her – as someone with athetoid cerebral palsy she has great difficulty controlling her arm and hand movements. However, as Gwen's mother indicates from her last point, even if Gwen's methods of communicating were fully recognised and maximised she would still have few options because our society does not offer much to young people with high levels of support needs like Gwen.

From our observations of her at school and at home, it would seem that Gwen is probably quite similar to Adam, in terms of how cerebral palsy affects her body and cognitive ability. However, their experiences around communication and having a say in their lives could not be more different. We were told that Gwen would not be able to participate in an interview, although it would seem that she does not have significant cognitive impairment, while we were told that Adam would 'speak' for himself, using clear methods of indicating 'yes' and 'no'. Adam's methods of communicating 'yes' and 'no' had been recognised from an early age by his parents, who had high expectations of his potential for communication. His school did not try to get him to communicate using switches or other methods that would not have suited him. And possibly most importantly he had, as discussed in the next section, been given many experiences of making choices and having a say in his life. When asked 'Do you feel you have a say in what happens in your life?' he responded, 'Yes'.

It seems to be quite common for young people to be encouraged to use methods of communication which are seen as socially acceptable, or which a professional has knowledge of, but which may not be best suited to their needs, while those methods which do suit them are ignored or belittled. Katherine, for example, was set an objective by her teachers of using two switches to indicate 'yes' and 'no' although she seemed much more able to communicate by facial expression.

We observed a number of young people at school and it was clear that some of them experienced situations where no-one understood how they communicated. Sometimes their inclusion in lessons – and their opportunities for learning – was tokenistic. One interviewer observed 16-year-old Lois and described how the teacher, using photographs in an exercise about different types of jobs:

> showed her two possibilities, taking care to try to get the photos into her eyeline by placing them vertically on the edge of her tray. Lois did scan these, but no methodology was employed to get her to make her choice – no eye pointing or other method. I had asked [the teacher] at lunch break about this. 'How does Lois make choices, what is her "yes" and "no"?' and she replied that she really had no idea.

Even when a young person is able to use a communication system such as Makaton, there often seem to be barriers. Philip, who uses Makaton signs as his primary means of communication, was visited one day when he had just moved from one bungalow to another at his residential school. The interviewer noted:

> As the morning went on it became apparent that no-one in the staff group was proficient at Makaton (the teacher who seemed to have the most knowledge was unsure of many signs and was also unaware of any 'peculiarities' Philip had).

There did not appear to have been any transition time between staff who knew Philip well from the last bungalow and present staff. There was also disagreement between the staff as to what the signs for certain words were.

There often seemed to be a distressing carelessness about maximising a young person's communication abilities. Sharon was observed to use Makaton at home. When the interviewer asked her teacher about her own use of Makaton she replied that she had just got BSL Stage One and tried to teach staff the 'odd word'. 'However' she went on, 'because we have so many supply teachers, we cannot use Makaton and in any case, they don't use it further down the school so there's no point using it in my class.'

So many times we were told by teachers or other workers that they had plans to do work around communication – when it seemed this should have been done years before (all the young people in the research project were between the ages of 15 and 20). For example, we were told, by his teacher, that 15-year-old Joseph is very effective in communicating with eye pointing and can recognise symbols for everyday objects. However the teacher also admitted that the school had not really 'done much with this' and they 'hoped to build on it next year'.

Sometimes, equipment was inadequate or had fallen into disrepair. Anjum is bilingual in Urdu and English but only has a blissboard in English. Her blissboard had not been updated and this forced her to use unnecessarily simplified language. Annette had a Liberator Talker which had been supplied to her five years ago and was now broken. Two of the young people interviewed had recently been assessed as needing a piece of communication equipment which was very expensive (£7,000 and £12,000) and which neither education, health nor social services were willing to pay for. Their parents were therefore trying to raise the money through charities.

It seemed to be quite common – particularly amongst those young people with the highest levels of communication and cognitive impairments – for passivity to be treated as a good thing. Philippa's support worker said, 'She's very pleasant, she'll go along with anything.' In contrast, young people's attempts to communicate are sometimes seen as troublesome – particularly in school. Philip was observed during a day at school and many times his attempts at communication were either ignored or suppressed. The interviewer wrote: 'Philip was often told off during the day for making a noise, going on about things. He seems to have a series of signs which he uses over and over again and this was described to me as being attention seeking.' In contrast, Philip's mother describes him as 'a great communicator'. Danny is someone who uses noises and body language to communicate. He readily establishes eye contact and is often 'reaching out' with his eyes to initiate communication. However, in class his attempts to establish contact with fellow students, support workers and with the teacher were usually seen as inappropriate and disruptive.

We interviewed or visited with a number of young people who had recently moved from school to a residential home. In some cases, the home had received useful and comprehensive information about how the young person communicated but in others they had either not received any information or the information turned out to be of little use. We were sometimes shown information, for example, which seemed to have been based on communication assessments made many years ago, and instructions that did not make much sense. Michael's keyworker, for example, said 'The school gave us information about communication – but it wasn't always accurate and some of it's quite old. It listed "key gestures to use when speaking to Michael" which didn't mean anything to us. Also it didn't tell us that he has clear ways of communicating yes and no.'

It was clear that, for many of these young people, a failure to maximise their communication potential meant that, once they moved out of a situation where someone knew them well, they were very vulnerable. They had no way of telling anyone if they had toothache, or were feeling unwell, or uncomfortable, or were being abused. This must be very frightening and at times could be life-threatening.

In only a few instances did we encounter a situation where a move from one service to another increased someone's potential for communication. This was Mark's experience. We had been told by his school and by his mother that Mark was not able to express preferences and had no method of communication. Indeed, observation at school and at home seemed to confirm this. In contrast, when he was visited at the day service he moved onto when he left school, the manager described him as 'one of our more able clients'. She went on to recount how he had received an assessment from a speech therapist over a six-week period, and described the work that had then been done with support workers on Mark's communication needs, and how each day his support workers were expected to fill in a form showing what choices Mark had made and how he had communicated his preferences.

Making choices

Perhaps one of the biggest barriers to making choices is when it is assumed that impairment means that it is not possible for the young person to make choices. Her sister and mother said that 19-year-old Tahiba was not able to make choices – 'It makes it very difficult, we have to think for her. To be honest with you, there's no communication there at all. It's difficult.' However, Tahiba was present during the interview and was communicating using body language and facial expressions – particularly when the interviewer asked about friends and what she liked doing. Indeed, her sister described situations where Tahiba communicated her needs and preferences very clearly: 'For example, if she wants a cuddle, she'll crawl up to you and sort of put her face near you and she'll initiate that she wants a cuddle.'

It is not always cognitive or communication impairment which gets in the way of exerting choice. Anjum's family allows her very little choice in her life. She told us that her mother keeps her benefits and her parents buy her clothes (without taking Anjum with them to the shops). She does not go out much. 'It's too hard' she said. 'The wheelchair and me are too heavy. If I had a specialist vehicle or chair, I might perhaps go out more but I don't have this opportunity.' Two care workers come into her home each morning and evening to help her but she has no influence or choice over the selection of carers who are sent by an agency. She would like to be able to choose. She told us that sometimes the care workers do things which she doesn't like and she tells her mother about this, as she wouldn't be comfortable complaining directly herself – 'they seem to be in such a hurry all the time.'

Sometimes a lot of attention is given to choices over day-to-day things like eating and drinking and little or no attention to the bigger things – like going out, or where the young person will move on to following school. When Katherine was visited at her residential school, it seemed that a lot of attention was given to going through almost a ritual of choice of whether to drink tea or coffee, but she was given no opportunity of choosing what to do after school or at weekends. She was also not able to choose to have a calendar of the Chippendales on the wall in her bedroom but had to keep it under the bed, to be brought out on 'special occasions'.

Ron's ability to make choices is very much determined by the ability of others around him to recognise the way he communicates preferences. This was illustrated in the disagreement between his parents and staff at the residential home as to whether he should go on holiday. His father said, 'We felt that the benefits were more in the mind of the staff. It would involve Ron spending long periods of time in his wheelchair, which he finds very uncomfortable, and being in an unfamiliar place that he doesn't like. But because he can't say what he is feeling they might think it's OK.' Ron's way of saying 'no' is that he just puts his head down and 'shuts out' the rest of the world: his parents feel this is easy to ignore.

Most of the young people involved in this research project spent time away from their homes, at boarding school, residential homes and/or in respite care settings. These were choices that others made for them. In some cases it was seen to be in their best interests (to attend a specialist school or college for example); in others it was for the benefit of others (primarily in order to give their parents a break for example); while in other cases this was seen to be the only way their needs could be met (for example young people who are considered to have nursing care needs). It was only rarely possible to discern what the young person themselves felt about these placements. Nicky's father reported that Nicky associated the theme tune to the television series Heartbeat with the time, on a Sunday evening, when his parents took him back to boarding school and told of how 'everytime he heard the music for Heartbeat he used to cry his eyes out'.

When young people do not have a say within a setting in which they spend time, this is reflected in the institutional 'feel' of, for example, the residential respite unit where 15-year-old Joseph goes on a Friday night. His bedroom, the interviewer noted, was 'very, very bare . . . no posters or anything bright and no toys'. Another interviewer, who visited 19-year-old Lawrence at the residential unit where he lives, commented: 'There was little evidence of an effort being made to make the place homely. It certainly does not feel like someone's home. There is a lack of art/pictures and colour. I remember seeing one vase of daffodils, but they were lost in such a large (sitting) room. There was a lot of clutter that made the place look unkempt, for example rubbish outside by the barbecue, equipment left in hallways. The exterior of the building also made me think of a hospital or doctor's surgery. The physical space therefore was enough, I thought, to make one feel down.'

Music is often very important to young people and even those with very little other choice in their lives make their preferences known when it comes to music. Gwen has little choice over the clothes she wears or over food, which are both chosen by her mother. However, when it comes to music she expresses her preferences very clearly and her choice of music is very different from her mother's. Anjum is able to express her preferences in terms of the music she likes – the radio station India 1 – and, like many teenagers, experiences her mother's disapproval of her taste in music. Rosalie was the only person who said that she had control over who gave her personal assistance. She also had clear ideas about having a home of her own, where she wanted to live and go to college. While she has a high level of personal assistance needs and uses augmented communication, she was one of the very few young people who came across as confident, and able to express her opinions and individuality freely. Physical dependency and communication impairment does not necessarily create passivity and a lack of independence.

Communication of needs

If young people are not able to say what their needs are, this can have a major impact on the quality of their lives unless those around them are able to understand whether they are in pain or are unhappy. We found that, for those with the higher levels of communication and cognitive impairments, it was common for those around them to feel that they cannot know what is going on for them. Philippa's headteacher reported that she had been through a period of 'crying and touching her eyes a lot'. She said that the staff had called a meeting to discuss this and 'felt it might be epilepsy and decided to monitor her'. After a while Philippa seemed better and they decided that it must have been that she was 'unwell or had some internal trauma'. Anna's acute appendicitis was misdiagnosed as 'pain associated with ovulation' because the doctor did not recognise Anna's communication of her symptoms – or did not pay much attention to the information her mother gave him.

Both Thomas and Ron had recently been diagnosed as needing glasses as a result of eye tests, which were done at the residential unit they moved into when leaving school. Their visual impairment had not been recognised at the residential schools they attended. Ron had recently started biting his lip, which, according to his mother, is a sign that he is in pain but no-one has managed so far to find out what is going on for him. We also picked up instances when those around them did not recognise that some experiences may be distressing. Philip, for example, had become distressed while on a visit to a museum when his group were being shown human bones on display. Philip has on occasion been extremely ill and had nearly died two years ago. The interviewer noted that she felt 'There's an awful lot to Philip that is just getting ignored.'

Sometimes, even when young people are able to communicate their feelings this seems not to be picked up by those around them. Jane boards weekly at her school and when she was interviewed, communicated that she does not like the boarding house. She indicated that she has no choice over things such as what she ate or what activities she does after school, that she did not like the people who assisted her there, and that the housemother shouts at her and tells her off. This information, which Jane communicated by a combination of indicating 'Yes' and 'No' and using Bliss Symbolics, came as a surprise to her support worker who was present at the interview. For some young people, a failure to maximise their communication abilities can make them very vulnerable to abuse. Paul's mother found out that the driver who picked her son up from school had been hitting him but it was only when a teacher saw this happen that anyone knew. Anna's mother also found out that another child had been hitting her daughter in the children's home they both lived in. 'I only knew about it because it happened one day I was there. Anna didn't react . . . I was just amazed that she didn't flinch.'

Some young people may use speech to communicate, yet other aspects of their impairment or experience make them vulnerable to not being able to communicate their needs. Darren's mother said that while Darren expresses his frustration and dissatisfaction with things at home, 'He tends to be very compliant at school. He's very vulnerable. He asks questions but he will never answer questions. You would have to know him very, very well before you knew whether he was unhappy with something.' Kamal said she was bullied at school, but didn't tell anyone about it – 'I didn't have a chance,' she said, although she has recently been able to tell her social worker about being bullied at college.

Sometimes, it is necessary to have access to specialist advice in order to understand someone's behaviour but this is not always available. Darren's autism was undiagnosed for some years and this meant his family had difficulty understanding why he behaved as he did. Having information about the nature and impact of someone's impairment can make a big difference to whether needs are recognised. Anna's mother found her habit of eating anything she could get her hands on very, very difficult to deal with. 'I really didn't know why she was doing it. I knew it wasn't hunger, I thought it was attention, and I thought, "Well I give you all the attention I can, why are you doing it?" I know it sounds ridiculous but it really did get me so annoyed. I thought, "Why are you doing this to yourself? It must be dangerous." After some years of this, a community mental health nurse became involved who – by monitoring Anna's behaviour – found that it manifested itself during the 72 hours leading up to an epileptic fit. Having received a diagnosis and a reason for her daughter's behaviour, her mother found that she was able to respond to Anna's needs more effectively: 'Once he told me it was just like a weight had been lifted.'

Unless channels of communication are opened up between these young people and those around them, it is difficult to see how they can experience ordinary human relationships. A denial of communication means a denial of so much of what it is to be human. It means being denied a say in what happens to you and creates a risk that needs will not be recognised. At best this results in a very poor quality of life; at worst it results in a threat to life itself.

Many of the chapters in this volume focus on how marginalised young people, with their allies, have struggled to make their own views heard. Jenny Morris' chapter shows that we still have a long way to go. We could see the chapter's title as an ironic reflection on their silence and exclusion. For the young people she writes about, 'having a say' is at best a distant dream. The chapter leaves us thinking about how participation and choice might be options for all young people.

CHAPTER 16

The struggle for inclusion: the growth of a movement

Richard Rieser

In this chapter, Richard Rieser, a disabled person, writer and trainer, describes how the commitment of a relatively small group of activists has had a major impact on the development of inclusive education in the UK. Grounded firmly on the principles of the Disability Rights Movement, the Alliance for Inclusive Education has used both political lobbying and direct action to challenge the barriers within society that prevent inclusion. Within the Alliance, the voices and experiences of disabled adults and children have been central in defining agendas for change.

Never doubt that a small group of thoughtful committed citizens can change the world: Indeed it's the only thing that ever has.

(Margaret Mead)

Introduction

Since 1989 a movement has developed in the United Kingdom that struggles for the inclusion of disabled children and students in mainstream schools and colleges as a civil and human right. It has set about changing the thinking throughout the education system; giving a voice to disabled children and their non-disabled peers and allies; supporting parents in coming to know it was the oppressive special educational needs system that was their problem and not their disabled children; changing thinking in the voluntary sector and government; creating a space for all those many professionals who influence the lives of disabled children so they can reconsider their beliefs and practices and thereby improve the life chances of disabled young people.

This has not been easy and even today, as will be shown, there is much resistance which maintains oppressive structures and practices in the education system and beyond. However, real change is occurring in schools and colleges, teacher thinking and government policy.

Here I will examine the development of the thinking, policies, practices and a few of the struggles which shaped the Integration Alliance. From 1989 the Alliance has developed a radical approach to the inclusion which has had impact well beyond the few dozen activists who make up the core of the Alliance. In 1996 the Integration Alliance changed its name to the Alliance for Inclusive Education. This was more than a change in name or image; it came from a growing understanding of the major differences between integration and inclusion. The former is a matter of location; placing a disabled child in a mainstream setting, usually with some additional support to access what was being offered in the school, changing the child to fit in with the social and academic life of the school. The latter is about valuing all children irrespective of their type or degree of impairment; of restructuring the institution to remove barriers so teaching and learning take place so all children can be valued for who they are, participate, interact and develop their potential. [...]

The Movement for Inclusion in the UK grew out of a range of groups and individuals who came from a range of perspectives, but all of them wanted to throw off the shackles of the past with its oppressive treatment of disabled young people, especially within the education system. They were guided by a principle of equality and human rights. For parents this was the idea that their disabled child had a right to belong to their local community and play a full part in their local playgroup, nursery, primary or secondary school and local college. For teachers and other professionals it meant a commitment to equality and civil rights which led them to question current segregative practices and the ideology of special educational needs with its oppressive origins and led to new practices of supporting inclusion. For disabled people the issue was an understanding of the damaging effects of their own schooling and a desire to bring civil rights for disabled people into education so that further generations of disabled young people would not have to undergo the alienation and isolation they had experienced. Civil rights organisations and activists saw the need for greater social justice and equality (Integration Alliance 1989).

The Integration Alliance

The Integration Alliance was set up following a conference in September 1989 of disabled adults, parents of disabled children and professionals and others who allied themselves to getting rid of segregated education for all children.

Parents of disabled children at the conference told of how the current special education legislation, practices and views of professionals prevented the integration of their children.

> You're told everyone wants integration, but only in an ideal world, not here and now. But we do want it here and now.

> Integrated placements should be a right not a privilege. It really is very odd that we have to go round asking – feeling we are imposing on the school.

Professional advice on statementing is a nation-wide joke: it is always designed to fit the kind of provision available, not the needs of the child.

Who are the most prejudiced people we encounter as parents? Not ordinary people, not other parents, but the providers of services.

(Integration Alliance 1989)

The initial impetus for the conference came from a linking up of Parents in Partnership, a Wandsworth, London, based group of parents of disabled children who fought for their belief that their children had a right to go to mainstream schools, with Micheline Mason, a disabled mother of a disabled child who brought the thinking of the disability movement to the question of integration. The Centre for Studies of Integrated Education, a small research and information-providing charity that had grown out of the Spastics Society but was now independent (CSIE), and Newham Council, which since 1984 had been developing integrated schools and closing special schools, were also important early key supporters.

Micheline had been educated at home until she was 14 and then sent to a special boarding school and was determined her daughter Lucy would not have to undergo the isolation that she had.

Children, contrary to the adult view, are not cruel. I have a daughter with a major physical disability. She has mixed with able-bodied children all her five years of life and is now in a mainstream primary school. The children's problems around her have been very easy to deal with. A bit of good information about her disability, a few guidelines about rough games and Lucy has been completely absorbed into school life. The children have come up with wonderful plans to overcome some of the problems caused by stairs, for example. Our problems in securing and keeping the integrated placement have all been with adults, and most particularly with bureaucrats, distant from the actual situation.

(Micheline Mason, Integration Alliance 1989)

Other disabled people attending spoke about the oppressive nature of their schooling.

Being separated at school was uncomfortable. I was being picked on and bullied quite a lot, made fun of, in the special school – which made me very aggressive towards people, even teachers. In an ordinary school, I wouldn't have seen the blackboard, but if I had closed circuit TV I would. And I would have mixed with ordinary people . . . Start young because then the kids would accept the other kids with learning difficulties or missing limbs and they would grow up with them.

(Simon Gardiner, Integration Alliance 1989)

The local disability movement in Lambeth – Lambeth Accord – and the London Boroughs Disability Resource Team, who provided advice and training on disability equality across London, were also at the conference.

> It really is about time you parents joined forces with us disabled activists, and perhaps together after sharing our expertise and strengths, we shall be able to blast a hole through what has seemed to be an impenetrable barrier of attitudes and inaccessible schools and teaching methods, and show what we really want and need, and also how to go about it.
>
> (Jane Campbell, LBDRT, Integration Alliance 1989)

Other disabled people at the conference spoke of the deeply harmful effects of being segregated, of not having a peer group, of being isolated. The following are examples of such perspectives:

> The experience of being isolated from our peer-group, and brothers and sisters, produced loneliness and isolation.
>
> No common schooling meant no common ground for play or association.
>
> We felt we were 'out of sight, out of mind'.
>
> We need more disabled teachers.
>
> We need disability equality training to be built into the training of teachers and educational psychologists.
>
> The difficulties for us in mainstream schools need to be tackled, not avoided. Integration needs to be on our terms! We are not the problem.
>
> (Integration Alliance 1989)

The conference was held in the run-up to the break-up of the Inner London Education Authority which, although the most segregated education authority in the country, with over 3 per cent of its pupils attending 105 of its own special schools and many others, was committed to developing more integration in the wake of The Fish Report Educational Opportunities for All (ILEA 1985). This document, which had argued for structural changes to develop more integration, had been largely blocked by the Teachers' Associations and the ILEA Inspectorate, but more and more parents were wanting an integrated school placement for their children. The conference developed and campaigned around the slogan 'Integration Now' to take to the 13 successor Inner London Boroughs and then, as the Alliance grew, across the whole country.

The trend for integration had started in the 1960s and 1970s, when more liberal ideas about education began to develop, and has continued to the present day among growing numbers of teachers and parents. For example, for England and Wales the number of ascertained (equivalent of statemented) pupils in mainstream schools including units and special classes rose from 11,027 (6.8 per cent) in 1973 to 21,245 in 1977, 12 per cent of all children requiring special provision (HMSO 1974 and DES 1977). The percentage of pupils with statements placed in maintained mainstream schools in England has continued to increase substantially, from 54 per cent (113,124) in 1995 to 60 per cent (152,800) in 2000 (DfEE 1999). However, in 2000 there were still 100,066 pupils with statements outside the mainstream in special schools, Pupil Referral Units and independent and non-maintained special schools in England (DfEE 2000).

Also at the founding conference were Linda Jordan and Chris Goodey who were part of a group of parents of disabled children in the London Borough of Newham who had fought since 1984 to close special schools in Newham and develop an integrated system where all children could go to their neighbourhood school. [. . .] Since that time Newham has continued developing its policy for inclusion and now has the lowest number of disabled pupils attending special schools in the whole country, only 0.33 per cent of all pupils compared with 1.3 per cent as an English average (DfEE 2000 Table 15). More interestingly, Newham schools continue to demonstrate that the changes in teaching and learning style that teachers have had to develop to include the full range of children in their classes has led to a general improvement in educational achievement. Newham secondary schools topped the improvement league tables over the last four years on A*–G GCSE grades (DfEE 1997–2000). In addition exclusion rates are the lowest in London with a growing emphasis on developing the emotional intelligence of all pupils (Jordan and Goodey 1996). [. . .]

The prospect of an integrated future for some disabled children had been raised by the Warnock Report (HMSO 1978) with the implementation of its thinking in the 1981 Education Act. However, there was much resistance in the educational and medical worlds to the integration of all children. Indeed the Warnock Report, while getting rid of the old categories of 'handicap' linked to particular types of special school, introduced the broader concept of 'special educational need' and put forward the idea that there was a continuum of special educational needs, some of which could be met through integration in ordinary schools, but that there were groups of children for whom provision at special school is particularly to be needed in the future. [. . .] This, together with the recommendation that LEAs should produce a special education review and plan led to a geographically discrete fixed continuum of provision in most Authorities, where pupils with mild impairments or needs were integrated and those with more significant needs were segregated in separate special schools or separated in units attached to mainstream schools (geographic or social integration).

Previously, the 1976 Education Act through section 10 had put on the statute book, as part of a move to wider comprehensive education, that subject to certain qualifications and from a date to be approved by the Secretary of State 'handicapped' pupils in England and Wales are to be educated in ordinary schools in preference to special schools.

The qualifications were impracticability, incompatibility with the efficiency of the school or the involvement of unreasonable public expenditure. However, ministers had given assurances that this was no threat to special schools:

> The new law . . . does not herald the precipitate dismantling of the very valuable work of special schools, particularly those for children with severe disabilities . . . a minority of handicapped children will always need the help that only a special school can give, and it will be important to ensure that integration does not force them into isolation.
>
> (Shirley Williams 1977: 122)

In the event the 1981 Act laid down three caveats which would make integration much harder to achieve as they could be used as hooks on which professional prejudice and fear could be hung.

This was later incorporated into section 316 of the 1996 Education Act as follows:

(1)   Any person exercising any function under this part in respect of a child with special educational needs who should be educated in school shall secure, if the conditions mentioned in sub-section (2) are satisfied, the child is educated in a school which is not a special school unless it is incompatible with the wishes of the parent.

(2)   The conditions are that educating the child in a school which is not a special school is compatible with
(a)   His receiving the special educational provision which his learning difficulty calls for,
(b)   The provision of efficient education for the children with whom he is educated, and
(c)   The efficient use of resources.

The Warnock/1981/1996 approach is fundamentally discriminatory and is based on viewing children with special educational needs as having individual needs which need to be met in the most appropriate setting regardless of how socially isolated this makes them. There is no conception of human rights here. At its heart it viewed children with special educational needs as needing to be subject to a multi-professional assessment which is predominantly based on a 'medical model' approach in which the impairment and fixing it is seen as more important than the ordinary needs of the child to be socially included and be valued for who they are.

Writing in 1989, Swann (1989) noted it was hard to discern anything that could be termed a national integration strategy policy since 1981. No clear steps had been taken by the DES to reduce the numbers going to special schools. They have not issued guidance to LEAs about how they should interpret the integration clauses in the 1981 Act. [. . .] The Integration Alliance aimed to address this inequity and since this conference has played a key role in developing the struggle for inclusion and its development in the UK. [. . .]

The organisation currently has a council which meets quarterly and this is elected at the AGM. It has an individual membership of around 200 families, individual parents, disabled people and professionals and some 60 affiliated organisations. A majority of the council are disabled people. This allows it to be part of the British Council of Disabled People which today has some 130 organisations which are run by disabled people representing over 300,000 disabled people. This distinction between organisations 'of' and organisations 'for' disabled people is important. The lives of many disabled people, especially in the world of education, have been determined by charities run by non-disabled people. They have often been patronising and disempowering to the disabled people they claimed to represent. Secondly, much of the disability movement has tended to be dominated by people with physical or sensory impairments. The Alliance set out to have representation from adults with learning difficulties on our council. We do not make a distinction between different impairments in defining disabled people because like BCODP we base our thinking on the social 'model of disability'.

Developing our thinking about inclusion

We start from the point of view that there is a real difference between our impairment and our disablement.

Impairment is the loss or limitation of physical, mental or sensory function on a long-term or permanent basis.

Disablement is the loss or limitation of opportunities to take part in the normal life of the community on an equal level with others due to physical and social barriers.

(Disabled People's International 1981, published in Mason 2000: 60)

Much of the confusion parents reported from schools faced with the demand for integration was based upon the non-appreciation of the difference between these two definitions and the implications for schools. The traditional thinking which had grown up around the identification and assessment of special educational needs was based upon a 'medical or individual model' of the child. What was needed was to view the child in a whole-school context. To identity and systematically reduce the barriers to their involvement in the full social and academic life of the school by changing the environment, communication, teaching and learning, attitudes and organisation to fully include the child. Our thinking was not as clear as this and it has taken the last ten years of testing our ideas in both training situations in schools and colleges and in struggles for inclusion for individual children to reach our present level of clarity, and this process will continue. [. . .] I will select a number of key moments to illustrate this development of our thinking.

As a disabled teacher in the 1980s I had become increasingly involved in the struggle to improve equality for disabled teachers (Rieser 1994). At the same time as my involvement in the struggle for greater equality for disabled teachers, I increasingly realised that the oppression we were up against was part of a wider ethos inside education that did not welcome difference and sought to exclude those who could not be assimilated into schools, as they were currently organised. In addition the curriculum content itself, by either reinforcing negative stereotypes of disabled people or by the absence of the experience of disablement from history, geography, English, science, maths, drama, PHSE, PE, art and music, was neither 'balanced or broadly based'. [. . .] My work while seconded led me to produce an internal document for the ILEA (Rieser 1989) which raised all these issues. My secondment had arisen from a battle against an unfair decision to force me to move from the school I had taught in for ten years based on my disability. I won my grievance appeal and the ILEA did not know what to do with me so they agreed I could look at disability and the curriculum. At the same time, the parents Consultative Committee for Special Needs, which had one parent from a special school and one from a mainstream in each ILEA area, was demanding ILEA did something from an equal opportunities perspective on disability in the last few months before it was disbanded. ILEA brought me together with Micheline Mason, a disabled parent of a disabled child in a mainstream school, and we were given ten weeks to come up with a document. We had never met before and coming from different backgrounds and perspectives we had an intense period of discussion, criticism and argument. Out of this highly charged atmosphere we both gained clarity and the result was not the pamphlet originally planned, but a fully illustrated, 260-page book, *Disability Equality in the Classroom: A Human Rights Issue* (Rieser and Mason 1990/1992).

From this work it became clear that the perspective of the 'social model' of disability and the Disability Equality Training that disabled people had developed themselves to promote this view was urgently needed inside the British education system. In 1991 Micheline and I were approached by Comic Relief to produce a resource and training for teachers for disability equality. We successfully argued that we needed to involve the Disabled Peoples' Movement in this project. With funding and support from Comic Relief we organised and ran two national Training the Trainers for Education courses for 60 disabled trainers. This was followed up by the writing of a booklet and the production of a video which provides ideas, arguments and visuals for the promotion of the 'social model' of disability in schools – *Altogether Better: From 'Special Needs' to Equality in Education* (Mason and Rieser 1994). This has been distributed widely and used to train many thousands of educationalists.

Some of our thinking developed the need to move from a 'medical model and integration/segregation' approach to a 'social model/inclusion' approach.

We try to get people in schools to understand that what we call the 'Medical Model' is more than just what doctors do to us. It started from what doctors do to us because it was looking at our impairment. We were no more than our impairment. In fact many children are still labelled by their impairment. A Down's Syndrome child, a child with spina bifida. However, we say: 'they are children first, we are people first'. Traditionally the focus is on the impairment and the cure or if we cannot get the cure we get shunted off to this 'special land' which is a different and parallel system. In fact it is very similar to mainstream in many respects but you are denied the rich social mix of peers available in mainstream. In 'special land' you have hydrotherapy, in mainstream schools we have swimming. In 'special land' you have art therapy, in mainstream, art. In mainstream schools you have literacy and language development, in 'special land' you have speech and language therapy. What is the difference between physiotherapy and an individual physical education programme? As integration has developed it is seen as essential that more of these medicalised therapies are made available in mainstream whereas the key issue for inclusion is to develop a diversity of teaching and learning strategies that encompass all pupils' needs.

Once you are in 'special land' you have few skills, you often have no qualifications, you have no self-esteem and no life skills, so then you have to be looked after for the rest of your life. More than a million disabled people (1.1 million) in the UK want work and cannot get it (Labour Force Survey DSS 1998). In schools it has led to a geographic development continuum of provision with the rarer your condition the more likely you are to be bussed or sent to board long distances from your home community. These schools are very far flung because that is where the 'expertise' resides. We spend a lot of money with psychologists and other people assessing the 'shape' of the child to slot them like a child's game into the 'right' peg hole. [. . .]

In the training we have developed we are saying this approach and treatment of disabled young people is an oppression, it is just as bad as other forms of oppression which have been outlawed and it has to go. The barriers are what disable us, not our impairment. It is the lack of access, the lack of communication, the lack of appropriate teaching methods, it is the way we reflect back to you what you do to us which leaves us with no self-esteem (Mason and Rieser 1994). It is the barriers in society which disadvantage and are discriminatory.

Therefore we get schools to identify the barriers which prevent inclusion and develop their practice to eradicate barriers. Barriers of access; barriers to communication arising from lack of British Sign Language, lack of Braille, information not in different formats such as tape, disc, pictogram or plain English; barriers in organisation; barriers in transport; or barriers in attitudes shaped by stereotypes. [. . .]

Our training and campaigning has been further strengthened by investigating and developing materials which expose the history of our oppression in education and society at the hands of the authorities, reformers, charities and eugenicists. Eugenicists who incarcerated many thousands of disabled children and adults for the whole of their life and set the seal on how disabled children should be educated in the first part of the 20th century and thus so influenced the development of special educational needs in the second half (Rieser 2000; Mason 2000). As labels and labelling increased, so has the population of our special schools. There was an inexorable rise in the special school population of England through most of the last century. [. . .]

Developing training for inclusion

We took a decision early on that our training should be separate from our campaigning work as schools, local authorities and government were often greatly challenged by the Alliance's campaigning role. From 1992 to the present we have sought to set up, train, market and develop a national trainers network of disabled disability equality trainers under a separate charity, Disability Equality in Education. DEE is as an educational trust, to provide training, consultancy and information and to publish curriculum materials to further develop equality and inclusion. In recent years, after a very hard struggle operating from my basement room, we have an office with three part-time staff and have trained 160 trainers in England and Wales, over 115 of whom are on our network. DEE is providing training for LEAs, schools and colleges across the country. Our leaflet has gone to every English school and we launched the network at the Department for Education and Employment in November 1999 with a government minister. Our funders have included Comic Relief, DfEE, Barrow Cadbury and the Platinum Trust, but it is still very difficult to get the funding and support we need (DEE 1999). [. . .]

During my secondment and since I have worked in a number of different classes in schools and colleges developing strategies for both teachers and children to raise disability awareness. Interesting observations arose from this work once I was talking freely to a group of children about how I was treated by non-disabled children when I was at school. First, they had a great sense of injustice and empathy for me. Secondly, a number of children began to volunteer information about themselves and immediate family who were disabled that the class teachers were very often not aware of.

This is very much backed up by the Office of Population and Censuses Study on Disability in Britain, Vol.6 (Meltzer et al. 1989), which shows that 66 per cent of children they define as disabled, some 240,000, are in mainstream classrooms. This is a gross underestimate as it does not include the some 800,000 children with a specific learning difficulty such as dyslexia, many children with emotional and behavioural problems, which create learning difficulties, or large numbers of other children with hidden impairments, such as Asthma, diabetes, fragile X, sickle cell anaemia and many others. In a classroom where difference is welcomed and valued, many impairments that have been hidden will be talked about freely and many children will feel happy to 'come out'.

Name calling and bullying will not be acceptable in such schools and classes and their life-threatening consequences and damage to children's self-esteem will be fully taken on board by teachers and other school staff. However, it is very difficult because people are surrounded with an image environment that is absolutely full of confusing stereotypes, and with disabled people there is not one single stereotype. There are at least ten identified by the 1 in 8 Group which the Alliance set up to influence the portrayal of disabled people in the media following a joint conference with Save the Children 'Invisible Children' (Rieser 1995) and you can probably think of more:

> Pitiable and pathetic; an object of violence; sinister or evil; atmosphere; 'Super Crip' or 'Triumph over Tragedy'; laughable; having a chip on their shoulder; a burden/outcast; non-sexual or incapable of having a worthwhile relationship; incapable of fully participating in everyday life.
>
> (1 in 8 Group 1996, in invisible child report, pp. 44–9)

What also became clear from this work was the unchallenging way that negative portrayals of disablement were routinely used in the school curriculum, displays and learning materials. There were very few books about and illustrations of disabled people just getting on with their lives in a non-stereotyped way. Children's book publishers, film and TV producers, writers and directors are still very much in need of re-educating on portrayals of disability. This led to 'Invisible Children: Joint Conference On Children Images and Disability' attended by 70 children's authors and some 100 image makers from radio, TV and film (Rieser 1995). There was a general consensus that things had to change and that disabled people were generally absent in the media, but when they did appear they were stereotyped. This process was not without resistance, as one children's author was heard to remark 'How can we show evil in our stories now we can't use disabled people?'! This led to a number of children's books that just included disabled children, a conference at the BBC, the setting up of the 1 in 8 Group and its Raspberry Ripple Awards 1997–99 and a broadsheet of which 20,000 were distributed throughout the media industry (1 in 8 Group 1996). [. . .]

The Alliance for Inclusive Education

So our journey to inclusion has involved us in developing training and challenging the media, but the primary role the Alliance played and continues to play is to campaign for inclusion. The Alliance does this through campaigning to change the law and bad practices and supporting a number of high-profile cases to gain publicity, change thinking and achieve inclusion.

In 1996 we realised we could no longer call ourselves the Integration Alliance. We needed to be much clearer about the difference between inclusion and integration. The development of our training and our campaigns had made us understand integration was just a necessary precursor of inclusion. It was just a starting point for a process of whole-school change that needed to identify the barriers that were preventing disabled pupils from accessing the teaching, learning and full social life of the school and to find solutions to overcome those barriers. We also learned that there were no children with categories of impairment or severity of impairment who could not be successfully included in mainstream school where the local authority was prepared to properly resource and the staff were prepared to change their attitudes and practices. 'All does Mean All' to quote People First (the self-advocacy organisation of people with learning difficulties).

We learned that inclusion was a process that started with integration, but went on changing the school so that all children in the local community could be valued and achieve success. This requires both the redistribution of resources from 'special land', the retraining of staff and the development of a pedagogy capable of meeting these diverse needs.

This thinking was important when members of the Alliance were on the working group which developed the Index for Inclusion. The index, which has been distributed by government to all schools in England, is a school self-review tool which encourages schools to ask questions and examine their policies, practices and culture or ethos to become more inclusive. The thinking of the school improvement movement had a synergy with our barriers analysis and this gave the index a firm basis and fitted the government quest to improve performance while developing inclusion (Ainscow *et al.* 2000). Often viewed as contradictory, there is much evidence to support the view that inclusion can improve the quality of education for all (Sebba and Sachdev 1997).

The Qualifications and Curriculum Authority have taken on board the barriers analysis as the key to delivering Curriculum 2000 in their General Inclusion Guidelines which all teachers are required to have regard to in the delivery of teaching and learning for all pupils.

> In planning and teaching the national curriculum, teachers are required to have due regard to the following principles:- ... Setting suitable learning challenges ... Responding to the diverse needs pupils bring to learning ... Overcoming potential barriers to learning and assessment for individual pupils or groups.
>
> (QCA 2000: 1)

In November 2000 OFSTED, despite some resistance, published guidance on inspecting schools for educational inclusion which all inspectors have to have mandatory training on. It lays emphasis on:

How well does the school recognise and overcome barriers to learning. This is about the schools understanding of how well different groups do in school; the steps taken to make sure particular groups are not disadvantaged in school and to promote their participation and success; its strategies for promoting good relationships and managing behaviour; what the school does specifically to prevent and address racism, sexism and other forms of discrimination And what it does about cases of discrimination that do occur.

(p. 6)

The compulsory segregation of disabled pupils against their wishes and those of their parents remains the most obvious denial of human rights against which the Alliance campaigns, both generally and in supporting numerous specific campaigns.

Sometimes we win and sometimes we lose for the individual concerned, but all the time we are shifting the climate of opinion. There have been many battles in our campaign but I will illustrate them with four.

Zahrah Manuel and her mother Preethi struggled for inclusion into both her local primary and secondary school.

It took over three years trying to convince the local authority that Zahrah could go to a mainstream primary school. By this time we'd sold our flat and had used all the money from the sale of the flat towards educating Zahrah at home, we'd even gone to a tribunal and won but the tribunal decision was not legally binding so not much came of that. After lobbying the Council the Alliance organised an occupation of the Education Offices and after some negotiation after three years Zah started at school. Zahrah thrived at primary school. Children would warm towards her and children learnt to communicate with her. Zahrah uses switches to communicate.

Zahrah is a happy thriving child as a result of inclusion. We can go down the street and there'll be a child running up to her 'look there's Zah'.

Recently we had a place for Zahrah at a secondary school which was resourced for £750,000 to include physically disabled children but the school refused to admit Zahrah using the three caveats. We went to court and challenged them with a judicial review. Minutes before the hearing the school agreed to admit her. Now Zahrah has been accepted by Hampstead comprehensive and she started in September 2000. What a contrast. The staff have all had disability equality training from DEE. They have spent £l40,000 over the summer holidays making enough of the school accessible for Zahrah to function and more work is planned. Zahrah and I have been made to feel welcome and part of the community.

(ISEC 2000)

Maresa MacKeith. We have found that the protest and voice of young disabled people and their peers can in the end be effective in a way that parents and their supporters cannot. The story of how Young and Powerful, a group of disabled and non-disabled young people supported by the Alliance, who campaign for inclusion, supported Maresa MacKeith in being included in a mainstream school is told in detail in 'Young Persons Guide to Changing the World, the Universe and Everything' (Comic Relief 2001). In brief Maresa, who is a non-verbal wheelchair user who has developed using facilitated communication, was categorised as having a 'mental age' of two years by psychologists and sent to a special school for six years, finally was integrated into a mainstream secondary school in Nottinghamshire. Here she was taught in a room on her own and said by the staff not to be ready for social contact with her peers. Young and Powerful as a result occupied the Director of Education's office and with much publicity and a further meeting got an agreement that Maresa would attend regular classes. Later Maresa moved to a different secondary school much more receptive to her needs and with greater understanding of the process of inclusion. Now Maresa has a circle of friends of other girls in her year, 'The Girls Gab Gang', and will do her GCSEs this summer (*Flying Pigs*, No. 1 1997). Listen to her voice:

> The most important thing is that I want to be part of ordinary life, and I want the same experiences as other kids. Also I want to be allowed to learn things that need thinking about and are challenging.
>
> I want to be able to contribute, and to discuss things that are important to me and other kids. We need to be together to do that.
>
> When we experience things together, we can learn about what we are each interested in, and about each other's life.
>
> It is important to educate schools so they change to make things better for kids who need a lot of help or get very tired.
>
> (Maresa MacKeith ISEC 2000)

The segregation of young people with a learning difficulty can often be the hardest to change. The whole education system is structured on a normative model of measured 'intelligence' and narrow academic ability. Many teachers and education officers cannot envisage how pupils with severe learning difficulties can be included in secondary schools. In other LEAs, however, such as Newham, Stockport or Barnsley, they are automatically included in mainstream secondary schools.

Chloe McCollum and Zelda, her mum, and her family were supported by the Alliance with high-profile lobbying of Lewisham Council and a picket outside the town hall but in this case we were unable to convince the council that this was a case of disability discrimination and they insisted upon placing Chloe in a special school most of the week using the efficient use of resources and appropriate education caveats. Listen to her voice:

> My name is Chloe McCollum. I am 16 years old and have Down's Syndrome. I love parties, having drinks, going to the market, stories and E.T.

I went to Lucas Vale, an ordinary primary school. I liked it there. I had many friends especially Nejula, Siobahn and Ellie. When I left Lucas Vale (after nine years) I wasn't allowed to go to ordinary secondary school with my friends. I campaigned to go, but the education authority said no. I stayed at home and my daddy taught me reading. He took me to museums and we had picnics together. I now go to Greenvale special school with kids my own age. I go to Deptford Green one day a week too.

Deptford Green is a mainstream secondary school with lots of children in it. I love it because it is good there. I like reading especially a book called 'Underground to Canada'. I like writing, Science, Maths, English and Humanities. I like the experiments best. I play with everyone in the play ground. Its great to go to an ordinary school and I like both my schools.

I wish I went to Deptford Green after Lucas Vale and there wasn't such bother. I hope there won't be such bother for other children in the future.

(Chloe McCollum Nov 1998, in Comic Relief 1999)

Anthony Ford's mother and father believed strongly that Anthony should go to his local primary school. Eventually, through their campaigning, Camden Council put in a lift and accessible toilet. However when it came to transfer, the local secondary school said they couldn't manage having Anthony even though they demonstrated that a stair climbing wheelchair would work. So the family moved to Harrow where Anthony is now attending Whitmore High School, which is accessible.

I went to Beckford Primary School in Camden from my first year of school. For two years first my mother and then a school assistant carried me up and down about one thousand steps a week to lessons. This was because the school refused to keep my classroom on the ground floor. I hated being carried because it made me very nervous. Eventually the school got a lift. This meant I could go in the lift to lessons. I was delighted.

At the end of my time at Beckford I wanted to go to Hampstead School, but the school refused to let me use a stair climbing wheelchair to go up and down the stairs. This stopped me going to the school with my friends.

I am now going to an accessible school in Harrow which has lifts. This has made me very happy and I have a lot of new friends who have made me welcome. But I have still lost my old friends.

I wish that other disabled children get their choice of schools.

(Anthony Ford aged 12, 1998, in Comic Relief 1999)

The battle that the Fords waged for Anthony made it possible for Zahrah to gain access to Hampstead school as the attitudes began to change, but this did not help Anthony who had to move.

Barriers of attitude, school organisation, curriculum, teaching, learning, communication and school environment each can exclude disabled pupils from being included. But where school staff are prepared to find solutions to these barriers then it does prove not only possible but beneficial for the school, its staff and pupils to include disabled pupils.

The Alliance launched 'Whose Voice is it Anyway' (Wilson and Jade 1999), a report into the views of young people on their education, and this was followed up with a conference in September 2000 into the sorts of support that young disabled people need to be included in mainstream. 'The Inclusion Assistant' (Alliance 2001) is a report and video of this consultation. The voice of young people is a powerful testimony to the effectiveness of inclusive education. This generation of young disabled people will not be invisible.

The Alliance has at the same time as supporting individual campaigns been seeking to both change the legal position and the attitude towards inclusion among politicians and educationalists both locally and nationally. The 1993 Act had again made integration conditional upon a child's needs being able to be met, not interfering with other children and being an efficient use of resources. The Alliance and linked organisations had objected to this formulation in the consultation on this Bill. Soon after this at the Council for Disabled Children, which represented the main voice of the voluntary sector, we were able to persuade them to set up a working party on integration. Because the working party left enough time to listen to the experiences and thinking of disabled people and parents of disabled children who wanted inclusion we were able to recommend that these caveats should go and for those parents who wanted a mainstream place they should have a right to get one (Council for Disabled Children 1994). The Alliance adopted the scrapping of the three caveats as a short-term objective. We sponsored an early day motion signed by 37 MPs in 1996.

This meant that when the School Standards and Framework Bill was being debated and the CDC set up the Special Education Consortium in 1997 it was able to sponsor an amendment in the House of Lords to get rid of the caveats. Responding, the government in 1998 said they would listen to what the Disability Rights Task Force said on this issue and they agreed that the caveats should possibly be amended as they were often used by local authorities to prevent inclusion. Under the consultation on the Disability Rights in Education Bill in 2000 the government agreed to get rid of the appropriate educational provision clause but wanted to keep the other two: efficient use of resources and not interfering with the education of other children. The Special Education Consortium, representing over 200 organisations, adopted the scrapping of section 316 and the three caveats as a principled position.

The newly formed Disability Rights Commission, which included Phillipa Russell of CDC and Jane Campbell of the National Independent Living Centre, agreed at its first meeting, after some lobbying by the Alliance, to recommend scrapping the caveats. The majority of voluntary organisations, parents and disabled people's organisations supported the Alliance position in the consultation. [. . .]

Conclusion

The Bill was enacted and two of the three caveats have been removed. We are now in a very different place from 1989. We have a Government Action Programme with an increase in inclusion at its heart. [. . .] The teaching profession and National Union of Teachers are more accepting of inclusion. Many more local education authorities are developing inclusion and more than 156,000 disabled pupils are now attending mainstream schools. Another 100,000 in England remain segregated and depending on where you live the local policies are very different. Now we have to build and strengthen a network of inclusion campaigners and trainers in every locality to make inclusion a reality for the benefit of all. It would be foolish to think that everything will be plain sailing from now on, but inclusion involving the wholesale restructuring of education to meet the needs of all pupils in mainstream schools is at least a real possibility and a reality for thousands of disabled pupils in no small measure due to the efforts of the Alliance for Inclusive Education and its members. A small group of thoughtful committed citizens has changed their part of the world. [. . .]

References

1 in 8 Group (1996) *Disability in the Media*. 1 in 8 Group, 78 Mildmay Grove South, London N1 4PJ.

Ainscow, M. *et al.* (2000) *The Index for Inclusion*. Bristol: CSIE.

Alliance (2001) *The Inclusion Assistant – A Consultant with Young Disabled People and their Parents*. Alliance for Inclusive Education, Unit 2, 70 South Lambeth Road, London SW8 1RL.

Comic Relief (1999) *The Best Lesson Plans in the World Ever*. Comic Relief, 5th Floor, 89 Albert Embankment, London SE1 7TP.

Comic Relief (2001) *Young Person's Guide to Changing the World, the Universe and Everything*. London: Comic Relief.

Council for Disabled Children (1994) *Policy Statement from the Integration Working Party*. CDC, 8 Wakley Street, London EC1V 7QE.

Department of Social Security (1998) *Labour Force Survey*. London: DSS.

DEE (1999) *Are You Prepared for the Future? Inclusive Education*. Disability Equality in Education, Unit 4Q, Leroy House, 436 Essex Road, London N1 3QP.

DES (1977) *DES Statistics 1977*. London: DES

DfEE (1997 to 2000) *Secondary School Performance Tables*, (November). London: DfEE.

DFEE (1999) *SEN Statistics Bulletin*. London: DfEE.

DfEE (2000) *Statistics of Education: Special Educational Needs Statistics January 2000, 9/00*. London: DfEE.

Flying Pigs, Journal of the Alliance for Inclusive Education, Unit 2, 20 South Lambeth Road, London SW8 1RL.

HMSO (1974) *Statistics of Education 1973 Vol. 1.* London: HMSO.

HMSO (1978) *Special Education Needs Report of the Committee of Enquiry into the Education of Handicapped Children and Young People* (Warnock). Cmnd 7212. London: HMSO.

ILEA (1985) *Educational Opportunities for All* (The Fish Report). London: ILEA.

Integration Alliance (1989) *Integration Now: Conference Report.* IA, Unit 2, 70 South Lambeth Road, London SW8 1RL.

ISEC (2000) *International Special Education Congress, Manchester Proceedings on CD-ROM.* Inclusive Technology, available at: inclusive.co.uk.

Jordan, L. and Goodey, C. (1996) *Human Rights and Social Change: the Newham story.* CSIE Bristol, 1 Redland Close, Elm Land, Redland, Bristol BS6 6UE.

Mason, M. (2000) *Incurably Human.* London: Working Press.

Mason, M. and Rieser, R. (1994) *Altogether Better.* London: Comic Relief.

Meltzer, H. *et al.* (1989) *Disability in the UK.* London: HMSO.

OFSTED (2000) *Evaluating Educational Inclusion.* London: OFSTED.

QCA (2000) *Curriculum 2000 Appendix on General Inclusion Statement.* London: QCA, 1.

Rieser, R. (1989) *Disability and the School Curriculum.* Curriculum Equality Discussion Paper. London: ILEA.

Rieser, R. (1994) Insider perspective: the voice of a disabled teacher. In L. Barton (ed.) *Course Reader M.Ed in Inclusive Education* Sheffield: University of Sheffield.

Rieser, R. (ed.) (1995) *Invisible Children: Report of the Joint Conference on Children, Images and Disability.* Save The Children, 17 Grove Lane, London SE5 8RD.

Rieser, R. (200) Disability discrimination, the final frontier: disablement, history and liberation; and: Special educational needs or inclusive education: the challenge of disability discrimination in schooling. In M. Cole (ed.) *Education Equality and Human Rights.* London: Routledge/Falmer.

Rieser, R. and Mason, M. (1990/1992) *Disability Equality in the Classroom: A human rights issue.* DEE, Unit 4Q, Leroy House, 436 Essex Road, London NI 3QP.

Sebba, J. and Sachdev, D (1997) *What Works in inclusive Education.* Ilford, Essex: Barnardo's.

Swann, W. (1989) *Integration Statistics: LEAs reveal local variations.* London: Centre for Studies on Integration in Education.

Williams, S. (1977) Speech of Secretary of State for Education and Science at the opening of Inkersall Green Special School at Staverly, Derbyshire on 21 January 1977 quoted in HMSO (1978) Warnock Report, para 8.6, p.122.

Wilson, C. and Jade, R. (1999) *Whose Voice is it Anyway?: talking to young disabled people at school.* Alliance for Inclusive Education, Unit 2, 70 South Lambeth Road, London SW8 1RL.

Young and Powerful (1998a) Letter in *Flying Pigs,* 3 (summer), 11. The Journal of the Alliance for Inclusive Education, Unit 2, 70 South Lambeth Road, London SW8 1RL.

Young and Powerful (1998b) Proposals to the Department for Education and Employment on developing inclusive education. *Flying Pigs,* (autumn), 8–9.

Throughout the Learning From Each Other course, we see inclusion as a process of change. In this chapter, Richard Rieser charts the impact that individuals and groups have had in bringing about change in the UK. In particular, the experience of the adult disability movement has been crucial, as he sees it, in challenging the exclusion of marginalised young people. This chapter shows that change is not easy: it can involve radical challenge to established practice. But the chapter offers hope for the future and indications of how change can be brought about.

CHAPTER 17

Accessing, through research interviews, the views of children with difficulties in learning

Ann Lewis

Gaining the views of children in an ethically appropriate and sensitive way should be a central part of research in the area of inclusive education. In this chapter Ann Lewis provides an overview of some of the key issues encountered when conducting research interviews with children who experience difficulties in learning. She concludes by illustrating one method that she has used to access pupils' views.

Michele started it. I'd been talking with children about their views concerning special and mainstream schools. I'd felt that it was going quite well; the children seemed open, relaxed and friendly. Then Michele, having shared her views with me, hurtled off, shouting to another child: 'Kim, the posh lady wants to talk to you'. The comment summed up her perception of the situation all too clearly and was certainly not as I had seen it.

The purpose of such conversations is to access children's views in an authentic, fair and accurate way. The inherent complexities are compounded when professionals or researchers are from different agencies, have various sets of professional knowledge (e.g. law, health, social work, education, psychology) and hold possibly contrasting value positions, but are all involved with decision-making around a particular child (Porter and Lewis 2001). One illustration of this situation might be when various professionals seek the child's views concerning special needs provision. This chapter focuses on interviewing, for research purposes, children who show difficulties in learning. The first part considers some ethical aspects of interviews involving these children; second, principles about such practice are reviewed; and third, building on these, a suggested approach is outlined. Many of the points will also apply to talking with other children and in other contexts.

Teacher researchers often include the views of children in reports about inclusion and integration. This shift has been triggered by various legislation and formal guidelines that have stressed the need to ascertain the views of the child. These span legal, social, medical and educational contexts, research and practice (e.g. France 2000). Significantly, the revised Code of Practice concerning special educational needs (DfES

2001a) has considerably strengthened its reference to ascertaining the child's views. [. . .] The revised Code notes:

> Pupils' views should be sought and recorded as part of the statutory annual review process where possible, as well as within the IEP and any other assessment and review . . . A child's views can be ascertained at other times as well as during consultation, formal choice and decision-making.
>
> (DfES 2001a, paras 3:15, 3:16)

Similarly, the accompanying SEN Toolkit (DfES 2001b) includes (Section 4) material on enabling pupil participation which addresses this in general and with specific reference to statutory assessment, annual reviews and transition plans.

Ethical concerns

There is, rightly, concern about the ethical aspects of interviewing children (Lindsay 2000; Moore, Beazeley and Maelzer 1998). Concerns have revolved particularly around six areas:

- access/gatekeepers
- consent/assent
- confidentiality/anonymity/secrecy
- recognition/feedback
- ownership
- social responsibility.

These may operate slightly differently in research, compared with professional, contexts. For example, in the professional context, the professional's position will lead to the involvement of a particular group; for researchers who are based outside the context, sampling issues and access become more critical and may shape findings significantly. The researcher perspective has relevance for professionals as it may highlight otherwise unexamined issues such as the distinctions between informed consent, assent, failure to dissent and informed dissent.

Access/gatekeepers

Unless the researcher is interviewing their own child then someone acts as a gatekeeper, providing or withholding access to the child to be interviewed. In most cases this direct (first level) gatekeeper will be the parent or carer. Somebody else may in turn act as an indirect (second level) gatekeeper to the parents and carers. In school contexts this may be the head teacher, school governors or LEA; but, depending on the focus of the research, it may also, or instead, be health, legal, and/or social service agencies.

There are ethical committees and protocols designed to protect children from unwarranted intrusion by potential researchers. These procedures and their interpretation will shape the nature of the group of children interviewed and hence the range of views ultimately collected. A clear illustration in the integration/inclusion context occurs when a school chooses to opt out of involvement in an evaluation, consequently removing a particular group from those whose views are accessed. This may also occur through tangential circumstances rather than by design, as when a school withdraws from the study due, for example, to staff illness or prioritising of inspection arrangements. Decisions about sample have repercussions for access (and vice versa), with consequent implications for the interpretation of the findings of the work.

Consent/assent

The continuum from informed consent – through assent – to failure to object highlights the distinction between consent and assent. *Consent* may be given by the child or by another on the child's behalf for (a) the child to be interviewed or (b) the researcher to ask the child to be interviewed. *Assent* refers to the child's agreement to participation in the process when another has given consent. In the more conventional context of interviewing adults these two aspects are conflated, that is the adult being interviewed both consents and assents to the interview.

Consent is not in itself sufficient; *informed consent/assent* is needed. In order to give informed consent the person giving this has to:

- have information about the chance to participate
- know about a right to withdraw from the activity
- know what the participant's role will be
- know what the outcomes are intended to be.

To be able to respond to all the above four aspects of informed consent the participant (or someone on their behalf) has to receive the information, understand it and respond to it (Alderson 1995). Spelt out in this way it can be seen that obtaining informed consent may be a considerable undertaking and daunting to achieve. Some writers have argued that, while involving children and young people in research and evaluation is important, it may be very difficult genuinely to obtain their informed consent (McCarthy 1998; Clegg 2001; Homan 2001).

There is strong agreement among commentators that allowing *informed dissent* is crucial. Children have a right to privacy that researchers have a moral responsibility to acknowledge (Homan 2001). A child's expression of informed dissent may not be easy to recognise. For example, there may be disagreement among adults about whether a particular behaviour by a child with severe or profound and multiple learning difficulties reflects dissent. Keeping an open dialogue with the network of people around the child helps to sustain checks on whether the child is continuing to assent to involvement (Kellett and Nind 2001; see also Porter, Ouvry, Morgan and Downs 2001 re: validating communication). Explicit continuation of assent enables a corresponding and genuine right to withdraw at any point.

In the legal context, much stress is placed on whether a person is competent to give consent: 'A child who has the capacity to understand fully a decision affecting his or her life automatically has the capacity to make that decision unless statute law states otherwise' (Masson 2000: 39). This is referred to, in short, as the Gillick competence test after the Gillick v. West Norfolk and Wisbech Area Health Authority (1985) case concerning under-16-year-olds' right to contraception without the permission of their parents. The court found in favour of the GP. This set a precedent in that it allowed under 16-year-olds to consent to medical treatment providing they could show 'sufficient understanding' and 'competence to make wise choices'. Lengthy debate has ensued around how such competence is to be defined. Regardless of this legal debate, lack of competence does not remove the right to express a view.

Confidentiality/anonymity/secrecy

Formal guidance on research methods usually stresses the importance of *confidentiality*. This seems right, proper and uncontroversial. However, it may be more difficult to sustain in practice, particularly if small or atypical groups are involved, than exhortations to sustain confidentiality suggest. Confidentiality may also not be sustained for different reasons – that is, if the child reveals information that the interviewer feels should be passed on in the child's best interests. It might be felt that it is preferable to exclude a particular type of data collection if its collection might place the researcher in an invidious ethical position (and hence jeopardise the relationship with the child) (see Oakley 2000 for an example).

A researcher may attempt to guarantee *anonymity* in any written documentation (that is, comments or views are not attributed in a way that could be traced to a specific individual). This may mean that some views have to be excluded from the report (for example, if only one child with cerebral palsy is included in mainstream schools in the sample then any comment reflecting that particular perspective could be traced back to an individual).

Another issue about confidentiality arises from procedures concerning conducting interviews; privacy has to be balanced with child protection procedures. Whether parents should be present at interviews with their children has been much debated and it has been argued that parents may want, but not need, to know what happens. Relevant bodies produce ethical guidelines for researchers (e.g. see BPS 1991; BERA 1992; BSA 1987) although the detail of these varies widely (see Lindsay 2000). Clegg (2001) argued that when interviews are conducted in a spirit of openness, then privacy/confidentiality is not an issue and the very notion of gatekeepers (see above) betrays a lack of trust between those involved with the children.

There is a distinction between confidentiality, given to people participating in the research, and *secrecy*. Secrecy applies to procedures, and in most cases such secrecy would probably be deemed inappropriate in educational research. However, there might be contexts in which it was felt legitimate to keep procedures secret (e.g. observation to monitor suspected bullying).

Recognition and feedback

Often when children are interviewed in schools this is presented as part of routine school activities with no specific 'reward' for participating. However, small token gifts such as holographic stickers given to all the children in a class whether or not interviewed seem to be popular and provide a modest 'thank you'. Alternatively, a group 'treat' such as a party may be organised. In more substantial projects researchers may give children gift vouchers or token payment in exchange for their involvement (with parental agreement). The basis of this exchange is respect for the children's time and efforts.

It is now widely recognised that participants should have the opportunity to receive feedback from researchers about the outcomes of the study. However, some sample groups move around geographically and make this sustained link difficult or impossible over a longer term project. With children, feedback may be provided through adults known to them. Little seems to have been written on this topic in published accounts of children's views about inclusion and it is potentially a sensitive area.

Ownership

In educational research data is generally presumed to belong to the researcher (although data protection measures apply, giving participants rights to access electronic data under certain conditions). Kellett and Nind (2001) propose the researcher as a banker, retaining data/information (e.g. video material or interview narrative) but giving others access to it. In the inclusion context, it might be argued that schools should have access to such information and the right to use it in certain contexts. One might make a distinction here between data and information. Information refers to what is collected (e.g. a piece of video film), while the process of conversion or extraction from information generates data – the units or material analysed. Thus the data are a subset of the information.

There may be unintended outcomes of using protocols intended to safeguard the interests of children interviewed. For example, notions of ownership whereby materials are returned to children interviewed may be interpreted as a rejection or failure. Jean Ware (personal communication) has noted that destroying confidential materials at the close of a project may be read as discounting of the material by some children, particularly perhaps those with difficulties in learning ('valuable' material would have been retained or even displayed).

Professional groups may take contrasting views, sometimes arising from particular legislative constraints, about what constitutes an authentic way to obtain children's views. A particular issue here is the use of facilitators. Ideally facilitators should be chosen by the child. Facilitators act as intermediaries conveying, or translating, the views of those interviewed. For example, a facilitator may interpret Makaton or British Sign Language (BSL) signs for the researcher. This enables views to be collected from people who might otherwise be excluded from those whose views are accessed. However, the filter of the facilitator may unwittingly distort the views held. If they are used, then any report needs to acknowledge how views were collected so that the reader/listener can make a judgement about whether the conduit for views may have distorted the evidence.

Social responsibility

One of the intellectual virtues embodied in the process of carrying out research is the pursuit of truth. This links with Lindsay's (2000) discussion about the social responsibility of the researcher. The strong rights arguments around inclusion and the strength with which personal value positions are held may make it difficult to sustain research endeavours that threaten to produce findings at odds with the prevailing orthodoxy. Researchers have a responsibility to acknowledge both their own value positions and whatever truth emerges from the research process.

Principles underlying the research process

Authenticity

The potency of research is in its authenticity. Research involving children with difficulties in learning increasingly seeks to check for the authenticity of the context in which views are collected; that is, these should be true to the child. Part of these checks are likely to be awareness of features that may distort the child's response in unhelpful ways (for example, reflecting who else is present, their relationship with the child, the child's tendency to be acquiescent, features of the context such as noise, etc.).

Validity/credibility

Validity, or in a similar vein credibility, draws attention to the fairness of the particular process leading to a child's response. This includes seeking responses that are about what we think they are about; for example, if we ask children about which schools they prefer when seeking *educational* preferences we may instead be obtaining comments about friendship patterns, as children tend to prefer the schools to which friends go. A loss of validity may arise more subtly when a child's interpretation of the situation leads them to make a particular (untrue) response. For example, when Nesbitt (2000) talked with children about religious beliefs she noted that the children sometimes applied terms from one sect to their own (e.g. a Baptist girl, against her normal practice, termed her church minister a 'vicar'), possibly reflecting what she believed the researcher would expect or understand. Such nuances are often lost but were highlighted here through the researcher's sensitivity and the use of language as distinctive markers.

Validation concerns ways of checking that responses are being interpreted in a fair way. There has been increasing discussion about validation of responses in interviews with children. Some researchers have used peers as interviewers or involved people with learning difficulties in validation (see projects by Triangle/NSPCC, the Children's Society and Joseph Rowntree Foundation, e.g. Ward 1996). Accounts in which researchers have sustained contact through friendships with those interviewed also help to show, through longer-term and personal involvement, whether interpretations were valid (Crozier and Tracey 2000; Booth 1998).

Reliability/trustworthiness

Reliability, or trustworthiness, encompasses the idea that the response is representative or typical of what the child believes. Two aspects of the many ways in which we may unwittingly distort children's responses to questioning are summarised here: questioning style and ways of prompting (elaborated in Lewis 2001).

A range of work with children has shown the value of making statements that prompt a response, rather than a direct question, to elicit views. The tendency for adults, particularly teachers, to use question–answer–feedback routines has been described by some writers as reflecting power relationships (Edwards and Westgate 1994). Through the use of questions, the adult keeps the 'upper hand'. Thus in the context of an interview, the use of questions rather than statements also reflects an implied power relationship. However, the use of statements as prompts (less overtly 'powerful') can occur naturally in small group interviews with children, when one child's comment may naturally trigger a response from another child in the group (Dockrell, Lewis and Lindsay 2000).

How much to prompt children, and the effects of this on the reliability of what is said, has been examined by various researchers. In summary, children with difficulties in learning seem to respond best to general open-ended questions such as 'What did you do in the playground?' (rather than free recall, such as 'Tell me about playtime' or specific questions such as 'Did you play with Pokemon cards at playtime?'). The level of general open-ended questions parallels the function of the cue cards described in the following section which are somewhat, but not overly, specific. More generally, children have a bias towards confirming what is put to them, so it is important to ask about both sides of an issue (e.g. not presuming a wish to stay in/leave the current school).

One approach: use of cue cards to structure narratives

One strategy used successfully with pupils with difficulties in learning, recognising the goals of authenticity, validity and reliability, is storying. This stems from research into script theory (Fivush 1991). A script in this context is a generic memory structure that guides the child's recall, retention and attention of stimuli. This links more broadly with notions about a narrative self; that is, each individual builds up a story reflecting continuity about the self. Stable events are important markers in the course of this narrative self, but they do not occur in isolation. They happen in a time and place, surrounded by particular feelings and in the presence of particular others. One interpretation about what we are doing when we interview children is that we are trying to access this narrative and, in the technique described here, we do this by hooking on to those (i.e. place, etc.) features.

The approach adapted here, originally developed in the United States in connection with interviewing children about suspected child abuse, involves using a set of cue cards to prompt a structured response from children with minimal interference (in terms of questioning) by the interviewer. The lack of interruptions with questions is an important feature of the approach in the light of evidence (summarised briefly above) about the ways in which certain styles of questioning and prompts inhibit children's full and fair responses.

A modification of this approach has been developed, and found to be effective, with pupils (ages 6–12) in a school for children with moderate learning difficulties (MLD). It was used as a way to encourage the children to talk more fully about general school-related events that they had experienced in the recent past. In summary, the technique involved training the children to recognise what each of the six cue cards represented. The cards acted as prompts for ideas about (in turn): people, talk, setting (indoor/outdoor variants), feelings and consequences associated with the particular event under discussion. The cue cards contained carefully selected, and trialled, symbol pictures that conveyed meaning in a neutral way (sample cards shown below).

Examples of symbol pictures

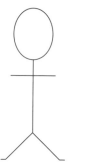

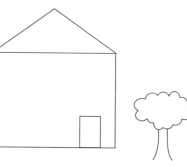

Cue card: people   Cue card: setting (outside)   Cue card: feelings

Teachers introduced the children to the cards through routine story activities such as the story told at the end of each day and through discussion around weekend events. The cards were presented in succession with minimum talk (if needed – 'Does this remind you of something else?') from the interviewer so that the child's narrative was prompted but not substantially interrupted. After practice in the use of the cards, the children became adept at retelling a series of events, or an incident, including significant and correct detail.

To try to ascertain to what extent the use of the cue cards was triggering fuller but not false accounts, children over a series of weeks recounted events to me, sometimes beginning with an unprompted account and at other times beginning with the cued approach. The event was always something that had happened in the class or school over the previous few weeks, as the intention was not to test memory itself but rather this facilitative technique.

The following extracts illustrate (account 2) typical use of the cue cards compared with an unprompted account. The event that provided the focus for these discussions was a visit to the school from Hannah, who had been away ill for a long period and had returned to visit the class the previous week. Various children (here, 6–8-year-olds attending an MLD school) were asked about what had happened on Hannah's return visit. The two accounts are by the same child (Tanya) in response to being asked: 'Tell me about what happened when Hannah visited last week'.

Unprompted account

Tanya: *It was sad.*
Hannah wanted go back home.

Here Tanya recalled just two aspects of Hannah's visit: a general sadness and that Hannah wanted to go home.

Prompted account – using cue cards

Tanya: *The first time Hannah didn't come.*
After this dinner playtime Hannah come.

(people card shown)
(I) helped Hannah
In the classroom
I was in there ... my coat on cos it was after playtime
Hannah come
Her Mom ... and her Gran

(talk card shown)
She went to hospital
And she went to hospital in car
(NB – the teacher later reported that Hannah's
mother had talked about this to the class)

(feelings card shown)
I was sad
Hannah sad

(setting card shown – no response)

(actions card shown)
She come in her wheelchair

(consequences card shown)
(She) went in a yellow car
(She left us) sweets
Two sorts
Smarties
Chocolate in the little one.

Here, as the cards were shown, more detail emerged. The prompted account clearly generated much more detail than did the unprompted account and, on checking with the class teacher, I found that the details given were accurate.

The advantage of the prompted (using cue cards) version in eliciting a more detailed and accurate account over unprompted accounts was sustained across a range of children and events. The only children with whom the approach did not work well were those with marked autistic spectrum disorders. Perhaps predictably, these children latched on to particular responses, repeating them across the cue cards. This technique seems to have potential in encouraging children to tell what they know even with an adult with whom they are familiar but do not know well. Interestingly, the school extended the approach into general use, employing it, for example, to explore details of playground or bullying incidents. The technique described here has potential but it needs more development to explore, for example, how effective it is across a range of contexts, how well it works with children using signing, the applicability to web-based contexts and its limits in terms of degree of accurate detail generated.

Conclusion

The ways through which the child responds in an interview (or less formal discussion) can he varied in a wide number of ways so that all children can potentially make an authentic, valid and reliable response. An increasingly wide range of techniques are being developed to access children's views, particularly in the context of fostering inclusion. Comparatively formal interviews may be constructed around sentence completions (Wade and Moore 1993), formalised assessment measures or attitude scales such as Harter and Pike's (1984) pictorial scale. In contrast, ethnographic interviews may be relatively unstructured, involve an interviewer known well by the children (Allan 1999; Billington 2000) and possibly use concrete activities or role play as the starting point for the conversation. (For further ideas, see Hill, Laybourn and Borland 1996; Christensen and James 2000; O'Kane 2000; Joseph Rowntree Foundation 2001; Morris 1998.)

Interviews may be, and increasingly are, supplemented with other approaches including drawings, diaries, simple questionnaires, grids for completion, multimedia and web-based approaches, or observational records. The use of drawings, while intuitively attractive, needs to be considered carefully as it is easy to misinterpret such information (Thomas and Silk 1990; Lange-Kuttner and Edelstein 1995).

The points raised here reflect a researcher perspective but are applicable also to a range of professional contexts. The Code's (DFES 2001a) stress on pupil participation (echoing parallel trends in relation to work with adults with learning disabilities) represents a significant challenge to professionals if the goal is to be taken seriously, not merely in a token way. Accessing children's views can never be achieved 'perfectly'. However we can endeavour to do this with the aim of reflecting children's views authentically, while acknowledging the limitations. The researcher or professional then has a responsibility to check that the views expressed seem to be a fair and typical response. One way of making such checks is to compare responses across different contexts and through a variety of means, one of which is the cue cards approach described here.

References

Alderson, P. (1995) *Listening to Children: children, ethics and social research*. Barkingside: Barnardo's.

Allan, J. (1999) *Actively Seeking Inclusion: pupils with special needs in mainstream schools*. London: Falmer.

Billington, T. (2000) *Separating, Losing and Excluding Children*. London: Routledge.

British Psychological Society (BPS) (1991) *Code of Conduct, Ethical Principles and Guidelines*. Leicester: BPS.

British Educational Research Association (1992) *Ethical Guidelines for Educational Research*. Edinburgh: BERA/SCRE.

British Sociological Association (1987) *Statement of Ethical Practice*. London: BSA.

Booth, W. (1998) Doing research with lonely people. *British Journal of Learning Disabilities*, **26**, 132–6.

Christensen, P. and James, A. (eds) (2000) *Research with Children: perspectives and practices*. London: Falmer.

Clegg, J. (2001) *Healthcare ethics from a hermeneutic perspective*. Paper to ESRC seminar series: Methodological issues in interviewing children and young people with learning difficulties. University of Birmingham, April 2001.

Crozier, J. and Tracey (2000) Falling out of school: a young woman's reflections on her chequered experience of schooling. In A. Lewis and G. Lindsay (eds) *Researching Children's Perspectives*, pp. 173–186. Buckingham: Open University Press.

DfES (2001a) *Code of Practice on the Identification and Assessment of Pupils with Special Educational Needs*. London: DfES.

DfES (2001b) *SEN Toolkit*. London: DfES.

Dockrell, J., Lewis, A. and Lindsay, G. (2000) Researching Children's Perspectives – a psychological perspective. In A. Lewis and G. Lindsay (eds) *Researching Children's Perspectives*, pp. 46–58. Buckingham: Open University Press.

Edwards, A. D. and Westgate, D. P. G. (1994) *Investigating Classroom Talk*, 2nd edn. Lewes: Falmer.

Fivush, R. (1991) The social construction of personal narratives. *Merrill-Palmer Quarterly*, **37**, 59–82.

France, A. (2000) *Youth researching youth: the triumph and success peer research project*. Leicester: National Youth Agency/Joseph Rowntree Foundation.

Harter, S. and Pike, R. (1984) The pictorial scale of perceived competence and social acceptance for young children. *Child Development*, **55**, 369–82.

Hill, M., Laybourn, A. and Borland, M. (1996) Engaging with primary-aged children about their emotions and well-being: methodological considerations. *Children and Society*, **10**, 129–44.

Homan, R. (2001) The principle of assumed consent: the ethics of gatekeeping. *Journal of Philosophy of Education*, **35**(3), 329–43.

Joseph Rowntree Foundation (2001) *Findings: consulting with disabled children and young people*. July. York: Joseph Rowntree Foundation.

Kellett, M. and Nind, M. (2001) Ethics in quasi-experimental research on people with severe learning disabilities: dilemmas and compromises. *British Journal of Learning Disabilities*, **29**, 51–5.

Lange-Kuttner, C. and Edelstein, W. (1995) The contribution of social factors to the development of graphic competence. In C. Lange-Kuttner and G. V. Thomas *Drawing and Looking*, pp. 159–172. London: Harvester Wheatsheaf.

Lewis, A. (2001) Reflections on interviewing children and young people as a method of inquiry in exploring their perspectives on integration/inclusion. *Journal for Research in Special Educational Needs*, **1**, 3. www.nasen.uk.com/ejournal.

Lindsay, G. (2000) Researching children's perspectives: ethical issues. In A. Lewis and G. Lindsay (eds) *Researching Children's Perspectives*, pp. 1–20. Buckingham: Open University Press.

Masson, J. (2000) Researching children's perspectives: legal issues. In A. Lewis and G. Lindsay (eds) *Researching Children's Perspectives*, pp. 34–44. Buckingham: Open University Press.

McCarthy, M. (1998) Interviewing people with learning disabilities about sensitive topics: a discussion of ethical issues. *British Journal of Learning Disabilities*, **26**, 140–5.

Moore, M., Beazley, S. and Maelzer, J. (1998) *Researching Disability Issues*. Buckingham: Open University Press.

Morris, J. (1998) *Don't leave us out: involving disabled children and young people with communication impairments*. York: Joseph Rowntree Foundation.

Nesbitt, E. (2000) Researching 8–13 year olds' perspectives on their experience of religion. In A. Lewis and G. Lindsay (eds) *Researching Children's Perspectives*, pp. 135–49. Buckingham: Open University Press.

Oakley, M. (2000) Children and young people and care proceedings. In A. Lewis and G. Lindsay (eds) *Researching Children's Perspectives*, pp. 73–85. Buckingham: Open University Press.

O'Kane, C. (2000) The development of participatory techniques: facilitating children's views about decisions which affect them. In P. Christensen and A. James (eds) *Research with Children: perspectives and practices*, pp. 136–59. London: Falmer.

Porter, J. and Lewis, A. (2001) *Methodological issues in interviewing children and young people with learning difficulties*. ESRC Seminar Series Briefing Paper. University of Birmingham, Summer 2001.

Porter, J., Ouvry, C., Morgan, M. and Downs, C. (2001) Interpreting the communication of people with profound and multiple learning difficulties. *British Journal of Learning Disabilities*, **29**(1), 12–16.

Thomas, G. V. and Silk, A. M. (1990) *An Introduction to the Psychology of Children's Drawings*. Hemel Hempstead: Harvester Wheatsheaf.

Wade, B. and Moore, M. (1993) *Experiencing Special Education*. Buckingham: Open University Press.

Ware, J. Personal communication.

Ward, L. (1996) *Seen and Heard: involving disabled children and young people in research and development projects*. York: Joseph Rowntree Foundation.

Ann Lewis suggests that the value position held by professionals and researchers might affect the process of accessing children's views in 'an authentic, fair and accurate way'. The sound ethical reasons why we need to construct appropriate means of accessing these views have been presented in this chapter and Ann Lewis leaves us with ideas for developing methods necessary if we are to take pupil participation seriously.

CHAPTER 18

Inclusion in mainstream classrooms: experiences of deaf pupils

Joy Jarvis, Alessandra Iantaffi and Indra Sinka

Joy Jarvis, Alessandra Iantaffi and Indra Sinka discuss what deaf children think about their school experiences and the issues that they see as important. The diversity of experiences and attitudes presented here reveal the existence of both significant barriers to inclusion and also successful examples.

The British Deaf Association has very strong objections regarding the widespread placement of individual children in local mainstream [schools].

(British Deaf Association 1996: 7)

This statement, from a major organisation representing Deaf[1] people in the UK, goes against the international and national move towards inclusive education. Currently over 85 per cent of deaf pupils in the United Kingdom are educated in mainstream schools (Lynas *et al.* 1997). Why are some Deaf adults against this practice and do the experiences of deaf pupils in mainstream classrooms reflect these concerns?

Cultural issues

The arguments against placing deaf pupils in mainstream classrooms, particularly against placing them individually in their local schools, fall into two categories: issues of culture and issues of access, and we examine the former first. The cultural issues are in relation to the Deaf community and the understanding of deafness, not as a disability, but as a difference. The main aspect of this cultural difference is the use of a different language: British Sign Language (BSL). The right of deaf children to be part of this culture, to have a deaf peer group, to have Deaf adult role models and to use BSL as a first language is advocated by many Deaf people (British Deaf Association 1996). Through membership of this community, it is argued, children will develop self-esteem and a strong first language and can thrive in a context where their access to

---

1 NB Here Deaf with a capital D refers to people who identify themselves as members of the Deaf community. A lower case d in deaf indicates a person with a hearing loss

communication and understanding about the world is not limited by their difficulty in understanding and/or producing spoken English. This then gives them a position of strength from which to operate in the wider, hearing community.

Deaf culture is nourished by Deaf clubs and community activities and by Deaf families. It is also developed in specialist schools for deaf children, although these are now fewer in number than in the past (Eatough 2000). One argument is that as most deaf children are born to hearing parents it is only when they are with Deaf adults and peers that they can access this culture and that this takes place most easily in special schools. A group of adults who attended mainstream schools and have subsequently formed the 'Deaf Ex-Mainstreamers Group' felt that attending 'hearing' schools meant that they did not develop an understanding of the Deaf community and its language and culture and were thus excluded from this. 'Deaf ex-mainstreamers are made to feel excluded from the Deaf community because their behaviour is different from other Deaf people . . . ' (DEX 1996: 5).

Access issues

It could be argued that as most deaf children are born to hearing parents and have hearing siblings and peers, then it is important that they can be part of the hearing community and culture. The issue of access is important here; to what extent can one be a full participant in a community if one has problems understanding its language? Most deaf children will have some difficulties understanding spoken language. Many will be able to achieve good comprehension and use of spoken English by using hearing aids, cochlear implants, radio systems, speech reading or a form of sign supported English. Most of these children are currently in mainstream schools where Deaf writers, such as Paddy Ladd (1991), argue that they may see themselves as inferior hearing people, unable to understand everything that is going on, misunderstanding information and jokes and feeling isolated from hearing children. One deaf secondary-aged pupil expressed this feeling of difference when she responded to a questionnaire about integration for the National Deaf Children's Society. She explains, 'At a hearing school you are always have to work towards being the same as the others, but you will always be different so you never get there . . . ' (NDCS 1990: 19).

For a minority of deaf children British Sign Language will be the language they are using to communicate and to learn at school. This implies either that teachers are delivering the curriculum in BSL or that it is being interpreted for them by support staff. It also implies that there is a deaf signing peer group to interact with, or that hearing children in this context are fluent sign language users. In practice, if BSL users are not attending special schools, then they are likely to be in a resourced school where there is a group of deaf pupils and where communication support workers interpret what the teacher is saying. In this case much of their teaching is indirect and is delivered by someone who may not be a specialist in a particular subject area. This raises the question of equal access to the curriculum.

Academic inclusion for deaf pupils in a mainstream school can be inhibited by lack of deaf awareness, teaching that is not related to pupils' preferred learning styles, inappropriate support and low expectations (Monkman and Baskind 1998; Powers *et al.* 1999). In many cases the deaf child's level of English is below that of hearing classmates, which can lead both to children failing to understand key aspects of the curriculum and to teachers and other adults providing inappropriate support for language development (Hopwood and Gallaway 1998). The need for many deaf pupils to have support with their English and, for BSL users, their development of sign language, can conflict with full access to the curriculum. If pupils are withdrawn for additional work then they are unable to attend all mainstream classes. A slower pace of communication due to interpretation may limit participation within the classroom. Difficulties with group work and classroom discussion arise owing to the rapid pace of conversation, deaf pupils being unable to understand individuals' contributions and having difficulties in hearing when there is background noise (Stinson and Antia 1999). In general deaf children perform less well academically than hearing pupils (Powers *et al.* 1998), although a minority of deaf pupils show good academic achievement (Lewis 1996). Factors supporting academic achievement would seem to be: high expectations of what deaf pupils can achieve, the involvement of specialist staff and the incorporation of their skills into mainstream practice, appropriate support for staff and pupils, team working by all involved and specific strategies to ensure classroom participation by deaf pupils (Stinson and Liu 1999).

Access to social interaction is seen to be particularly problematic for deaf pupils in mainstream schools. Communication difficulties between deaf and hearing children can leave a deaf pupil isolated (Baldwin 1994; Jarvis 2002). Problems of loneliness and frustration seem likely if a child is the only deaf pupil in a setting (Gregory *et al.* 1995). Difficulties with communicating on an equal footing, misunderstanding information, missing jokes and being unable to understand in group settings can lead to low self-esteem. Baldwin (1994: 165) argues that 'full inclusion denies the deaf child access to an environment that addresses his/her unique social and emotional needs.'

Identifying pupils' experiences

So far, the potential negative aspects of inclusion have been outlined, but what do those deaf pupils currently being educated in mainstream schools really think of their school experience? Taking into account the views of the pupils themselves is vital if successful inclusion is to be achieved and children have a right to be consulted about their education (DfES 2001). A research project by The University of Hertfordshire and the Royal National Institute for Deaf People (UH/RNID 2002) interviewed 61 deaf pupils and 22 hearing pupils being educated in mainstream secondary schools in

England. Both Deaf and hearing researchers were involved in the process of data collection. The project aims were: to document and disseminate deaf pupils' experiences of inclusion and to identify barriers and factors facilitating the effective inclusion of deaf pupils into mainstream schools.

The deaf pupils covered an even spread across the range of hearing losses, from moderate to severe to profound, including pupils who had received a cochlear implant. Figure 18.1 shows the numbers of pupils according to communication mode used during interviews and degree of hearing loss.

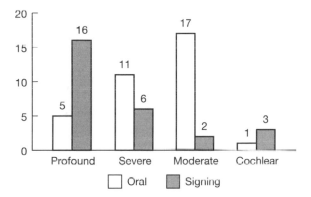

Figure 18.1 Communication mode and level of deafness

The research team visited 25 schools, in 16 different educational authorities. Fifteen schools had specialist provision for deaf pupils, such as hearing impaired units; seven schools had no specialist provision beside the peripatetic services of a teacher of the deaf and three schools had special educational needs bases but no dedicated provision for deaf pupils.

Both individual interviews and focus group discussions were carried out. A variety of methods ensured that the pupils had an opportunity to express their views in detail and in the manner that best suited them. These included the use of mindmaps, which children could draw, write or ask the researcher to write under their dictation; brainstorm exercises; question and answer scenarios; role-playing and the exploration of metaphors. This approach generated a wealth of qualitative data and its analysis identified the following key themes: identity, pupils' views on deafness, school ethos, staff roles, academic inclusion, social inclusion. The rest of the chapter outlines these themes and highlights their implications for policy and practice.

Pupils' views on being deaf in a hearing school

Identity was an issue that emerged spontaneously from the pupils' comments about themselves and their hearing peers. This issue was closely related to that of the school ethos. Some pupils were very confident about deafness as being part of their identity, while others saw it as something to hide. Similarly, in some schools the profile of deafness was high, with the use of visual images of deaf people, such as posters, issues related to deafness as part of the curriculum – for example, looking at hearing aids when studying sound – and identification of the special needs of deaf people within the school environment. In other schools the deaf pupil became invisible under an 'all children are special' blanket philosophy, where the particular issues raised by deafness may not have been identified and therefore addressed. The pupils quoted hereon are all deaf unless noted otherwise. The findings can be studied in more detail in the UH/RNID (2002) report.

Identity

The deaf pupils were asked to choose the terminology they would normally use to describe themselves, which led to discussions around whether they would willingly disclose their hearing status to others. Some of the pupils felt that, if they could 'pass' as hearing, then they would and that they would only disclose their hearing loss on a need-to-know basis. The following quote from a Year 8 pupil with a moderate hearing loss exemplifies this stance:

> I tend not to tell people I'm deaf unless they find out . . . and when they asked me I'd go 'yeah, I am', but I wouldn't tell them.

Another year 8 pupil with a profound hearing loss had similar views:

> I wouldn't unless they needed to know – if they spoke really quietly or didn't look at me and I needed to.

Most of the deaf pupils interviewed chose to label themselves as either partially hearing or partially deaf, but overall the replies spanned a range of terms including hearing, hard of hearing, a little bit deaf, Deaf and profoundly deaf. Different labels were used by different individuals and their choices were not necessarily related to their degree of hearing loss. For example a pupil with a moderate loss might readily identify as deaf, whilst other pupils with severe or profound losses might see themselves as hearing or partially hearing. Some also felt that there were disadvantages in being identified as being deaf as they might be teased, bullied or just treated differently:

> I prefer sometimes people not to know 'cause some people tend to act strangely . . . They kind of talk overdramatically and say H-E-L-L-O and it's easier if they just talked normally. I just say, 'Please don't do that. I prefer it if you talk normally. I'm not stupid.'

> (Year 8 pupil, severe hearing loss)

One Year 9 pupil with a cochlear implant pointed out that posters displayed in school, promoting good communication with deaf people, might be the cause of some hearing people's behaviour.

> There's actually a couple of posters about, telling people to, like, t-a-l-k l-i-k-e t-h-i-s and I don't really like it when people do that.

Other pupils felt that it could help with communication if people understood that they were deaf and that other people would notice anyway.

> Don't pretend there's not a problem, there is. Well, it's not a problem but you have to explain to people, otherwise they don't understand and that causes a big problem.
> (Year 8 pupil, moderate hearing loss)

Interestingly, some hearing pupils commented quite emphatically about the need of deaf pupils to have deaf peers as a means of feeling more secure in their identity.

> If it's only one person in the entire school who has a hearing aid, that person is like, left out. He or she might say things like ' Oh why am I the only one? Why am I like this?' It's like they start to get upset about who they are because they are the only one that needs a hearing aid.
> (Year 9, hearing pupil)

> Because you want to talk to someone who is deaf . . . you want someone who knows what you're going through, how you're feeling . . . It's alright for us because there's lots of hearing people . . .
> (Year 8, hearing pupil)

Most deaf pupils also said that they liked having other deaf pupils in the school as they could communicate more easily with them and it meant that there was someone else with similar experiences. Nevertheless, they also liked having hearing pupils in the school as this could lead to understanding each other's worlds and to wider experiences.

> We can talk about things, we're the same. Like. In my primary school, people didn't really understand and it's much easier to talk to my friends who are hearing impaired . . .
> (Year 7 pupil, severe hearing loss)

> It is good that it is mixed here, you can have more friends. Deaf pupils can teach hearing to sign and hearing pupils can teach deaf to speak. It will help for the future when you work with hearing or go out with hearing friends.
> (Year 8 pupil, profound hearing loss)

School ethos

The majority of pupils spoke positively about their school and mentioned particular arrangements made for them, such as counselling or structured peer support (these were often open to hearing students as well). They also noted activities designed to encourage deaf and hearing pupils to communicate and socialise together, such as sign language clubs, open to all pupils, and deaf awareness sessions for hearing pupils. The acknowledgement of the particular needs of deaf pupils was usually seen as positive.

> I like the way they can arrange stuff like this to happen, so, like, they don't just treat me like, 'oh, I'm another person.' They don't just say, 'oh, you're deaf,' whatever, 'you can carry on.' They actually say you can come up here and you can talk to someone about it. I'm treated a bit more than other people are, which I don't think it's very fair but it's still quite good for me. They're just not acknowledging me like another person, they get to arrange other things for me and stuff. Good special needs arrangements.
>
> (Year 7 pupil, moderate hearing loss)

Some pupils, however, reported negative experiences and found themselves excluded from activities hearing pupils were undertaking. This raises the question as to the extent to which the needs of deaf pupils are considered in the initial planning for school activities.

> I couldn't go [on the school trip] because the man might give us instructions like how far to go [in the water] and without my hearing aids on I wouldn't understand it.
>
> (Year 7 pupil, moderate hearing loss)

Deaf awareness, of both staff and hearing pupils, is a key aspect of inclusion. This includes awareness of the particular communication needs of deaf people and therefore using appropriate strategies and equipment such as radio hearing aids. It also means being sensitive to the desire of many pupils not to be overtly identified as needing special treatment. The level of deaf awareness varied between schools involved in the project and within the schools themselves and it significantly affected the pupils' experiences.

> It's really embarrassing 'cause sometimes teachers tend to go, 'Oh can you be quiet. We've got deaf children in the class!' and how you should be quiet and how you shouldn't be noisy otherwise they won't be able to hear and everything. And you're like 'Why did you do that? You've just embarrassed me so much, why did you have to?'
>
> (Year 8 pupil, moderate hearing loss)

Everybody used to pull them out [hearing aids connected to radio aid]. This teacher even pulled them out and he never said sorry or anything. He thought it was a stereo and it wasn't.

(Year 7 pupil, profound hearing loss)

Pupils' access to the curriculum and staff roles

Access to the curriculum is facilitated by a variety of people: the mainstream teacher, teachers of the deaf working within the classroom or withdrawing the pupil for separate tuition, support staff and peers. Pupils expressed a range of perceptions in relation to curriculum access, ranging from very poor to very good. Some pupils highlighted the need for more support in mainstream lessons and felt that they were otherwise unable to access them. Many pupils found that mainstream teachers in particular used inappropriate teaching styles, such as talking when moving around the room or facing the blackboard, talking quickly and without using any form of visual aid and allowing noise levels to rise so that deaf pupils found it uncomfortable.

I like the way teachers always make sure that you've understood things.

(Year 7 pupil, severe hearing loss)

I would tell [a new pupil] that school is horrible and pointless. People will mess about and they would need more support at school.

(Year 9 pupil, profound hearing loss)

I prefer teachers here, at the Unit, than the mainstream teachers. Here they help me to understand the meaning. The mainstream teachers don't, they talk way too fast.

(Year 7 pupil, profound hearing loss)

This teacher is always angry and shouting in my radio aids. When he shouts my radio aid is hurting me.

(Year 7 pupil, profound hearing loss)

The role of support staff was seen as to aid deaf pupils' communication with mainstream teachers, help them to understand their work and ensure that they stay on task. Deaf pupils appreciated that support staff facilitated communication with mainstream teachers, encouraged them with their work and were there when they needed them. But they also commented on how support staff might over-explain things and be intrusive by over-helping or by interjecting in the deaf pupils' social interactions with hearing pupils. Of course, the balance between giving adequate, but not too much, support can be difficult to achieve and it requires particular skills and knowledge. Below are some of the comments that pupils voiced on this topic.

This school is very helpful, I got a communicator help me do some work. They help me with the subjects I don't understand.

> (Year 9 pupil, moderate hearing loss)

If I'm stuck, like on a question, she helps me out and gives me a little example of it. If I'm struggling she's there.

> (Year 7 pupil, moderate hearing loss)

Some of them always help me so they can annoy you because you don't want them to help you a lot.

> (Year 8 pupil, profound hearing loss)

At school, helpers, in lessons, keep prodding me and asking me if I'm alright, that sort of thing, they try to do my work for me! I mean, I think if the LSAs get bored, they just try to help me; they don't like sitting there with nothing to do. The teachers, they've got a whole class so they tend to leave me alone but the LSAs are trying to help just me so I don't get a lot of peace.

> (Year 9 pupil, profound hearing loss)

Sometimes when I stop writing realising that I have made a mistake, she would leap to the rescue, asking if I wanted any help. Often I said no but she would push me aside and take my work to check. I wish I could conjure up something that would freeze her at least for a few minutes!

> (Year 8 pupil, profound hearing loss)

Pupils' social inclusion

Having friends and being part of a group was, for most of the pupils, the most significant aspect of school and what they commented on the most. The following quote by a Year 8 pupil with a moderate hearing loss exemplifies the feelings shared by the vast majority of the pupils interviewed:

> It's my mates that make me go through school. If I'm having a bad day, it's friends who talk to me about what I can do. Friends are the best thing.
>
> (Year 8 pupil, moderate hearing loss)

The deaf pupils in the project had a range of experiences, both positive and negative, regarding social inclusion. The key factor seemed to be the ability to communicate, which required strategies to be used by both deaf and hearing pupils, and above all, the willingness to use these strategies.

With a group of hearing people talking I feel left out. One girl signs for me but the others wouldn't wait and carry on talking. They say I talk like a baby.

(Year 7 pupil, profound hearing loss)

Sometimes when they say a joke and we don't hear it and they all start laughing and then they don't say the joke again. I do fake laughs. Sometimes I pretend I understand and then, to my best friend maybe, I might go and say, 'I didn't quite get that joke.'

(Year 7 pupil, severe hearing loss)

Here lots of people are hearing and don't want to speak to deaf people. Here lots of hearing people just say, 'I don't know what he's saying.'

(Year 8 pupil, profound hearing loss)

It was hard because they didn't understand us at first but, after a while, they got used to how we talk and it was a lot easier.

(Year 9 pupil, profound hearing loss)

No problem. I like both deaf and hearing. I have made lots of new friends and they're being very nice. I like sitting with them and it's nice to make new friends.

(Year 7 pupil, moderate hearing loss)

They don't treat us like outcasts, they just treat us with respect and that's fine.

(Year 8 pupil, profound hearing loss)

Because friendship was such a vital part of their school lives, the pupils felt that being able to work alongside their friends enhanced the quality of lessons and made them more fun, as well as helping them with their work. Friends were therefore seen as a resource, which could facilitate academic, as well as social, inclusion. Unfortunately teachers often had a different opinion on the matter and separated groups of friends in lessons in order to reduce distractions.

I can work better when I'm around friends.

(Year 9 pupil, profound hearing loss)

You actually can make more friends [working in a group]. You're basically working and then you know what people are doing, their ideas and that.

(Year 7 pupil, moderate hearing loss)

Hearing classmates are not nice and I don't feel right. It would be better if I had my deaf friend with me. The teacher said she had to separate us. I was angry inside.

(Year 9 pupil, profound hearing loss)

They [teachers] give you seating plans, which is bad because you can't sit with your friends.

(Year 7 pupil, severe hearing loss)

Pupils were asked about social activities both within and outside school and their responses revealed that, as well as valuing individual friendships, most of them took part in a range of sports and social clubs. These activities encouraged further the socialisation of deaf and hearing pupils.

Conclusions

There is no easy answer to the question of whether inclusion in mainstream schools is the right educational choice for deaf pupils. However, one of the pivotal elements that should not be overlooked is what deaf pupils themselves think and feel. This research highlights that while for some pupils mainstream placement might be the best solution, for others it may not be so. The following two quotes, both from pupils with profound hearing loss who prefer signing as a mode of communication, illustrate the opposite poles of a continuum of experiences within the field of mainstream education for deaf pupils.

I'm not interested in school. Lots of people, hearing, they group all together and I'm left out.

(Year 8 pupil)

I wish all schools mixed deaf and hearing. My mom thinks about that I should go to my brother's and sister's school but no, they're all hearing. There are so many hearing schools and few deaf and hearing mixing very few, and we need many schools that are a mixture of deaf and hearing, ideally I would like every school!

(Year 7 pupil)

If inclusion in mainstream schools for deaf pupils is to be successful, services, schools and teachers need to think carefully about the resources, strategies and training necessary for all involved. An issue that requires careful consideration is whether the deaf pupil will be included individually in a school with no dedicated specialist provision and no deaf peers or adult role models available, as such an arrangement could have a significant impact on his/her sense of identity. Solutions to these issues are already being sought and trialled by some services. For example, one education authority has established an e-mail network of deaf pupils, who are placed in different mainstream schools, in order to foster peer support, while another brings hearing aid users from different schools together for discussion of mutual concerns (Moore *et al.* 1999). Access to D/deaf adults, in relation to developing a sense of personal identity, also needs planning and consideration. Deaf pupils have needs, which are specific to the fact that they have a hearing loss and these must be addressed rather than glossed over. Therefore, mainstream teachers will need support in developing, adopting and maintaining the use of relevant strategies that, while facilitating the inclusion of the deaf child, respect the child's desire to be seen as being 'normal' by his or her peers. New and supply teachers, as well as students and trainees, in particular, need to be provided with appropriate information so that deaf pupils' education is not disrupted by staff changes. Support staff also need to be aware of the boundaries of their roles and need to receive adequate training to develop the skills required in order to provide effective support for both mainstream staff and pupils.

Our research project revealed that deaf pupils linked the success or failure of their educational experiences to their experiences of friendship within their schools. These experiences, however, were not just personal and, as such, separate from school life. In fact, those deaf pupils interviewed who expressed positive views on friendship were located in school environments that celebrated diversity and where deafness had a high profile amongst both staff and student bodies.

Currently in the UK there is no clear conception of what inclusion means and it is often associated merely with placing a deaf child in a mainstream context (Powers 2002). For some children inclusion in a wider sense would best be supported by placement in a specialist provision. If mainstream placement is the preferred option then the range of issues discussed in this chapter must be considered if the experience and the outcomes are to be positive for all concerned.

References

Baldwin, S. (1994) Full inclusion: reality versus idealism. *American Annals of the Deaf, Selected Topics of Interest, 1994: Full Inclusion*, **139**, 147–71.

British Deaf Association (1996) *The Right to be Equal*. London: BDA.

Deaf Ex-Mainstreamers Group (1996) *Mainstreaming Issues for Professionals Working with Deaf Children*. Barnsley: DEX.

DfES (2001) *Special Educational Needs Code Of Practice*. London: DfES.

Eatough, M. (2000) Raw data from the BATOD survey England January 1998. *British Association of Teachers of the Deaf Magazine*, (May), 1–8.

Gregory, S., Bishop, J. and Sheldon, L. (1995) *Deaf Young People and their Families*. Cambridge: Cambridge University Press.

Hopwood, V. and Gallaway, C. (1999) Evaluating the linguistic experience of a deaf child in a mainstream class: a case study. *Deafness and Education International*, **3**(3), 172–87.

Jarvis, J. (2002) Exclusion by Inclusion? Issues for deaf pupils and their mainstream teachers. *Education 3–13*, **30**(2), 47–51.

Ladd, P. (1991) Making plans for Nigel: the erosion of identity by mainstreaming. In Taylor, G. and Bishop, J. (eds) *Being Deaf: the experience of deafness*. London: The Open University.

Lewis, S. (1996) The reading achievement of a group of severely and profoundly hearing-impaired school leavers educated within a natural aural approach. *Journal of the British Association of Teachers of the Deaf*, **20**, 1–7.

Lynas, W., Lewis, S. and Hopwood, V. (1997) Supporting the education of deaf children in mainstream schools. *Deafness and Education*, **21**(2), 41–5.

Monkman, H. and Baskind, S. (1998) Are assistants effectively supporting hearing-impaired children in mainstream schools? *Deafness and Education*, **22**(1), 15–22.

Moore, M., Dash, J. and Bristow, L. (1999) A social skills programme with primary aged isolated hearing aid users. *Deafness and Education International*, **1**(1), 10–24.

National Deaf Children's Society (1990) *Deaf Young People's Views on Integration: a survey report*. London: NDCS.

Powers, S. (2002) From concepts to practice in deaf education: A United Kingdom perspective on inclusion. *Journal of Deaf Studies and Deaf Education*, **7**(3), 230–43.

Powers, S., Gregory, S. and Thoutenhoofd, E. (1998) *The Educational Achievements of Deaf Children*. London: DfEE.

Powers, S., Gregory, S., Lynas, W., McCracken, W., Watson, L., Boulton, A. and Harris, D. (1999) *A Review of Good Practice in Deaf Education*. London: RNID.

Stinson, M. and Liu, Y. (1999) Participation of deaf and hard-of-hearing students in classes with hearing students. *Journal of Deaf Studies and Deaf Education*, **4**(3), 191–202.

Stinson, M. and Antia, S. (1999) Considerations in educating deaf and hard of hearing students in inclusive settings. *Journal of Deaf Studies and Deaf Education*, **4**(3), 163–75.

University of Hertfordshire/Royal National Institute for Deaf People (2002) *Inclusion: what deaf pupils think*. London: RNID.

This chapter most valuably places students' views at the foreground of the discussion. Once again we see that we can learn from each other and that deaf students have particular experiences that need to inform our understanding of inclusive outcomes as well as intentions.

Part 4

Looking from within classrooms and schools

CHAPTER 19

Learning Support Assistants talk about inclusion

Caroline Roaf

In this chapter Caroline Roaf allows us to consider the role of the Learning Support Assistant from their perspective. Here we can gain an insight into the LSA's developing role within the classroom, the school and beyond. We are able to consider their relationships with students, teachers and families, and the impact this has on learning and communication. By listening to their voices we are offered their view of the skills they bring to the learning environment and how these skills should best be used and developed. We can clearly see how the inclusion of a wide range of individuals within the learning environment can generate school improvement and effectiveness.

Introduction

This chapter, written in 2002, draws on a discussion within the team of Learning Support Assistants (LSAs) of The Cressex Community School, a coeducational secondary school for 900 pupils aged 11–18 years, set adjacent to a business park in High Wycombe, Buckinghamshire. In socio-economic terms, Ofsted (2001) had this to say: 'Many pupils experience financial disadvantage. The proportion of pupils known to be eligible for free school meals, two pupils in every five, is well above the national average. A very high proportion, more than one pupil in every two speaks English as an additional language. A very large proportion, three out of every four pupils, are of non-white ethnic background' (Ofsted 2001).

The context

Everything about this time and place is significant in terms of the concept of inclusion as a journey and the role of school support staff in that journey. For example, the school is a secondary modern in an authority that continues to select at 11+, and this group of practitioners is referred to as Learning Support Assistants, not yet as Teacher Assistants. Both, in different ways, are indications of debates being waged in the United Kingdom as a whole about the principle of inclusion. The size and nature of the team too is significant at this time. Eighteen LSAs, compared with a teaching staff of 49, cover a range of skills and operate in a range of modes (in-class support, withdrawal, small group work) and a range of specialisms, e.g. behaviour. In addition, a separate Ethnic Minority Achievement Service, with three LSAs and two teachers, supports pupils with English as an Additional Language. The Learning Support team is based in a specially designated part of the school, with a range of resources at its disposal. The discussion among this group of LSAs about the nature and purpose of their work speaks of changes recently experienced and of those anticipated.

Enquiry among a group of Special Educational Needs Coordinators (SENCOs) on a training course held at about the same time in the same authority showed that the majority of schools employed roughly half as many LSAs as teachers – a trend reflected nationally. According to Phil Revell, writing in the Guardian (23 October 2002), 'Spending on support staff has been rising for the last five years, and in the last recorded year the number of non-teaching staff in English schools rose by 15%. [. . .] There are 213,000 support workers in English schools, for 437,000 teachers of whom 70% are classroom support staff.'

Expanding role

Although LSAs first came into mainstream schools during the mid to late eighties, their numbers were low overall. Numbers grew slowly as mainstream schools gradually opened their doors to a wider range of students. The role of the LSA was crucial in promoting this process in the classroom. As Rhona Seviour, head of a 520-pupil middle school in Hertfordshire, (quoted in Haigh 2002) points out:

> The original belief was that only teachers should be involved with children in the classroom. It took a long time to win people over, and it was the quality of the LSAs that did the trick – their effectiveness in working with young people.

So successful were they, indeed, that in many Local Education Authorities (LEAs) learning support assistant hours became the 'currency' in which support for children with statements of SEN was calculated.

Since 1997, growth has been rapid, in response to government support for inclusion, and the increasing shortage of teachers. At such a time, the growth in numbers of support staff has, indeed, been such as to draw comments from teacher unions. They have expressed unease, in particular, about the adequacy of training, pay and the lack of clarity as to role. Two reports on the subject of school support staff coincide, as it happens, with the discussion recorded here. The first was a research study (Lee 2002) that provides an overview of existing research and commentary on the roles of teaching assistants in schools and the issues arising from the ways they are employed and deployed. This report comments, for example, on the 'plethora of job titles ... used to describe people who assist in classrooms' (p. 4) for which the government's preferred generic term is 'teaching assistant'. The second was a government consultation paper (DfES 2002) which, it declares, 'heralds a revolution in both the nature and the extent of the contribution made by our support staff in schools' (ministerial introduction). The proposals focus on providing a new legal framework to govern the supervision of support staff, and the development of training opportunities and a career structure. The discussion that follows illustrates the importance of these issues to LSAs.

Also reflected in the discussion is the wider debate about the developing relationship between professionals and paraprofessionals found in many services. Teachers are only one of a group of professionals (doctors provide another example) now working together and sharing skills in teams rather than in isolation. A consequence has been a much closer analysis of the proportion of non-teaching tasks carried out by teachers at a time when they are in short supply. If, it is argued, teachers are carrying excessive workloads, with term-time teaching loads in excess of 50 hours per week and half of that time spent on non-teaching tasks, then there would appear to be a role for non-teaching support staff to carry out some of those non-teaching tasks. There has also been greater interest in sorting out what some of these non-teaching tasks are. While approximately two-thirds of support workers are classroom-based teaching assistants, the remaining third fulfil roles in administration, as personal assistants, secretaries and bursars (figures which do not include caretaking, cleaning and catering staff).

In relation to special educational needs: the 2002 figure of around 50,000 SEN support staff constitutes roughly a quarter of all full-time-equivalent teacher assistants currently employed. These practitioners are among those most closely involved in the progress and process of inclusion, and their rapid growth mirrors the development of the government's espousal of inclusion since 1997.

In this new situation, in which support staff roles are undergoing governmental, professional and union assessment of their potential, it seems an appropriate time to listen to a group of LSAs talking about their work and how they would like to see the role develop in the future. A team meeting of about an hour and a quarter was specially convened for this discussion.

The LSAs in this team were mainly local residents. Some of them had been brought up in the area and had themselves been to Cressex. Three members were from local Asian and Afro-Caribbean communities. There was also a range of professional background with, for example, an ex-police officer and an ex-youth worker. At least two others were hoping to gain unqualified teacher status.

The concept of inclusion

We began with a short discussion about how the concept of inclusion was interpreted among them.

> I suppose inclusion is changing the situation so that everyone can be part of it as opposed to trying to change people so that they fit into certain situations – so that you create an educational establishment that caters for all children would be inclusion – probably impossible actually to include everyone!
>
> (Helen, Senior LSA)

There seemed to be general agreement as to the basic thrust of policy promoting inclusion, suggesting that the idea of inclusion as a journey was accurate, reflecting a developing personal experience in which new perspectives were being tasted and tested:

> You've got to decide do you actually agree with the policy of inclusion . . . or are there other ways of dealing with it [i.e. the development of inclusive practice]? Having worked in a special EBD boarding school – that's at the other political end of what we're doing – it's a complete turn around for me. But that's not to say I don't feel fulfilled in what I'm doing.
>
> (Andrew, LSA)

There was some ambivalence, too, about the extent to which a school could be 'inclusive' and whether inclusion could be interpreted more widely to include other forms of provision made elsewhere than in the school. The possibility that a school might 'care' beyond its own boundaries 'hangs in the air' in this discussion.

> There comes a time when you have to say that you cannot keep a child in this establishment because of behaviours or that the establishment cannot include that child for one particular reason or another. So long as you can recognise that it is including them in education – just not that particular venue at this time, not excluded in the sense of being expelled, that's it, they don't get any more education, that's exclusive. If they then go to another school that maybe caters for their needs, that's still being included in the education system.
>
> (David, LSA)

Listening to children and young people

The progress of inclusion seemed to be linked clearly with an increased value placed on the children's voice, and the space and time given to this. These ideas were introduced internationally through the 1989 United Nations Convention on the Rights of the Child, notably in Article 12. In the UK, the 1989 Children Act made it obligatory to listen to children about all matters affecting them, and this principle appeared to have become embedded in this school's practice.

> You can also take as inclusive . . . the fact that you have involved the child in every stage of the process.
>
> (Sonia, SENCO)

> And that includes not just the child but peers, parents and significant others.
>
> (David)

> It used to be a system whereby you decided what was best for the child and then informed the child about what was going to happen. Now the child is much more involved in the meetings as we go along, so they have a voice.
>
> (Sonia)

> That way it's much more effective. They don't feel out of the system. They are actually involved in the process and have a say. So therefore the outcome is more valid because they've made a contribution. And if they decide not to participate then you can turn around and say well look, you agreed to this, this is what you wanted, what's happened to change?
>
> (David)

Accepting diversity

Inclusion sometimes seemed too much to ask of classroom teachers on top of all the other demands made of them.

> I think one of the difficulties is that you are asking staff to include all the students like learning difficulties, behaviour, speech and language and communication and a whole range of students at a time when they are also being pressured from the other end to get exam results, SATs results, GCSEs. It's almost as if their job is becoming wider but you are setting much, much higher targets for them to achieve.
>
> (Sonia)

There was also the possible effect on the majority of the class of including some young people.

> The downside is people like X who is barely literate. He's included in lessons and sometimes he holds back the other students because he doesn't understand so he then goes off at a tangent or tries to become the centre of attention and distracts from the learning of others. He's being included but at the expense of the others who could get further forward.
>
> (Natalie, LSA)

It was recognised that these debates were still open and ongoing, with a strong sense of policy being made and challenges being faced in relation to the principles and values underpinning inclusive practice. The thrust of the following discussion will be recognised among practitioners in schools and among teacher trainers and policy-makers across the UK.

I think there are issues there that ought to be talked about whether people like that are included in another way. Like an education system or a school within a school for especially needy – that would be inclusive because at the same time something like that I think would be a good thing.

(David)

But do you think a child like that would feel included if they didn't spend any actual lesson time with their peers? Would they actually mix with their peers at breaks and lunchtime?

(Helen)

That's an interesting thing to say but I think most kids go off to different sections and lessons and sets and provided you put it in that context I think they'd understand that and wouldn't feel excluded.

(David)

Let's say we change the school here and have one-to-one here [in the Learning Support Base] on a full time basis. The other children know where they are and they would not feel part of the community of the school, because even though theoretically they are included in the school they are excluded in what the children take part in.

(Helen)

This doesn't mean every single day they are here, there are other things, Youth Award, PE . . . There are lots of networks they can tap into. Their needs could be specially addressed.

(David)

I think they would be stigmatised.

(Joy, LSA)

They're stigmatised now, aren't they, because they are outside the system.

(Mary, LSA team leader)

Not sure that here [Cressex] it is seen as a stigma. One of the strengths of this school is that the withdrawal system . . . works in such a way that they all want to be here [Learning Support Base].

(Helen)

They come here when they are not supposed to.

(David)

It's a fine line to tread.

(Helen)

The final point in this part of the discussion raises an interesting and significant matter in relation to the role of disability as a catalyst, hastening the progress of inclusion. Although not specifically mentioned, the Special Educational Needs and Disability Act 2001 (SENDA) is likely to have raised awareness of the question of access, for students with both short and long term disabilities. The lack of physical visibility of students with disabilities highlighted the importance of a genuinely whole-school inclusive culture in the sense proposed in, for example, the *Index for Inclusion* (Booth and Ainscow 2001).

Inclusion in its purest form would involve none of that [withdrawal] but I'm not sure it's right for the children. Children who are struggling in lessons do need extra support. It's not always possible to give them that support in class. At this school we don't have many physically disabled because the site isn't suitable . . . When we do have children who break legs and ankles, it is very difficult for them to be in school, when they can't get about the site.

(Helen)

Children seem to be much more accepting of each other at schools like Y, you don't get the name calling or the lack of acceptance because the whole ethos of the school is set up to take these sort of students from the word 'go' – it hasn't been something imposed on the school late and I don't think they have the same problems.

(Sonia)

Making a difference: mediation

Overall, the LSA role was strongly associated with helping others on their journey towards inclusion on a daily basis and often in seemingly small ways.

I've got a child in class who is quite withdrawn and isolated from the others. Making an effort to find strategies of getting that child involved in the work of the group . . . ways to help kids with MLD [moderate learning difficulties] to assimilate them into lessons without too much difficulty. So there's lots of things that we do to include children in everything.

(Mary)

LSAs could give many examples of times where they felt that their presence had made a difference, perhaps helping a teacher to accept a child and to make both teacher and child feel valued.

You can act as a mediator between children and their teacher where there's been some misunderstanding or the children don't understand, where they don't understand what's expected of them and how to interact to produce work or how to behave themselves sometimes and that takes the strain off the teacher as well which is helping them on their journey.

(Joy)

The other way as well – we have discussions with the teacher about what the children have learnt and what the child would like to do with the teacher as well – that can work both ways. You can feedback to the teacher how the pupils have been in class and how they are pleased with themselves. You might be discussing with the teacher the work that needs differentiating.

(Shahida, LSA)

Making time for planning and communication with teachers

LSAs were pleased that they now had the time and opportunity to discuss strategies and lesson plans with the teachers.

We're doing something now with long-term impact . . . a planning sheet. We have discussions termly and ad hoc and everybody's got those sessions to have with the teacher they work with.

(Mary)

(My query 'So you have time for this?' was greeted, predictably, with laughter . . .)

We do have to make time so we'll prepare the sheet beforehand by filling in the details of the children. We may have worked with them before and the teacher may not have done. So we'll know e.g. behaviour problems, whether they're going to need a laptop, if their works needs differentiating, provide starter activities, seating plans . . . So we can give advice to the teachers. So it's a general planning document – as a basis for discussion.

(Mary)

Looking back, they could see how rapidly changes in attitude and closer working relationships between teachers and LSAs had come about.

We could negotiate non-contact time.

(Mary)

It's taken a while actually. I've been here 18 months and I've never had a problem but there has been sort of animosities over LSAs coming into class – so that's the process of evolution isn't it?

(Andrew)

It's changing that. You'd be surprised how much they value us. That meeting I had with the new teachers last night to explain what my role is – one of them said 'I love it when you're in there because you know those kids and you can control them.' You know she's still trying to get the behaviour management structure in there so that helps her especially when the new teachers are newly qualified.

(Mary)

Teachers accept that now.

(Husna, LSA)

I've never had any personal problem but 6 months ago there would be LSAs moaning about certain teachers who didn't want them to do this or do that and that seems to have died the death.

(Andrew)

It comes to negotiation – a question of communication.

(Sonia)

This is what I said to the new teachers yesterday – the key to it is talking. If you talk on a regular basis and we try and timetable people so that they're going to be there on a regular basis and follow a subject on three or four days a week so that they have that continuity. If the teacher at the end of the lesson says we're going to do this . . . they're going to be providing us with lesson plans (laughter . . .). The key is communication between teachers and LSAs and once they've built up a relationship it's very valuable.

(Mary)

Advocacy and pupil participation

To what extent, I asked, do you feel inclusion would fall apart without you? The inspection report speaks very highly of the contribution you make to the students' progress (this was said of the EMAS/EAL team).

> I'd say it would be very difficult to manage a class of say 20–25 students, 6 or 7 of whom have special needs of one sort or another, like behaviour or learning difficulties or something. For one teacher to teach those children without help in the classroom is just a management issue on its own. I think personally it would be very, very difficult to manage on your own. Even if it's to take a kid out because he's misbehaving you have another adult in there it makes all the difference.
>
> (Andrew)

> I think it helps the children to have someone who's there for them because then the teacher can take charge of teaching the class and you can make sure that the children who need help are actually keeping up to speed with things. I think it's the children that suffer because although the teacher would control the class and run the class not all the children would actually be participating in the lesson.
>
> (Helen)

LSAs were adept at understanding student apprehension over loss of face and fears about the possible reactions of teachers. They regularly 'modelled' alternative behaviours for their students – approaches which secured the student's participation and engagement with the lesson.

> Quite often a child will ask you what they have to do rather than front up to the whole class and say 'I don't know what to do.' The strategy I've used in the past is to put my hand up and say, ' I didn't understand that,'or, ' I didn't hear that can you say that again please' and the impact comes back to you and you can see half the class going 'whew'.
>
> (Sonia)

> It's quite hard to have the guts to do that!
>
> (David)

> A child can't do that. Or you can say, 'I don't know that, I'll have to go and ask' – that's acceptable.
>
> (Joy)

Sharing your experience with kids is very valuable – saying, 'This looks really hard doesn't it – let's have a go at it.' Because you can see them thinking it, so all right – they can see that I'm accepting that it does look hard but I'm willing to have a go and we'll start to break it down into bits together – and it's team work.

(Mary)

So often a child thinks, and teachers say, 'You've got to do this on your own' – well how often in life do you do things on your own? If you can't do something you go to someone who can help you

(Sonia)

In these instances it seemed that inclusion was as much a journey for the children as for the teachers and support staff. They too have to learn how to learn. They have to discover that relationships, particularly the power relations between teachers and students, can change. They have to accept that teachers can accommodate individual learning styles, become more sensitive to diverse modes and paces of learning and more responsive to a wide range of different people.

I think it helps them on their journey as well through the way we are behaving and what we are doing. If we are shouting at the teacher – if our behaviour wasn't acceptable then they could justify behaving badly too. The way we talk to the teacher even if we don't understand is important for them on their journey.

(Shahida)

Any of the children can ask for help and be given it and we work with all the children so they see you being there without the stigma.

(Mary)

In Science, and I'm not that brilliant at it, but I'll say 'We'll do this and we'll put our hand up and ask Miss S to come and check and see if it's OK before we go on'. They feel if Miss isn't sure, it's OK for us not to be sure.

(Husna)

I asked the LSAs how they felt the children recognised the school's willingness to change. How did they feel the children recognised the school's attempt to become more inclusive?

Raise expectations, raise sights, aim high. The teachers do do this – in Maths, the teacher deliberately gave them a hard task 'This is what you can do.'

(Mary)

Give them steps to achieve Maths skills – build on this skill to get there. Doing a lot of detailed work, self-esteem – go round and praise, often non-verbal.

(Joy)

Because of the 11+ a lot come here feeling like failures – never been good at anything in their whole school careers. Giving them praise and encouragement but be genuine!

(Sonia)

'Helping youngsters do better than they might'

The LSAs clearly felt they had made a clear difference to the pupils' academic performance, and their acceptance within the classroom by staff and pupils.

Last year I worked in the behaviour unit and there was one child whose Maths teacher refused to have him in the lesson any more unless he was supported and because of the way the timetable went I went into his Friday Maths lesson. I just went in and sat with him and I thought, 'Oh well this is going to be easy.' I mean Maths is not my subject at all and I thought, 'Well obviously if he's not going to do anything in Maths we'll just sit there and struggle together.' But he was actually very capable. All it took was for me to be there and say to him, 'I can't do this – show me how does it work? I can't understand – how do you work this question out?' And he would SHOW me, and he would do pages and pages of work to teach me how to do these particular problems. And by the end of the half term we showed the teacher and he didn't believe that it was this child's work. I had to say to him, 'I *can't* do this, it's *not* my work! I'm not capable of that level of work – this is the child's own work.' And after that he was perfectly happy to have the child in the class on his own, and he was accepted in the class and his behaviour, which had been a problem, ceased being a problem in that particular class because he was accepted by the teacher. But the teacher hadn't realised his capabilities because all he saw was the behaviour.

(Helen)

That's interesting because that teacher – an excellent teacher – never had behaviour problems and maybe that was part of the problem because he didn't expect behaviour problems and he found it difficult to respond to someone he couldn't control. Faced with a similar situation he would think again.

(Sonia)

It was a personality clash – it wasn't like him but for whatever reason, he couldn't see beyond the behaviour to see the child but I gave the child the opportunity to produce the work so he was raised in the teacher's estimation and that changed their relationship then. It was an opportunity I gave the child and it was a discovery that we all three learnt.

(Helen)

What about the other students, I asked. How did it affect them?

Difficult to say because once he was working and the teacher was happy, I wasn't there any more! But I think the other children were surprised at how good this particular boy was at Maths. I don't think they realised and I don't think he realised how good he was.

(Helen)

Two further examples illustrate the attention to detail, the determination to help students follow through to successful outcomes, and the serendipity that characterises so much of LSA practice.

Last year I was helping an MLD [moderate learning difficulties] kid in Technology. Some of the other SN [special needs] children were sat at the table with us where their issue was behaviour. Just seeing me get on and work with this lad – they actually ended up getting involved in trying to help him as well, which ended up increasing their performance and their self esteem. It was an interesting by-product.

(Sue, LSA)

It was an SSA [support staff assistant] we had. We had a pupil was a school refuser but very bright but she worked with him on his Science GCSE and he was a few marks away from an A" which for him was such a boost – down to the work she had done with him and because she produced work for him to do whether she was there or not. He knew he could come in and just get the work on the table and go home and do it if he wanted to. Although he didn't always turn up, he turned up for all his exams, which we were really worried about because we'd ring him up and say 'get out of bed and come in' because we'd allow him to come here and gave him cups of coffee and stuff. Lots of students come here for pastoral care really who don't feel safe in a classroom because they feel looked after and listened to.

(Mary)

Supporting the curriculum

Our discussion turned to the academic curriculum – that heartland of educational activity in which LSAs play out arguably the most important aspect of their role. The tension, mentioned frequently in the literature on Learning Support Assistants, between whether to follow the students or stick with a curriculum subject is apparent.

I know new teachers that I've been working with are trying very hard to make work accessible, so they are providing differentiated work across the range – on the same subject and maybe extension work. When you are in a school like Cressex, the ability of the students is so diverse so you have to be able to keep up with the ones who are brighter as well as challenging those that maybe need motivating.

(Shahida)

Secondary teachers are gradually cottoning on to something primary staff always knew and secondary staff always resisted.

(Sonia)

An LSA is key in that role really to let the teacher know. In my class the teacher asks you, 'How do you think I should approach this?' We ask LSAs for their preferences [of subjects to support] and I find that really good this year.

(Shahida)

People are allied to departments and go to meetings. The link person can take things to the meeting and bring stuff back to us.

(Mary)

Had the presence, and growth in numbers, of LSAs encouraged teachers to try new approaches?

We've grown. Five years ago there were a few of us poked into a little office – we never discussed anything with the teachers. Now we've got dialogue. The SMT [senior management team] will say, and have done recently, 'You are going to be giving your LSAs copies of your lesson plans and we will ask the LSAs if you are getting them.' 95 per cent do take them seriously. They are a valuable tool.

(Mary)

This team of LSAs had a strong sense of self worth, part of which they attributed to support from the head teacher, reinforced by a recent, and very positive, Ofsted inspection.

They do regard us as valuable.

(Mary)

When people come to this school they are shocked because there are no notices on the staff room saying no LSAs in here.

(Lynn, LSA)

When you work with the teachers in the classroom you strike up a bond, a friendship and the children see that friendship is there and when we're out of the classroom the friendship is also there so even if they are the teacher and you are the LSA we're always included; staff outings, training days.

(Cara, LSA)

Our Head is very, very supportive of what we do and without her help there'd be a big gap.

(Andrew)

We were losing staff but she gave us a lot back, listened to all our ideas about a career structure – paid holidays. Increase in pay made us feel important and she valued us. She's carried out all her promises.

(Mary)

LSA skills

Given the high value placed on the work of LSAs by teachers and young people, what skills and attributes contributed to this?

Mediation mentioned earlier – people skills.

(Mary)

When I first started here I remember the person who took me under her wing. She said all you really need to be an LSA is to be a jack-of-all-trades – you need to be able to do everything from the subject to listening – and have a sense of humour.

(Lynn)

But, I suggested, the reality is that it is very hard to be a jack-of-all-trades. Appropriate training and a commitment to teamwork in which experience and strategies could be shared were important features.

We do the City and Guilds training for all LSAs – that's a requirement – and we do get trained in helping children to read, MLD, dyslexia, behaviour, visual impairment, hearing impairment – basic stuff so you are given those skills which can then be used in any subject.

(Mary)

One of our strengths is working as a team to share information, share problems and strategies we might use. So if there's a problem with a particular child that will be shared and I might say, 'Well I try sitting with so and so, we do this or that' – shared strategies as well.

(Mary)

Sometimes staff won't do that because they see it as a sign of weakness – not that someone has a strategy that might work.

(Sonia)

The strength of this school is working together.

(Shahida)

You have to be willing to learn.

(Joy)

Since I've been here I've done Science for the last two years and next year I'm going to do the exam as well! If you've been here for a while you've been in a certain subject for a while and you know what's coming or you can bring existing skills – you might have a degree in something – that helps as well.

(Mary)

Role in the community

Given the nature of their work and particularly its low pay, the majority of LSAs live in the communities in which they work. As Hilary Wilce (2002) points out, 'They know the children and their families. And they tend to stay, providing the familiarity and consistency that so many pupils badly need.' It is tempting therefore to see LSAs as a form of community worker. How did the group react to this?

I've lived in the area – there are certain children that one knows – it's followed through from when they were at school with my children that also builds relationships.

(Cara)

A lot of children followed me up from the nursery and knowing the parents and when they see me here they're a bit more relaxed if they've got the kids to talk about.

(Husna)

I think it helps to identify you. You're in the community, living down the road. The parents are sometimes afraid to talk to teachers whereas I live in the area and I see a lot of parents and when I'm in town the kids will say 'Hi' and the parents are with them.

(Shahida)

I'm now teaching kids whose parents I taught!

(Sonia)

We're talking about key workers now . . . Some children have got either severe behaviour problems or, well, like Tom – who needs one-to-one support and we have links with their families. So like Tom that I look after, I'm in a lot of his lessons, or I speak to his mum regularly and I write her little reports every now and then so she knows how he's getting on and I send her little notes home as well and when she comes up I'm involved in the meetings and annual reviews meetings I'll be involved in those. So she knows she can pick the phone up to me at home or here and say what's Tom been up to? We do have strong links with parents.

(Mary)

The existence of other professionals coming in to school with roles overlapping in some respects with the role of the LSA was acknowledged to be confusing. It was by no means clear what effect, if any, these new roles would have on the still-developing role of the LSA/TA.

I think another aspect overlaying all of this is that you get more and more people coming in now. We've got Learning Mentors now who are coming in at a different layer. I'm not totally convinced that bringing in these different layers is productive. Sometimes it's better having one person and widen our role because you see the people in the classroom, have a relationship with parents. The Learning Mentors are not in classes.

(Sonia)

The future

Finally, the conversation moved on to a consideration of the future development of the role. Where were LSAs going professionally?

Having that relationship with the teacher. I think LSAs might work only with two or three teachers and they would plan and their input will be as much as two-thirds of the teacher input in terms of deciding how a lesson will be taught – I'm not talking about team teaching, just talking about more input . . . More qualifications for LSAs on different levels. I know this is coming . . . And a more pastoral role i.e. the counselling area, qualifications in counselling to enable us to work with the families of the pupils as well as the pupils themselves and their teachers. So we have a role that goes a number of ways. More responsibility for what we're doing.

(Mary)

The clear differentiation of role between teachers and LSA/TA was regarded as mutually supportive but distinct. This was reflected in the guidelines teaching staff were offered for working with the team of LSAs. These emphasise the distinctive role of the LSA in supporting the pupil, the teacher, the curriculum and the school and stress the need for close cooperation.

It takes the load off the teachers as well if we're able to communicate with the parents and that, to do with pupils. That spares them the time to do other things which they only can do and we can't.

(Husna)

A teacher only sees a child in one subject.

(Sonia)

We see them in a variety of subjects. I think that's one thing that might happen in the future. I'm not sure it's a good thing is that. LSAs would become subject specific, so that people will also have their own subject but I think you lose one of the strengths we have as LSAs in seeing the same child in different lessons with different teachers . . . which enables us to actually make suggestions.

(Helen)

I see you as cross-fertilisers.

(Sonia)

You actually have a better relationship with a child if you see them in more than one subject. You can build up the relationship. You can improve their self-esteem in a subject where they're not doing very well, if you know they are doing better somewhere else.

(Helen)

But another aspect of it is that children will compartmentalise: this is Maths, this is Science, this is English and you say, 'Why aren't you using that skill in this lesson? Why can't you do this in Science when you could do it in Maths?'

(Sonia)

I think it's key to follow the pupil and not the subject. Often a child will be disruptive in one lesson and not in another and if you only see them in that lesson that's the only picture you've got of them. But in another lesson they might be doing some extension work or whatever and you've got a better overall picture of how to help them and how to include them.

(Shahida)

There was discussion about the extent to which LSAs could take responsibility for areas of student care and welfare. There was speculation as to how far these keyworker and community worker roles could be pushed.

I think wouldn't it be nice for parents with kids with a problem, wouldn't it be nice for them to go to an open evening with their child and their child's keyworker to go round the different teachers and have their positive input as well.

(Mary)

Having a keyworker going round with the child at parent's evening you would have to be very careful in that situation you weren't going to antagonise the teacher and destroy the working relationship.

(Sonia)

As an LSA you are part of the school, and although community work is a huge asset, if you are working in a school you have to be in the community as a representative of the school, instead of turning yourself into a representative of the community. There are community workers who do that.

(Helen)

End word

The SENCO summed up with what can also stand as an appropriate conclusion to this discussion:

One of the messages to get across in what you write is that now LSAs are in an incredibly strong position to start changing things the way they want to go.

(Sonia)

Acknowledgements

This article could not have been written without the help and participation of the Learning Support team at the Cressex Community School. I am deeply grateful for their time, support and interest.

References

Booth, T. and Ainscow, M. (2000) *Index for Inclusion: developing learning and participation in schools*. Bristol: CSIE.

DfES (2002) *Developing the role of school support staff: the consultation*. London: DfES.

Haigh, G. (2002) Clear challenge of blurred boundaries. *Times Educational Supplement*, (6 December).

Lee, B. (2002) *Teaching Assistants in School: the current state of play*. Report 34. Slough: NFER/Local Government Association.

Ofsted (2001) *Inspection Report: The Cressex Community School*. London: Ofsted.

Revell, P. (2002) New Model Army. *The Guardian*, (23 October).

Wilce, H. (2002) Let's stick together. *Times Educational Supplement*, (6 December).

Caroline Roaf's chapter has underlined the need to make the best use of everybody's skills within a school. It is a clear reminder that we all have multiple social voices and roles, which can help in the inclusion and exclusion of others. If we merely fit people into pre-established parameters we will always miss opportunities to listen to those voices and maximise their roles.

CHAPTER 20

Learning in context: identifying difficulties for learners

Susan Hart and Penny Travers

In this article Susan Hart and Penny Travers ask us to develop a more sophisticated, interactive view of learning difficulties. We are encouraged to move away from a model where the concern is 'accurate identification' of perceived difficulties within an individual to a model where an 'adequate analysis' is made of the individual and the context of their learning. This requires us to become used to questioning our own impact on the child's learning. The original article was written against the backdrop of the 1994 Code of Practice, which only made a passing reference to the importance of the learning context. In the 2001 Code of Practice this emphasis is greater, but nonetheless we have still to meet the challenge of truly re-examining our categorisation of need.

Following the introduction of the Code of Practice on the Identification and Assessment of Special Educational Needs, there have been growing concerns amongst teachers of bilingual learners* about its impact and implications.

One central issue has to do with decisions about whether to place bilingual pupils on a register of concern. The law specifically states that children should not be regarded as having a learning difficulty simply on the grounds that they are learning English as an additional language; therefore, teachers are concerned to avoid the mis-identification of bilingual learners as having special educational needs. But teachers are concerned that many bilingual children who would benefit from additional learning support are losing out because they are being denied the extra help available as of right to their monolingual peers.

These two sets of concerns have given rise to a growing conviction that the most urgent task in the current context is to develop methods and procedures for the conduct of assessment that will facilitate *accurate identification* of those bilingual learners who do have *special educational* needs, as distinct from specific *linguistic* needs arising from their status as learners of English as an additional language. This article questions this interpretation and suggests an alternative view of what needs to be done to safeguard the entitlements of bilingual children whose progress gives cause for concern.

Is 'accurate identification' the key issue?

One problem associated with the focus on 'accurate identification' is that it risks perpetuating, if not actively encouraging, a narrow view of 'learning difficulties' as products of within-child deficits. The idea that it is possible, with appropriate technology, to differentiate between those children who do and those who do not 'have' learning difficulties downplays the impact of context and tends to equate learning difficulties with inherent intellectual limitations.

In fact, this within-child view of 'learning difficulties' has been rejected by many teachers in favour of a more interactive view: that 'learning difficulties' arise through the complex interaction of a multitude of factors associated not only with children themselves but also with the immediate and wider learning environment. It was this interactive view of learning difficulties that led many teachers and schools, in the 1980s, to concentrate on bringing about developments in the mainstream learning environment as the most appropriate, effective and equitable means of offering 'support'. Providing support in this way made it unnecessary to identify and label a distinct group of children as 'having special educational needs', and there was a recognition that the difficulties experienced by individuals could be indicators of possible areas for development for the potential benefit of *all* children.

No matter how comprehensive and culturally sensitive the procedures and methods adopted, it will not serve the interests of those bilingual children identified as 'having special educational needs' if their perceived difficulties are viewed narrowly as products of individual deficits and all they become entitled to is a discrete package of work to be pursued alongside the mainstream curriculum, rather than a re-examination, adaptation and development of teaching approaches that will enhance the child's progress and participation *within* the overall curriculum provided for the class. The mainstream classroom, offering a supportive learning environment, has come to be recognised as the key context for curriculum access and language acquisition. [. . .]

It is the trend towards individualisation of support, and its implications for narrowing the learning environment for bilingual children (Hall 1996), that has made some teachers all the more reluctant to identify bilingual children as having special educational needs.

If not 'accurate identification', what is the key issue?

A group of teachers in the London Borough of Enfield were convinced that there was scope for developing a more inclusive approach to support for bilingual learners whose progress was giving cause for concern, and that this would not be facilitated by a focus on 'accurate identification'. They wanted to explore the implications for practice of combining an interactive view of learning difficulties with their own understandings of current 'good practice' in support for bilingual learners (LCAS 1995). To create time for collective reflection, they set up a research-based INSET course.

The participants were eleven mainstream class teachers and subject teachers (Key stages 1–3) working in partnership with Section 11 support teachers. Each chose to focus on one or more bilingual children whose learning was giving cause for concern. They set out to look for ways of enhancing the child's learning *within* the mainstream classroom by maintaining an interactive view and focusing on children's engagement with learning experiences provided, by seeking to understand this in the context of the immediate and wider learning environment, and by looking for ways to adapt, adjust or develop aspects of existing provision in the light of their understanding.

> . . . What is more important than anything else is an *attitude of mind*. The key to effective assessment is . . . in the realisation of the importance of *learning from the experience* of working with pupils in the classroom.
>
> (Ainscow 1988, p. 152, our emphasis)

In addition to their own existing guidelines regarding conditions for teaching, learning and assessment that are supportive of bilingual learners, they also drew on the 'framework for innovative thinking' outlined in the book *Beyond Special Needs* (Hart 1996). This framework proposes five 'moves' which can help teachers to question existing understandings, and open up thinking and practice to new possibilities (see Fig. 20.1). The teachers decided to use these moves in whatever way seemed appropriate and helpful to support their *own* processes of reflection about what might be done to enhance the children's learning.

- *exploring connections* between the child's response and features of the immediate and wider learning environment;

- *re-examining the norms and expectations* that shape our interpretations and judgements;

- *taking the child's eye view*: stepping outside one's own frames of reference and trying to see the situation from the point of view of a child's understandings and meanings;

- *noting the impact of feelings*: how our feelings affect our interpretations, or offer clues to others' feelings;

- *suspending judgement*: in recognition of the limits of our available knowledge, and taking steps to learn more.

Figure 20.1

Importance of interactive analysis

Their collective work over the year testifies to the critical importance for children that teachers' judgements and assessment practices should be structured by a genuinely interactive analysis of perceived difficulties, as the following examples seek to illustrate.

Revising negative judgements

The first example illustrates how important it is that teachers search for interpretations beyond those that immediately spring to mind, especially when the immediate interpretations are negative and tend to reinforce an existing concern about a child. An interactive analysis implies a conscious commitment to take into account all the features of the situation that may have a bearing on the child's learning and behaviour, including the teacher's interpretations of the child's response, the child's own meanings and interpretations and the many influences that shape both of these.

There was an occasion, for instance, when one of the KS1 teachers (Elin) was frustrated to find that Costas (the child she was studying) had failed to carry out a 'perfectly clear' instruction to take a game back down to the library and put it on the table. Her immediate reaction was to interpret this as further confirmation of her view of him that he 'never listens to instructions'. When she asked him what he should be doing with the box, he started explaining how to play the game. He seemed to be utterly confused although he successfully carried out the instruction when she explained again.

It was only afterwards when Elin started thinking some more about what had happened that it occurred to her that perhaps, when she had asked for a volunteer, Costas had thought that he was offering to play the game, not put it away. She realised that she had assumed that Costas knew it was lunch time. But how would Costas know this? Had it actually been stated? Do young children know how to judge when the end of a session is near? Moreover, there was a lot of noise and bustle in the classroom at the time, so it was quite likely that Costas did not actually hear what was said. Elin knew that the particular game was Costas' favourite, so his desire to play may have helped to shape what he thought was going to be said by his teacher. Also, the library was a place where Elin frequently took them to do group work; why would she have sent two people, if the task was to put the game away rather than to play? Elin found that, as a result of this additional thinking, a very different perception of Costas' response to her request began to open up. It gave her an encouraging new sense of Costas acting competently within his own frames of reference, and a heightened awareness of how communication can break down when adults take for granted that children share their own assumptions about the situation.

This is, in one sense, a trivial interaction – one of thousands of encounters that take place during the course of a school day, week or year. Yet it is far from insignificant. It is through such interactions that children's identities are continually negotiated, identities that will shape and affect subsequent responses to school learning. It only took Elin a few moments to do the thinking described here. Yet doing it fulfilled a vital responsibility towards Costas, enabling her to question rather than reinforce a negative view of his learning, and leading to a subtle shift in the dynamics of her own relationship with him.

Re-thinking curricula to enhance learning and inclusion

In a second example, a class teacher and support teacher discussed a shared concern about a Year 7 girl, Ayse, who often seemed to be lost, confused or distracted during lessons. They hoped that, if they could develop their understanding of what was leading Ayse to respond in this way, they would be able to find ways of supporting her learning more effectively. Recognising that the terms 'lost, 'confused' and distracted' represented *their perception* of Ayse's response to learning activities, they determined to reconsider the evidence upon which this perception was based and to try to see the learning situation with fresh eyes, from Ayse's point of view.

The support teacher negotiated an opportunity to shadow Ayse's class for a day, and was surprised to discover how demanding and confusing she herself found the sequence of different lessons, not just with their different topics, but with the different expectations and requirements of different teachers, and the different systems of management, marking and feedback that they used. Walking along a corridor between lessons, she met a colleague who remarked (not knowing what she had been doing): 'You look lost!'.

Although most teachers do, as a matter of course, include activities to allow students to re-orient themselves and re-connect with ideas already discussed in previous lessons, her observations brought home to her how much more remote the previous lesson and previous learning may be to the student than to the teacher (who has planned and prepared the lesson); and how important it is therefore, at the start of lessons, that activities do actively engage all students in reformulating the knowledge that is a pre-requisite for learning in the current lesson. It also caused her to reflect on what might be done to reduce at least some of the confusing variation between learning (without losing the variety and distinctiveness that adds interest to lessons) – by having, say, a common system for laying out and responding to written work.

The experience provided some new perspectives on Ayse's seeming confusion and distractedness, and recognition of some specific steps that teachers might take in response to their concerns. However, discussion with Ayse herself showed that this was by no means the whole story. Her teachers began to realise that Ayse did not *see herself* as 'disengaged'. Her agenda was a different one from that of her teachers. In her terms, she was engaged: doing what she knew how to do well and could be sure of being successful at, namely being a helpful and co-operative pupil. She volunteered for classroom tasks such as collecting books and cleaning tables and the blackboard. She was rewarded by friendliness and appreciation on the part of her teachers, which ensured that each lesson offered opportunities for personal recognition. This feedback suggested to her that she was being 'successful', but unfortunately obscured from her that her *learning* was seen by her teachers as a cause for concern.

Acknowledging the difference between their own agenda and Ayse's led the two teachers to reconsider the extent to which there actually *was* scope within the curriculum activities currently provided for Ayse to experience success as a *learner*.

Were activities linguistically accessible and meaningful to her? Did they encourage her to recognise the contribution that she could make to the work of the group, to recognise, value and use her own resources for learning? Did they activate her *desire* to engage intellectually?

It was these questions, the teachers concluded, that needed to inform their planning, if they were to encourage Ayse to engage more fully, on their terms, as an active learner. Indeed, they felt that the questions encompassed aims that could legitimately inform and enrich their planning for the whole class group. They set out to re-think and plan afresh a unit of work that the class could engage in together, as a shared experience, but with various forms of visual support, collaborative peer support and 'scaffolding' (LCAS 1997) built in to ensure that the activities were appropriate and accessible to all. From Ayse's point of view, the evidence of the success of their thinking and planning would be reflected in a more sustained engagement with learning activities, as well as the quality of the work produced.

The example shows how an interactive style of analysis helps teachers not only to re-examine existing perceptions and practices, but also to *move beyond* existing understandings, and open up new possibilities for enhancing children's learning within mainstream classrooms. These teachers believed that, if they could create the right circumstances, Ayse *would* engage more actively with learning activities; and they found clues to the circumstances required by exploring the meaning of her responses to learning activities currently provided. The strategies that they came up with, unlike individualised work, were designed to enhance not only her learning but also her *participation* and *inclusion* in the work of the whole class. Moreover, the teachers found that thinking specifically about Ayse's needs also provided a stimulus to creative thinking about the curriculum that enriched learning opportunities for everyone.

Acknowledgement

An unanticipated by-product of teachers' commitment to an interactive understanding of perceived difficulties was that they found a *new quality* developing in their relationship with the child they were studying. It was only in retrospect that they were able to appreciate how faint and two-dimensional their perceptions of the children had been at the outset, even though they felt that they already knew a deal about them and, in most cases, had formed positive relationships with them. The studies brought a new quality to their perceptions and interactions by bringing about both a more appreciative, multifaceted awareness of the individuality of the child on the teacher's part, and a perceptible blossoming on the part of the child who picked up on, and responded to, the teacher's sustained interest.

Searching for a word to represent this new sense of value and being valued, the teachers felt that the notion of 'acknowledgement' discussed by Pye (1988) in relation to the 'invisible children' in schools that concerned him, most closely corresponded to what had clearly emerged as a common experience across all the case studies. Acknowledgement involves *two-way recognition*: on the part of teachers, it is a recognition of the interesting individuality and complexity of the child, which is *communicated to* the child; on the part of the child, it is an active awareness of and response to the sense of being recognised as an interesting, complex and unpredictable individual whom the teacher considers important and wants to continue to get to know.

However, a sense of 'acknowledgement' on the part of the child is a product of genuine regard; it cannot be fabricated and communicated if it is not genuinely *felt* and experienced by the teacher. As the example of Elin and Costas shows, a necessary condition for the development of genuine acknowledgement between teacher and child is an openness that allows existing perceptions to be reconsidered. It requires a commitment on the part of teachers to searching out the reason and competence underlying the child's response, even when this is different from what the teacher expects or desires.

The teachers' conclusion was that an enhanced sense of 'acknowledgement' might be more important to children's progress in the longer term than any specific strategies used to enhance their learning. Indeed, without it they might well fail. As Cummins argues:

> The interactions that take place between students and teachers and among students are more central to student success than any method for teaching literacy or science or maths . . . When students' developing sense of self is affirmed and extended through their interactions with teachers, they are more likely to apply themselves to academic effort and participate actively in instruction.
>
> (Cummins 1996: 2)

From 'accurate identification' to 'adequate analysis'

The examples have shown not only why a focus on 'accurate identification' may be an unhelpful distraction but also why it is so important *for children* that teachers are committed to achieving an interactive understanding of perceived difficulties. Such an approach to assessment – and indeed to the interpretation of classroom events more generally – safeguards children's interests and entitlements by affording children an automatic right of appeal against negative judgements; by creating conditions for genuine acknowledgement; and by ensuring that whatever can be done *is* done to overcome barriers to learning and enhance children's participation and inclusion within mainstream classrooms. [. . .]

Attention needs to remain focused on features of the immediate and wider context because these are *essential to achieving an adequate understanding* of perceived difficulties and to the provision of 'appropriate' support. It is by looking more closely at what is going on, and how it is perceived and understood by both teacher and child, that we reach new insights into what might be done to foster more successful learning. As Ayse's story shows, by setting our sights wide, even when focused on an individual child, we remain open to the possibility that perceived difficulties manifested in the responses of an individual child may be alerting us to possibilities for development within the curriculum for the whole class – or developing aspects of organisation and provision within the school as a whole. It is such *wide-frame* thinking that is an essential pre-requisite for developing schools' capacity for inclusion (DfEE 1997: 44). [. . .]

A priority task must be to develop some practical guidelines to support teachers in carrying out interactive analysis of children's classroom responses: giving appropriate thought to all the various features of a situation, but within the constraints of ordinary teaching. The situations that we seek to analyse are enormously complex. There is so much to think about and understand that no analysis can ever be exhaustive. How then can we be sure that we have taken the essential features of the situation into account, even though it is impossible to consider everything? How can we have confidence in using the new ideas arising from our analysis to inform our teaching?

Within a more inclusive approach, then, concerns about 'accurate identification' give way to concerns about '*adequate analysis*'. We realised that the reflective framework used by these teachers offers one way of representing the features of a situation that, as a minimum, any adequate analysis would need to take into account. These include:

- the relationship between children's learning and behaviour and features of the classroom and overall school context
- how the teacher's particular resources, beliefs and values shape the meanings constructed from the evidence
- the child's own meanings, purposes, agendas
- how the teacher's own feelings affect the meanings bestowed on the situation
- how the inescapable limitations of the information and resources which the teacher currently has available affect these meanings.

The example of Elin and Costas has shown that such an analysis need not be impossibly time-consuming. Indeed, the teachers in our study found themselves increasingly using the various moves spontaneously with other children as part of their everyday classroom teaching. Nevertheless, there may be other ways of formulating the essential features of any analysis that teachers find more helpful. Or maybe there are other important dimensions that need to be considered, including – for bilingual children – an awareness of their knowledge and use of other languages and the wider context of culture and community in which they live and operate. Perhaps there is a need to define minimum requirements in terms of essential *knowledge* that needs to inform teachers' thinking, including the perspectives of other adults involved with the child, as well as these different *dimensions* of the interpretive task.

Establishing the necessary elements of a workable framework for interactive analysis is an important development task, and one that is of relevance not just to bilingual children but to *any* children whose progress or behaviour gives their teachers cause for concern. Indeed, it may be that the time is now ripe to move beyond the unhelpful compartmentalisation of thinking that assumes that qualitatively different forms of provision are needed according to whether or not a child – monolingual or bilingual – is identified as 'having special educational needs'.

The time may also be ripe to re-think the principle that has for so long been taken for granted: that bilingual learners' specific linguistic needs are not to be confused with special educational needs or learning difficulties. This principle seeks to protect *one* group of children from discrimination and from the social stigma associated with these labels, at the expense of a wider group of children perceived to have difficulties. Yet surely those of us who are committed to equality in education have a responsibility to challenge the perpetuation of such discriminatory attitudes on behalf of *all* children? With inclusion officially on the political agenda (DfEE 1997), we may be poised now to move beyond these old divisions and boundaries, and develop ways of fruitfully *combining* new insights and expertise drawn from both fields to empower and strength our efforts to develop a more inclusive, anti-discriminatory approach.

References

Ainscow, M. (1988) Beyond the Eye of the Monster. *Support for Learning*, **3**(3), 149–53.

Cummins, J. (1996) *Negotiating Identities: education for empowerment in a diverse society.* Ontario: California Association for Bilingual Education, distributed in UK by Trentham Books.

Department for Education and Employment (1997) *Excellence For All Children: meeting special educational needs.* London: DfEE.

Hall, D. (1996) *Identifying Needs. Language Matters.* Centre for Language in Primary Education.

Hart, S. (1996) *Beyond Special Needs: enhancing children's learning through innovative thinking.* London: Paul Chapman.

Language and Curriculum Access Service (1995) *Making Progress: teaching and assessment in the multi-lingual classroom – a guide for class and subject teachers.* London: LCAS.

Language and Curriculum Access Service (1997) *Making Progress in Humanities: scaffolding learning in the multilingual classroom.* London Borough of Enfield.

Pye, J. (1988) *Invisible Children: Who are the real losers at school?* Oxford: Oxford University Press.

Note

* We do not regard 'bilingual' learners as a homogeneous group; nevertheless we consider that the arguments in this article are relevant to all those to whom this term is generally applied.

Acknowledgements

We would like to thank the members of LCAS staff, and teachers and pupils in Enfield schools, for their contribution to the ideas presented in this article.

> Susan Hart and Penny Travers force us to question the notion that people come in categories or can be effectively placed within them. Effectively defining the support we are going to offer someone involves taking fundamental consideration of the impact of our situations, our systems and ourselves.

Part 5

Looking in from outside

CHAPTER 21

Viewing inclusion from a distance: gaining perspective from comparative study

Tony Booth

In this chapter Tony Booth steps outside of the immediate context to look at inclusion from a different, comparative perspective. He explores the contribution that comparative study can make to the theory, policy and practice of inclusion, illustrating the discussion with two studies. The first is a study of perspectives on inclusion in economically richer countries, sometimes called countries of the North, and the second is a study involving collaboration with researchers in economically poorer countries of the South. He suggests that the shift in perspective and development of concepts required to study inclusion in other countries is helpful for the critique of inclusion policy in England.

Engaging terms

The use of the term 'inclusion' is growing in popularity in official documents in England but it is not clearly or consistently defined within them (DfEE 1998, 1999a). If we are to think and act clearly in education, we have to take control of the definition of our concepts.

Defining inclusion/exclusion

I define inclusion in education in terms of two linked processes. It is the process of increasing the participation of learners in and reducing their exclusion from the curricula, cultures and communities of neighbourhood mainstream centres of learning. My definition recognises the reality of exclusionary pressures in education and the need to identify and counter them, if the participation of learners is to be increased. I have begun to call this project 'inclusion/exclusion' to encourage the keeping of both processes in mind. Inclusion/exclusion is an unending project, applying to all learners who are vulnerable to exclusion from their local schools and to the construction of an education system that recognises and is responsive to learner diversity within common groups. Like Mittler (1995), I emphasise locality in my definition, even though this runs counter to current educational policies in England, which encourage people to choose schools outside of their neighbourhood, according to their position in league tables.

Learners with impairments and others categorised as 'having special educational needs' are only some of those subject to exclusionary pressures. It is counterproductive to tie a notion of inclusive education to only some of the learners vulnerable to marginalisation. The participation of real learners, who all have multiple group membership, requires schools that are responsive to all aspects of learner diversity. Inclusion/exclusion is a broader and different field from 'special needs education' (see Booth 1998). I argue that inclusion should be about revitalising the comprehensive ideal and replacing the current selective approach to raising achievement and improving schools. Inclusion is not about a marginal part of the education system but constitutes a framework through which all educational development can take place.

The limitations of special needs education

'Special needs education' has severe limitations as a way of approaching the resolution of educational difficulties. Despite the attempts of some to argue otherwise (Norwich 1990), it remains locked into the attribution of educational difficulties to learner deficits and deflects attention from the barriers to learning that exist in all aspects of the system. At its heart is the concept of 'special educational needs', which almost 20 years ago Mary Warnock argued should be jettisoned (Warnock 1982). The use of this concept continues to be confused. Government documents make the assumption that all such categorised learners will have difficulty with 'literacy and numeracy' (DfEE 1997), thus demonstrating, like many others, the difficulty they find in incorporating, within their definition, both learners with impairments and others who experience difficulties in education which may or may not result in relatively low attainments. The concept focuses attention on the difficulties experienced by some learners and deflects attention from those experienced by others as well as the developments in school cultures, policies, curricula and teaching approaches that will minimise educational difficulties for all. It deskills teachers by encouraging them to think that many learners need specialist teaching. Its use helps to marginalise inclusion policies from general education policies and to further fragment them in documents about special educational needs, *social* inclusion and exclusion, and ethnic minority education (DfE 1994, DfEE 1998, 1999a, 1999b).

Inclusion and 'education for all'

The application of the concept of special educational needs is problematic for the development of inclusive practice in countries of the North but even more so in countries of the South. In contexts where there is no mass education, and there are low rates of literacy and vast exclusionary pressures on the education of particular groups such as girls, the deflection from the task of providing community-based education for all can have particularly damaging consequences. In many countries of the South,

254

there are basic education policies, special needs education policies and inclusive education policies often supported by a wide range of different government and non-government organisations (see, for example, Khan 1998). What is required is a single set of policies that support communities, schools and education systems in reaching out and responding to the full diversity of learners.

'Education for all' is the term adopted within the United Nations Organisations to signal the movement to the recognition of a universal right to education supported within the Jomtien Conference of 1990 (World Conference on Education for All 1990, Little, Hoppers and Gardner 1994). It is usually taken to mean the provision of primary education for all, the provision of early childhood education and the provision of basic adult education, though it has to be formulated in a way that does not preserve the right to secondary and higher education within particular elites. The separation of special and general policies on education perpetuates the exclusion of disabled learners from education, shown in India by Alur (1998). It fosters the notion that all marginalised groups will be looked after by special interventions. In my terms, 'education for all' is the same project as inclusion/exclusion, which incorporates and transforms the task of special needs education. Both are concerned with overcoming barriers to providing community based education for all learners.

Approaching comparative study

The comparative study in which I am interested recognises and respects cultural difference and the effort that is required to make sense of the meaning of practice to others. It involves making the strange familiar and the familiar strange, using an immersion in the perspectives of others to challenge what is taken for granted in one's own system. It requires taking the anthropological perspective into the 'villages' of others and bringing it back to one's own. My view of comparative study is not about the search for 'good practice' but about finding instructive lessons in all practice. It requires extreme caution about the imposition of models created within a particular set of home circumstances in the education systems of other countries, and this applies both to imports and exports. We should be much more wary than we are of amalgamating research gathered in different cultural contexts and more aware of the parochial nature of many of our concepts, including those used to define categories of educational difficulty (see Hegarty 1993).

Exploring perspectives on inclusion in countries of the North

In one study in which I was involved, we asked a researcher or team of researchers to explore the processes of inclusion and exclusion in one school or a small group of schools in each of eight countries (Booth and Ainscow 1998). The participating countries were England, Scotland, Eire, the Netherlands, Norway, the USA, New

Zealand and Australia (the last two revealing one of the problems with the term 'countries of the North' to describe economically richer nations). We asked the researchers to give meaning to the practices they described in schools by explaining what an international audience would need to know about the local and national cultures and policies in order to make sense of local practices of inclusion and exclusion. We asked them to link the concepts of inclusion and exclusion and provided guidelines for the collection of information about the schools, but in all other respects we wished them to reflect their own perspectives and those of the children, young people and adults within the schools they studied and the wider educational systems.

We need not have worried about imposing our views on the other participants, for we found that even our initial suggestions were greatly modified by the perspectives that they brought to the study. Researcher perspectives were very resistant to change. Apart from our study (Booth, Ainscow and Dyson 1998), very few linked the processes of inclusion and exclusion. Almost all concentrated on the inclusion of disabled learners or others categorised as 'having special educational needs', even though such a formulation was challenged by some teachers and learners within the studies. Some used categories given meaning within a particular country as if they were universally understood. We called the book *From Them to Us*, to indicate both the exchange of gifts that comparative work offers and the extent to which researchers may see some learners as a focus for inclusion and a group apart, or as part of the diversity that includes us all.

The studies showed the subtle shaping of the practices in schools by national and local policies and cultures. But they also demonstrated, through the voices of policy makers, researchers, students, parents and teachers, that there is no single national perpective on inclusion or any aspect of education. Perspectives differ almost as much within as between countries.

In all the countries in the study, some people took for granted ways of grouping learners together that others challenged. For example, mixed-attainment grouping is the orthodoxy in Norway, while within England there is strong pressure to set according to ability, and in the Netherlands and the USA, the idea of grade repetition is accepted by many (Nes Mordal and Strømstad 1998; Reezigt and Pijl 1998; Ware 1998). Some issues were equally ignored in all studies. Religion was referred to as a shaping feature of education by most researchers but none of the studies dwelt on the selective nature of religious denomination schools. Equally, gender issues were hardly examined even though most of the studies alluded to the high proportion of boys identified as having difficulties. This neglect of the over-representation of boys or of ethnic minorities provides powerful evidence of the limitation of special needs education to account for and respond to difficulties in learning, and of using it as the lens through which to view the development of inclusive practice (Booth 1998). This has led one group of writers in the USA, concerned to preserve 'special education' from the reconceptualisation of the field associated with inclusion, to refer to arguments about over-representation as a 'smoking gun' (Semmel, Gerber and MacMillan 1995).

Learning with countries of the South

The second study has gradually emerged following several visits to South Africa. My intention on my first visit was to sit in on classrooms and staffrooms, gradually immersing myself in educational practices, but within a very brief period I became involved in policy discussions. I could have resisted and pleaded that I had insufficient knowledge of educational practice in South Africa. However, my concern was not to impose a model from England, or from any other country of the North, but to support the argument that such a practice would be counterproductive, and try to gather my knowledge and spend time in schools when I could (see Enslin and Pendlebury 1998; Sedibe 1998). In the post-apartheid era, many of those with influence had either gained their qualifications and views of professional practice within an education system established for the benefit of the white population or had studied in Western countries on courses in which South African education was not part of the curriculum.

The new regime inherited a special education system which provided special schools for 5 per cent of white students and 0.1 per cent of black students (NCSNET, NCESS 1997). In one province, there were no specialist professionals who could speak the language spoken by 80 per cent of the population. While many disabled learners do not attend any form of education, other groups and often whole communities are equally vulnerable to exclusion from education. Many learners attend centres of learning where the language of instruction is different from their home language. Such observations reinforce the idea that the special needs education solution to educational difficulties is entirely inappropriate in the South African context. I learnt that the task throughout South Africa is for local administrations to work with communities to overcome the barriers of the past and the present, and to create and support education centres so that they are increasingly able to respond to all learners within their communities. Such arguments led the National Commission on Special Needs Education and Training (NCSNET) to substitute the term 'learners who experience barriers to learning and development' for 'learners with special educational needs' in their report. The report became concerned with removing all barriers to learning, and participation, at all levels of the system, not just those associated with learners with impairments or others categorised 'having special educational needs'.

I prefer the term 'barriers to learning and participation' to 'barriers to learning and development' because the former refers explicitly to more than access to education and because the latter term can link thinking back to learner deficits. A list of groups of learners who may experience barriers to learning and participation is given in figure 1. The list is not comprehensive. All chronic illnesses are relevant, but AIDS has been included in the list because of its immense impact in Africa and in many countries. In Kwazulu/Natal it has been estimated that 50 per cent of young women of child-bearing age are HIV positive and AIDS has a dramatic effect not only on the people who have it but on family members – for example, children orphaned when their parents die (NCSNET, NCESS 1997).

- Learners in poverty
- Learners affected by war
- Learners affected by environmental degradation and change
- Learners who are victims of abuse and violence
- Street children
- Children being brought up by the state
- Child labourers
- Disabled learners
- Girls
- Learners affected by HIV and AIDS
- Learners whose home language is different from the language of instruction
- Nomadic learners
- Learners from oppressed minorities
- Learners who have inadequate schools or inappropriate curricula and teaching
- Learners who are pregnant or have young children

Figure 21.1 Learners who may experience barriers to learning and participation

I was aware that people within countries of the South have much to learn from each other. South Africa had shifted from a system in which the state was prepared to favour one section of the population with a disporportionate amount of its resources to a more equitable system of state funding. In other countries of the South, there is more experience of the pressures to create a different version of the two-tier system of education based on private wealth. However, I felt that countries of the South and the North can also contribute to each other's development. As a result, I initiated a collaborative, research, development and dissemination project, linking small areas of South Africa, Brazil, India and England. It is concerned with 'developing sustainable inclusion policy and practice' and links the development of practice to local, provincial and national policies and administrations. In each country, the local team of researchers has identified one or two development areas, each containing a small number of centres of learning. They have set about describing and analysing the exclusionary pressures and inclusionary possibilities within these areas starting from a common set of questions:

- Who experiences barriers to learning and participation?
- What are the barriers to learning and participation?
- How can barriers to learning and participation be minimised?
- What resources are available to support inclusion and participation?
- How can resources be mobilised to support inclusion and participation?

Barriers can prevent access to education or limit participation within a particular centre of learning. Barriers, as well as the resources to reduce them, may be found at all levels of the system, within communities, centres of learning and local and national policies and administrations. We are setting our analysis of our areas within the local and national context to make it understandable to others and to ourselves. The analysis will be followed by work with local stakeholders in education to draw up priorities for development within each area, the implementation of the development plan and its evaluation. Interventions are to be integrated into local practice so that they are sustainable and do not depend on limited project funding. Dissemination of what we have learnt and opportunities to learn from the practice of others, locally, regionally and internationally, are essential parts of the project. We see each study as supplemented by a fifth element, which is the additional benefit we gain from sharing and commenting on each other's experience.

Addressing local priorities

In examining barriers to learning and participation, we try to limit our assumptions about what barriers will be identified in advance of meeting with administrators, staff in centres of learning and community members, and our own observations. A primary school in South Africa illustrates the process. It is in a township in Gauteng province in South Africa, in one of the two South African development areas for the project. The township has had little international attention compared with the more famous Soweto. There are 2,080 pupils aged approximately 7 to 13, although every such school has many over-age students. There are fifty teachers. Half the school attends from 8.00 to 12.30 and the other half from 12.30 to 16.30.

Slowly, conditions are improving in both the homes and the schools but unemployment is very high and the people remain poor. The school has had its windows broken and these are left shattered. It is impossible to leave anything of value within the school overnight. Partly because of the distrust of state education during the apartheid divisions, it has been hard to create a new attitude to ownership of local schools in some communities (Christie 1998).

The Gauteng administration have taken on the 'health promoting schools' concept, and in this district this is seen as a cornerstone of the development of inclusion within the schools (NCSNET, NCESS 1997). All the staff are involved in discussing barriers to learning and participation for the students and identifying ways of mobilising more resources within the school and the community. They then decide on priorities for intervention. The inclusion team within the school meet regularly with representatives of the district support team to assign priorities for development.

At an early meeting, it was decided that a first priority should be ensuring that the learners can come safely to school. To get from their home to the school, they have to cross a swamp area with tall reeds and on several occasions girls have been assaulted on their way to school. The staff and members of the community met and planned to clear the area to make an open, safe path through the swamp. The learners, girls and boys, held a demonstration about their rights to come to school without being molested. The school staff and the district support personnel aim to build on this community action to develop a greater sense of partnership and shared ownership in the school.

Sharing a common framework

The common framework that we share with the countries of the South in our study seems to be of positive benefit in analysing barriers to learning and participation in England. Our development area has a high proportion of students originating from Bangladesh. Particular issues have been identified for us, by the community, about the effects of cramped housing conditions on opportunities for home study and in encouraging young people into joining street gangs. There is an issue of community representation within schools, of opportunities for first language teaching and the suitability of the literacy hour to support learners with the kinds of linguistic resources that this group brings. We have been considering the resources within the community, within the teachers and particularly within the learner population that might be drawn on to support learning and participation. We have been looking at the co-ordination between the various groups of teachers and assistants providing support to learners in schools, how this appears from the office perspective and for learners in classrooms. At the level of government interventions, a head of one of the schools in the area made a plea for recognition of a need for initiatives to be *sustainable* and not to be ended because the local education authority loses out on a particular round of bidding for targeted funds.

Lessons for policy development in England

It seems that the shift away from the special needs framework for understanding inclusion and exclusion is already implicit in the separation of official policies on 'inclusion' confined to documents on 'special educational needs' and 'social inclusion' policies addressing other learners vulnerable to marginalisation. It would not take much of a step to understand all forms of exclusion and inclusion as 'social' and to create policies which addressed them all together. It is an irony that neither version of official inclusion is addressed within general education policies and both appear to run counter to the selective approach to improving schools and achievement that is taken within such documents. The excluding pressures within the competitive school system are commented on frequently, and any reasonable inclusion policy has to address them (Barton and Slee 1999; Halpin 1999; Booth, Ainscow and Dyson 1998). However, the excluding pressure that is tied to the concept of special educational needs is more rarely addressed. The consultation on revisions to the *Code of Practice on the Identification and Assessment of Special Educational Needs* claims it is to be revised so as to reflect 'a more inclusive approach' (DfEE 1999b). To reflect a more inclusive approach, it would have to be transformed into a document which is about supporting teaching for diversity and its basic concepts revised. It would have to free itself from the identification of educational difficulties as arising from learner deficits and replace individual educational plans with teaching and learning plans. It would define support as part of ordinary teaching and learning designed to minimise the difficulties that arise for learners rather than being brought into action once problems have been identified. At the very least, a fundamental rethink of the document would be called for, rather than the minimal revision that is currently envisaged.

Concluding remarks

Comparative study involves us in attempting to understand the meaning of policy and practice in another country while recognising that we do so from within our own frame of reference. We can do this best when we subject our own way of viewing the world to careful scrutiny. Attempting to understand inclusive educational development in the countries of the South has revealed the irrelevance of the special needs education version of inclusion to increase the participation of learners in those countries. However, the shortcomings of a view of inclusion which concentrates solely on issues of disability and learners categorised as 'having special needs' can be shown to be just as glaring in the countries of the North.

References

Alur, M. (1998) *Invisible Children: a study of a policy of exclusion*. PhD thesis, University of London, Institute of Education.

Barton, L. and Slee, R. (1999) Competition, selection and inclusive education: some observations. *International Journal of Inclusive Education*, **3**, 3–12.

Booth, T. (1998) From 'special education' to 'inclusion and exclusion in education': Can we redefine the field? In P. Haug and J. Tøssebro (eds) *Theoretical Perspectives on Special Education*. Oslo: Høyskole Forlaget.

Booth, T. and Ainscow, M. (eds) (1998) *From Them to Us: an international study of inclusion in education*. London: Routledge.

Booth, T, Ainscow, M. and Dyson, A. (1998) Inclusion and exclusion in a competitive system. In T. Booth and M. Ainscow (eds), *From Them to Us: an international study of inclusion in education*. London: Routledge.

Christie, P. (1998) Schools as (dis)organisations: the 'breakdown of the culture of learning and teaching' in South African schools. *Cambridge Journal of Education*, **28**, 283–300.

Department for Education (1994) *The Code of Practice on the Identification and Assessment of Children with Special Educational Needs*. London: DfEE.

Department for Education and Employment (1997) *Excellence for All Children: meeting special educational needs*. London: DfEE.

Department for Education and Employment (1998) *Meeting Special Educational Needs: a programme of action*. London: DfEE.

Department for Education and Employment (1999a) *Draft Guidance, Social Inclusion: pupil support*. London: DfEE.

Department for Education and Employment (1999b) *Special Educational Needs: consultation document on the proposed revision of the SEN code of practice*. London: DfEE.

Enslin, P. and Pendlebury, S. (1998) Transforming education in South Africa. *Cambridge Journal of Education*, **28**, 261–8.

Halpin, D. (1999) Democracy, inclusive schooling and the politics of education. *International Journal of Inclusive Education*, **3**, 225–38.

Hegarty, S. (1993) Reviewing the literature on integration. *European Journal of Special Needs Education*, **8**, 194–200.

Khan, F. (1998) Country Report: Pakistan. *European Journal of Special Needs Education*, **13**, 98–111.

Little, A., Hoppers, W. and Gardner, R. (1994) *Beyond Jomtien: implementing education for all*. London: MacMillan.

Mittler, P. (1995) Special needs education: an international perspective. *British Journal of Special Education*, **22**, 105–8.

NCSNET, NCESS (1997) *Quality Education for All: overcoming barriers to learning and development. Report of the National Commission for Special Needs in Education and Training, National Committee for Education Support Services*. Cape Town: NCSNET, NCESS.

Nes Mordal, K. and Strøsted, M. (1998) Norway: adapted education for all? In T. Booth and M. Ainscow (eds) *From Them to Us: an international study of inclusion in education*. London: Routledge.

Norwich, B. (1990) *Reappraising Special Needs Education*. London: Cassell.

Reezigt, G. and Pijl, S. J. (1998) The Netherlands: a springboard for other initiatives. In T. Booth and M. Ainscow (eds), *From Them to Us: an international study of inclusion in education*. London: Routledge.

Sedibe, K. (1998) Dismantling apartheid education: an overview of change. *Cambridge Journal of Education*, **28**, 269–82.

Semmel, M., Gerber, M. and MacMillan, D. (1995) A legacy of policy analysis research in special education. In J. Kauffman and D. Hallahan (eds) *The Illusion of Full Inclusion: a comprehensive critique of a current special education bandwagon*. Austin: Pro-Ed.

Ware, L. (1998) USA: I kind of wonder if we're fooling ourselves. In T. Booth and M. Ainscow (eds) *From Them to Us: An international study of inclusion in education*. London: Routledge.

Warnock, M. (1982) Children with special needs in ordinary schools: integration revisited. *Education Today,* **32**, 56–62.

World Conference on Education for All (1990) *World Declaration on Education for All and Framework for Action to Meet Basic Learning Needs.* New York: UNDP, UNESCO, UNICEF, World Bank.

In the introduction to this volume we argued that much of what is familiar and ordinary in education is a legacy of past thinking and practice that seems amazingly resilient. Tony Booth's chapter has shown the importance of stepping outside of the familiar parameters so that we might see them better for what they are and begin to challenge them. As the next chapter also illustrates, there is much to be gained from looking at the big picture, or from looking at the everyday from a different perspective.

CHAPTER 22

Costing the future

Sally Holtermann

In 1995, Sally Holtermann was commissioned by the children's charity Barnardo's to review the impact of government spending on children. Her project looked at long-term implications for all children, not just the poor and disadvantaged. This chapter is based on her findings. There have been major changes in policy since the chapter was written and many of its recommendations have been acted upon. However, its fundamental challenges remain relevant to the ongoing questions we continue to ask, in particular, to questions about how much voters are prepared to pay towards investment in projects with social value.

[. . .] The central hypothesis of the review (Holtermann 1995) was that Britain is underinvesting in its children, that far more could with benefit be done in the public sphere to foster the present and future well-being of children, and therefore of society as a whole; that in some policy fields less was being done than in the past and in other policy fields actions were being taken (or not as the case may be) that would reduce the well-being of children.

The work had three parts:

(1) examination of the recent record on public spending in the UK;
(2) review of a number of key areas of childrens' lives and the related public policies to see where there would appear to be significant gains to be made in the well-being of children, and to provide costs where possible;
(3) consideration of the feasibility of spending more on children, or regearing public policies for their benefit, if the conclusion was that that was the way to go.

Spending on children

Examination of trends in the aggregates of the main public welfare spending programmes – education, health, housing, social services and social security – showed that in many programmes there had been some increase in the last decade or so, and this was the case even after allowing for general inflation, and for increases in the pay of public service workers, and for changes in client group numbers (Hills 1993).

Figure 22.1 shows the trend in the share of gross domestic product (GDP) over the medium term by taking 2 years, namely 1980–1 and 1991–2, that were at similar stages in the business cycle (HM Treasury 1993). It shows that education has declined slightly, health increased slightly, housing has dropped significantly and there has been a major increase in social security spending. Housing benefits, which are included here in social security, have risen substantially because of real rent increases, and if these were included with housing the decline in housing spending would appear less marked (Department of Social Security 1993; Hills 1993).

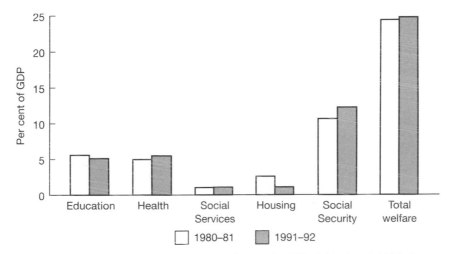

Figure 22.1 Public welfare spending as per cent of GDP in the UK, 1980–1 and 1991–2 (*Source*: HM Treasury 1993).

Disaggregated data on spending identifying the part spent on children and young people (generally this review covers young people up to the age of 18) are quite limited, but they also showed that many programmes had experienced a slight volume increase per head over the medium term: within education there has been a significant fall in per capita spending in further and higher education, a fall in spending per secondary school pupil and a small rise for primary school and the under fives (Department for Education 1993; Hills 1993). Within a rising volume of spending in the health service there seems to have been no decline in the spending on children when the fall in the number of children in the population is allowed for (analysis of spending figures in Office of Health Economics 1992). Social security benefits for families have had some real increase (Department of Social Security 1993), though it is possible to point to individual benefits, such as child benefit, which have fallen in real terms.

In international comparisons it is possible to point to many industrialized countries that spend more on their children than Britain, but Britain ranks in the middle range in terms of its generosity in spending on children and welfare programmes, and not at the bottom (Bradshaw *et al.* 1993; Hills 1993).

But these facts about spending trends coexist with widespread dissatisfaction at the amount that is being spent on children, and there is a widespread impression of cuts in services and serious underfunding. This apparent contradiction needs some explaining, but the reasons are elusive. Some of the discrepancy can be explained by an effective diversion of resources away from services and into the new management techniques and financial regimes that have been introduced into the public services. These are intended to produce a better allocation of spending within services, but they have costs of their own: administration costs are higher and there is an incentive to spend on things that are needed for the functioning of a market system but avoided in a planned system, such as publicity and promotions, and the extra capacity required to cope with variations in customer demand. Although services have been given some earmarked funding to cover the cost of the 'internal market' it seems that this has not been enough, though despite much research on the benefits and costs of the working of the new systems the evidence remains inconclusive (see for instance Le Grand and Bartlett 1993; Robinson and Le Grand 1994).

Part of the explanation for the perception of underfunding seems to be that services have been given new responsibilities – the *1989 Children Act* is a case in point – that have not been fully funded. There has also been some geographical redistribution of spending, both in National Health Service and local authority spending, which has required cutbacks in some areas. There have been programmes funded for short periods by specific grants such as Grants for Education, Support and Training (GEST), which sometimes mean the withdrawal of services when the funding ends.

The well-being of children and young people

Even if more is being spent on children this does not mean that spending is at its optimal level, given the state of the national economy. This review examines how children have been faring, and looks at various aspects of children's lives to see where additional public spending, or alterations in taxes and benefits, or other changes in economic policies, would bring benefits to children.

The approach adopted was that of conventional welfare economics, which has many applications in social policies (see for instance Le Grand *et al.* 1992). In each policy area evidence on the costs and benefits of policy changes was sought and the impact on the distribution of income or of well-being among various groups of people were examined. A broad interpretation of the term 'investment' was taken to include not just public spending on services, but action to promote a social and economic environment in which children and young people can better realise their potential. [. . .]

The report looks in turn at family life – considering changes in family structure, employment experience, and the extent of poverty and inequality; it looks at the special features of life for teenagers; and it looks at housing, health, education, the environment and social services.

This review discovered that in many aspects of life conditions have generally been improving for children and young people: life expectancy has continued to increase;

infectious diseases and many forms of ill-health have declined; more young people are gaining educational qualifications and continuing with their education after school-leaving age; housing conditions for the great majority are satisfactory; and average real incomes have continued to grow (Central Statistical Office 1993, 1994c).

But not everything is so positive. Life expectancy is higher in many other countries; some forms of ill-health are on the increase, notably those connected with air pollution; unemployment and job insecurity have risen among young people; homelessness among young people and families with children has risen; the number of children living in poverty has increased; and the improvements in education and training are considered to be insufficient to meet the needs of a modern industrial economy. More children are experiencing the separation of their parents and life in a single parent or step family, and these children are more at risk of poor outcomes (Central Statistical Office 1993, 1994c; Department of Social Security 1994; Kumar 1993).

In many of these less favourable conditions children from all walks of life have become more at risk. Some of these are not just problems of the poor and disadvantaged. Children from rich as well as poor families are suffering from the rising incidence of asthma; children all over the country, from all occupational groups and from all ethnic communities have been affected by the increased risk of their parents being unemployed; children from all sections of the community have become more likely to see their parents separate; unemployment has risen among young people at all levels of educational attainment. No one can be complacent.

Inequality and children

It does, however, remain the case that there are marked inequalities of outcomes from children according to their ethnic origin, according to which part of the country or what type of neighbourhood they live in, and, most noticeable of all, according to their social class background. Children from poor homes have lower life expectancy and are more likely to die in infancy or childhood; they have a greater likelihood of poor health, a lower chance of high educational attainment, a greater risk of unemployment, a higher probability of involvement in crime, of enduring homelessness, and in the case of girls a greater risk of teenage pregnancy (Kumar 1993).

The association between adverse outcomes and absolute poverty is well known, and the increase in relative poverty and inequality is well documented. There is now growing evidence that inequality itself is associated with adverse outcomes for children over and above the effect of absolute poverty (Wennemo 1993; Wilkinson 1994). The rise in inequality in the UK has gone along with a rising incidence of social ills such as poor health, depression, crime, drug abuse, suicides and a decline in some areas of educational attainment. The pathways linking these things are complex, but if there is causality in the connection, the implication is that a reduction in inequality is not just a matter of social justice, it is also a matter of economic efficiency (Glyn and

Miliband 1994). It would seem that without some success in reversing the growth in inequality of the last 10–15 years, some potential for improving outcomes for our children and young people will be forgone. Inequality has grown as a result of the rise in unemployment, a widening in the distribution of earnings and a restructuring of taxation (Joseph Rowntree Foundation 1994). All of these will probably need to be tackled if inequality is to be reduced.

Programmes and policies for significant benefits for children and young people in the UK

The review of policies produced a long list of suggestions for redirections of policy where there appears to be a likelihood that the benefits would be significant in relation to the cost, or where there could be a reduction of inequality. Each of these suggestions is a major topic of research in its own right, and this review was necessarily superficial. There are few certainties and there is room for lengthy debate about which things should be included, and which left out, and how they are best implemented.

Family policy

- Additional **family support services**, delivered through a variety of means including an expansion of family centres and outreach work, to help in strengthening family relationships and preventing family breakdown.
- A national programme of opportunities for **parent education**, to increase the skills of parents from all sections of society.
- **Counselling services** for parents and children when relationships are at risk of breakdown, expanded to reach more of the people who could benefit, and better funding for voluntary and statutory organizations.
- **Comprehensive mediation services,** readily available through a national programme, with better funding for local and voluntary services, to reduce the conflict between separating parents and to reduce the trauma for children.
- A national programme of subsidized quality **day care services** integrated as far as possible with education, to provide children with access to good quality care and to enable parents on low earnings to increase their family incomes through paid employment.
- **Support for lone parents**, including in particular help with child care, and a maintenance disregard in Income Support, to lift many lone parent families out of poverty and make it feasible for more to enter paid employment.

Employment policy

- The **reduction of unemployment** given greater weight in the aims of macroeconomic policy, and more measures to help the unemployed into work.
- Measures to tackle the widening **differentials in earnings**, including consideration of an incomes policy and minimum wage.
- Improved **employment rights** for parents in paid employment – paternity leave, longer maternity leave, parental leave, leave for family reason, maximum length of the working week and full employment rights for part-time workers.
- Expansion of effective programs to tackle **youth unemployment**, as part of a coherent strategy for education and training of 16- and 17-year olds.

Poverty and inequality

- An increase in universal **child benefit and child allowances in Income Support,** and a restructuring of taxes and benefits to alleviate child poverty.
- Extension of **eligibility of 16- and 17-year olds to Income Support.**

Housing

- Additional funding for investment in **affordable rented housing** to reduce the incidence of homelessness.
- Additional funding for **housing improvement** to combat disrepair and poor insulation standards.
- Reforms to **means-tested financial support for housing** to reduce the unemployment trap for families, especially owner occupiers, through a reduction of the taper on housing benefit and the introduction of a mortgage benefit.
- Extension of the **rough sleeper's initiative**.

Youth policy

- A **coherent policy for young people**, which ensures that policies emanating from the wide range of government departments affecting young people are consistent and constructive in their impact.
- **Health education** to combat smoking, drug taking and excess consumption of alcohol, supported by a **ban on tobacco advertizing and promotion**.
- Effective **sex education** in schools to help young people to a healthy sexuality and to avoid unwanted pregnancies, backed by an expansion of **confidential contraceptive advice and supplies** in well-publicized clinics for young people.

- Support for family life as a means of combating **juvenile crime**, and an emphasis on **community service and non-custodial sentences** for young offenders.
- An expansion of funding for the statutory **youth service**; practical and financial support for youth services provided in the voluntary sector.

The physical environment

- judicious use of regulations and **environmental taxes** and subsidies, especially in **transport and energy**, to ensure that growth and development are sustainable in the long term.
- Adjustment of social security benefits to **protect low-income people** from the income effect of environmental taxes.
- Better funding and stronger regulation for **wildlife conservation** and incentives to encourage environmentally friendly farming practices.

Education and training

- Additional funding for **primary and secondary schools**, to help children meet their full educational potential, and to raise educational standards to those needed by a modern industrial economy.
- Funding for **children with special educational needs** enhanced and safeguarded within the changes being made in the financial arrangements for schools.
- **Nursery education** for all children aged 3 or 4 whose parents want it, integrated with day care where there is demand, to give children immediate and lasting benefits in both educational and developmental terms.
- **Education and training opportunities for 16- and 17-year olds** need maintenance of funding and continuing efforts to provide a suitable and coherent range of choice, with the aim of 90 per cent of the age group achieving a nationally recognized qualification.

Policies for health

- A reduction in **inequality in health and life expectancy between socioeconomic groups** could be made a target of Government policy, backed by measures to reduce poverty, inequality and unemployment.
- **Hospital and community health services for children** to be brought up to the standards deemed essential by professionals.
- More action to reduce **accidents** among children, especially road traffic accidents involving pedestrians, without constraining children's freedom of movement, and to improve access to **play and recreational facilities.**

Social services for children

- Enhanced **funding for children's social services**, to enable local authority social services departments to implement the Children Act in full, and to give more attention to preventive services.

[. . .] Taken as a whole this package can be seen as a coherent programme of change: each part has its own rationale and the parts are mutually consistent. But what are the implications for public finance? A key feature is that this is not a fanciful and unrealistic wish list. The programme as a whole is capable of being implemented in a way that is self-financing without the need to search for sources of funding, which is where proposals for additional public spending usually founder. Many of the proposals will require significant additional public spending but some of them, in particular environmental taxation and redistributional taxation, require additions to taxation in their own right, and the package could be implemented in a way that is neutral in terms of the public spending borrowing requirement.

Some of the policies (for instance employment measures, housing investment and subsidized day care) should also result in some offsetting reduction in social security benefits for the unemployed and some increase in revenues from tax and national insurance contributions. It should allow savings in some public spending programmes such as the health services, but these second-round effects are generally hard to quantify with any certainty and no assumption of their magnitude is made.

Public finance implications of increasing investment

Full implementation of the package would, however, take the economy to a balance of tax and spending where both are higher than at present. What is the feasibility of this? First, an idea of the scale of change in taxation and spending is needed. The additional public services suggested in the report involve an extra £8 or £9 billion in spending, and the additional social security benefits might amount to an extra £7 or £8 billion. (This is all in terms of 1992–3 prices, the latest year for which public expenditure data were available at the time that the full report was written.)

These are large sums of money but must be placed in perspective. Altogether this £16 billion or so of additional public spending is less than 3 per cent of GDP (which in 1992–3 was £600 billion). On the other side of the account would be an additional £12 or £13 billion of tax revenue from income tax, national insurance contributions and abolition of tax allowances such as mortgage interest tax relief, and £3 or £4 billion of environmental taxes. [. . .]

A restructuring of UK taxes and benefits of this order could be done only with strong public support, and this has been lacking even though social surveys indicate that many people are willing to pay higher taxes for the sake of having better public services, and many are prepared to see taxes on the well-off increased (Jowell *et al.*, 1993).

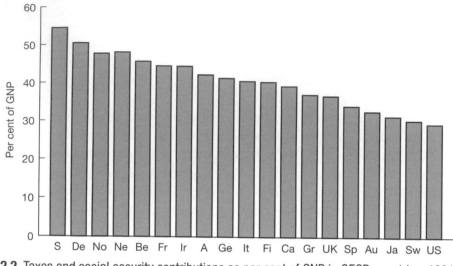

Figure 22.2 Taxes and social security contributions as per cent of GNP in OECD countries, 1991 (*Source*: Central Statistical Office 1994b).

Conclusion

The evidence assembled in this work lends support to the view that Britain is under-investing in its children. There are many more things that could be done in the public sphere to promote the well-being of children and to build up the human capital that they embody. But if things are to be changed there must be a greater willingness to spend more on public services for children than in recent years, and to give higher priority to promoting a social and economic environment in which all children can reach more of their potential. The measures considered here will require many to forgo some present consumption – that is the definition of investment – but without moving in that direction it will have to be acknowledged that what is being done for the future of Britain's children and young people is limited.

References

Bradshaw, J., Ditch, J., Holmes, H. and Whiteford, P. (1993) *Support for Children: a comparison of arrangements in fifteen countries*. Department of Social Security, Research Report 21. London: HMSO.

Central Statistical Office (1993) *Social Trends* 23. London: HMSO.

Central Statistical Office (1994a) The effects of taxes and benefits on household income, 1992. *Economic Trends,* **483** (January) 100–9, 122–3.

Central Statistical Office (1994b) Taxes and social security contributions: an international comparison 1981–1991. *Economic Trends,* **484** (February) 92–103.

Central Statistical Office (1994c) *Social Trends* 24. London: HMSO.

Department for Education (1993) *The Government's Expenditure Plans to 1995–1996. Department Report.* Cm 2210. London: HMSO.

Department for Education (1994) *Education Statistics for the UK 1993.* London: HMSO.

Deparment of Social Security (1993) *The Growth of Social Security.* London: HMSO.

Department of Social Security (1994) *Households Below Average Income: a statistical analysis 1979–1991/92.* London: HMSO.

Glyn, A. and Miliband, D. (eds) (1994) *Paying for Inequality: the economic cost of social injustice.* London: Institute of Public Policy Research/Rivers Oram Press.

Hills J. (1993) *The State of Welfare: a guide to the debate.* York: Joseph Rowntree Foundation.

HM Treasury (1993) *Public Expenditure Analyses to 1995–96: statistical supplement to the autumn statement.* Cm 2219. London: HMSO.

Holtermann, S. (1995) *All Our Futures: the impact of public expenditure and fiscal policies on Britain's children and young people.* London: Barnardo's.

Joseph Rowntree Foundation (1994) *UK Income Distribution during the 1980s.* Social Policy Research Findings 49. York: JRF.

Jowell, R., Brook, L., Prior, G. and Taylor, B. (eds) (1993) *British Social Attitudes Survey: the 9th report.* Aldershot: Social and Community Planning Research.

Kumar, V. (1993) *Poverty and Inequality in the UK: the effects on children.* London: National Children's Bureau.

Le Grand, J. and Bartlett, W. (eds) (1993) *Quasi-Markets and Social Policy.* London: Macmillan.

Le Grand, J., Propper, C. and Robinson, R. (1992) *The Economics of Social Problems.* 3rd edn. London: Macmillan.

Office of Health Economics (1992) *Compendium of Statistics.* London: HMSO.

Robinson, R. and Le Grand, J. (eds) (1994) *Evaluating the NHS Reforms.* London: King's Fund Institute.

Wennemo, I. (1993) Infant mortality, public policy and inequality – a comparison of 18 industrialised countries 1950–1985. *Sociology of Health and Illness,* **15,** 429–46.

Wilkinson, R. (1994) *Unfair Shares: the effects of widening income differences on the welfare of the young.* London: Barnardo's.

This chapter shows that it is public attitudes that in the end determine the kind of society we wish to have. The services and social infrastructure that we have depend on how much we are prepared to pay. We might go on from this chapter to think about how public attitudes are shaped and the role of the media in that process. We might conclude, as we read the next chapters in this volume, that inclusion is both a political and a personal struggle.

CHAPTER 23

The news of inclusive education: a narrative analysis

Bruce Dorries and Beth Haller

The development of inclusive education has involved confrontations between parents and the State. In this chapter Bruce Dorries and Beth Haller analyse one confrontation that turned into a public debate concerning the best method of educating disabled children. They examine the way in which distinct narrative themes within the news media competed to persuade the public about the costs or benefits of inclusion.

[. . .] News coverage of education issues in general has improved over the years (Hynds 1989), and with that has come more attention to high-profile cases of inclusive education. In 1999, Haller confirmed that in general coverage of disability issues, the news media most often focus on topics related to disabled children (23%) and inclusive education (17%). General education issues were also a popular topic in disability-related stories at 10% (Haller 1999).

One explanation for the current news media interest in inclusive education is that 20 years after it was first passed the Individuals with Disabilities Education Act (IDEA) was updated and re-authorised in 1997. The result of IDEA has been taking disabled children out of institutions and segregated special education settings and integrating them into regular classrooms and school activities. [. . .]

However, inclusive education is controversial. When inclusive education programmes were only directed at children with minor learning disabilities, such as slight hearing impairments, the issue was less controversial. However, parents of non-disabled children have long been concerned that children with more severe disabilities, such as autism, can be disruptive to their child's education. Others worry about finite educational resources, if large amounts may be needed for severely disabled children. Studies show that although approximately one third of children in the United States with special education needs receive an education in standard classrooms, few of these children have severe disabilities (Pae 1994). The controversy has grown as these severely disabled children and their families fight for inclusive education.

One high-profile case rocketed the topic of inclusive education to national media attention in the mid-1990s. Beginning in 1995, Hartmann v. Loudoun County Board of

Education tested whether or not schools must include severely disabled children in regular classrooms. Because of their 3-year legal battle in Northern Virginia, the Hartmanns and the inclusion movement became almost synonymous. Mark Hartmann, who is autistic, became a symbol in a national debate over whether, and how often, disabled youngsters should be educated alongside their non-disabled peers (Wilgoren & Pae 1994).

[. . .] This paper analyses 4 years of the extensive media coverage of the Hartmann story to provide a synopsis of the narratives that address the central issues of inclusion. Through the press, competing interests told their stories to the public, hoping to win the moral high ground and persuade others of the 'good reasons' that support their understanding of the costs or benefits of inclusion. Pedagogical issues concerning students with disabilities, who represent 11% of the school population in the United States, raise complex questions of finance, ethics and academic standards. Varied state standards for the education of disabled children further complicate the discussion. Furthermore, as the inclusion debate continues, the diagnosis of disabled children steadily increases (Lewin 1997).

Given the importance of this issue and the notoriety of this case, the narratives about Hartmann v. Loudoun warrant scholarly attention. Understanding these narratives also adds to the growing academic analysis of disability discourse (Corker & French 1999), which challenges preconceived 'readings' of disability-related texts. Narratives told by the Hartmanns, their allies, and the stories of those opposed to inclusion, constitute stories that present 'good reasons' for adopting a point of view (Fisher 1984). The narratives are more or less persuasive, offering positive values that constitute 'good reasons' to accept a claim. The narrative themes offered by the parties involved in the inclusive education controversy reveal that, although the Hartmanns lost their court battle, their narratives and others on behalf of inclusion resonated more persuasively in the news media's court of public opinion, thus advancing the national inclusion movement.

. . . Rather than being an evaluation of inclusive education, this study focuses only on news media narratives about inclusive education as a policy and its implications for the US education system.

The Hartmann case

The following section outlines the facts of the Mark Hartmann story as reported by US media, both local and national. After moving from a suburb of Chicago in 1994, Roxana and Joseph Hartmann enrolled their 9-year-old son in second grade at Ashburn Elementary School in Loudoun County, VA. Officials of the northern Virginia school district reported that Mark hit, pinched, screeched and threw tantrums when placed in a standard classroom. Despite having reduced the class size and having an aide work individually with Mark, his behaviour made learning and classroom management problematic, according to school authorities. By the school year's end, officials concluded that the autistic youngster should be removed from a regular class and placed in a Leesburg school with four other autistic students in a 'mainstream' programme. In this type of 'mainstream' programme, the Leesburg school placed students with autism in regular classes only for music, art and gym classes.

Mark's parents refused to accept this decision (Lewin 1997; Wilgoren, 1994a,b,c). They agreed that their son's experience at Ashburn had been a disaster:

> but they blamed the school system for not providing enough training to Mark's teacher and full-time instructional aide. They pointed to Mark's progress at an Illinois school, where he attended kindergarten and first grade, and they argued that it was crucial to Mark's social development that he go to school with his non-disabled friends.
>
> (Pae 1994: Cl)

So began a lengthy battle 'that stands as a troubling example of how bitter placement disputes can become' (Lewin 1997: Al).

The Hartmanns believed the law supported their case. In line with historic American values of equal access to education by all, IDEA was created to guarantee disabled children the right to free and appropriate education in the least restrictive environment (US Department of Education 2000). [. . .] However, when Loudoun County did not receive the Hartmann's approval to remove Mark from a regular classroom, the school district asked the State Supreme Court to appoint a hearing officer to decide Mark's academic future (Rosen & Jones 1994). The officer ruled that the boy's educational needs were not served by inclusion and gave school officials permission to transfer him to Ashburn. A spokesperson with the American Federation of Teachers indicated this was the first time any school district was allowed to remove a disabled child from classes since passage of IDEA (Rosen & Jones 1994). The Hartmanns appealed.

Although the legal battle had just begun, within months Mark's story had appeared in *People* magazine, on network morning news programmes and in numerous newspapers as far away as Costa Rica, his mother's native country (Wilgoren 1994d). During the next 3 years the enmity between the Hartmanns and Loudoun county school district officials took on the character of a difficult divorce (Abramson & Chadwick 1997a). Meanwhile, the Hartmanns sought out another public school system that promotes inclusion in Montgomery County. [. . .]

Finally, the Hartmann's attorney filed a petition with the US Supreme Court, arguing that Mark's case has significance for the nation (Abramson & Chadwick 1997a). Again the story made national news (Suarez 1997; Abramson & Chadwick 1997a,b), but the high court declined to act on the case (*Washington Post* 1998, January 14). The Hartmanns, who spent more than $200,000 in legal fees arguing for inclusion for Mark (Lewin 1997), vowed to continue their struggle for the inclusive education movement (Lu 1998).

After the legal battled ended, three commentaries, numerous letters to the editor and a lengthy story on inclusion (Applegate & Lu 1998) appeared in the major daily newspaper that serves Southwest Virginia, *The Roanoke Times*. One opponent of inclusion added to the discussion by writing a commentary that said he was:

> distressed to read that the recent court decision not to allow autistic and other learning-challenged children into regular classrooms applied to a Northern Virginia school district but not to Montgomery County Schools. In this regard, I recently questioned my daughter about her experiences with such children. Her words were shocking.
>
> (Holladay 1998)

The writer's commentary apparently shocked a number of readers. Over the next month Mark's mother responded to the attack with a long commentary for the paper (Hartmann 1998), followed by seven letters to the editor supporting her and berating the earlier writer's point of view. The Montgomery County Schools superintendent and school board chairman also contributed a lengthy piece on the issue (Klagge & Morton 1998).

The Hartmann v Loudoun County Board of Education case focused national attention on the inclusive education issue, placing the narratives of competing points of view before the general public. Therefore, the narratives of this case merit closer critical analysis.

Readers may notice one specific narrative is missing from the media coverage – that of Mark Hartmann's own stories told in his own voice. We can only speculate that some of the legal and ethical issues the media face may have caused them to avoid interviewing an autistic person who is not a legal adult. Media law specialists warn journalists that children cannot give legal consent to be interviewed; only their legal guardian can give the consent. Whatever the cause for 'exclusion' of Mark's voice in the coverage of the case, it suggests a significant issue in the discussion about inclusion and education in general: most media stories about any education issue fail to include the 'voices' of those most affected by the issue, children and teens. We suggest this might be a fruitful area of future research, investigating children's own narratives about education that do not appear in the media. However, that topic is not part of the scope of this article.

Narrative analysis as method

. . . Narrative inquiry emphasises an interpretive thrust. Interpretive research seeks to expand understanding of how meaning emerges and is used by people in specific contexts. The approach discovers how people create meanings through stories by interpreting their texts. Although there are many methods for conducting narrative analysis, in general the researcher seeks to discover how social actors perceive reality and evaluates the respondents' stories about their reality. Narrative analysis provides critical standards for interpreting stories; it is especially well suited to the study of subjectivity and identity because narrative analysis highlights human agency and imagination (Kohler Riessman 1993).

. . . the most contemporary and extensive work in the field related to this paradigm has been that of Walter R. Fisher (1984, 1985a,b, 1989a,b, 1993). Fisher regards humans as, first and foremost, storytellers . . . He argues that our reality is composed of sets of stories from which we must choose (Fisher 1989a). Storytelling is seen as central to all human discourse and interaction. Narratives include all symbolic actions, all 'words and/or deeds – that have sequence or meaning for those who live, create, or interpret them' (Fisher 1984: 2). Our stories aid us in interpreting and understanding our reality, giving meaning to our experiences and creating bonds between those who share stories. Through stories we find order, purpose and guidance in our experience, we create common ground or rapport with others, we establish and maintain cultures. [. . .]

Reality then is composed of stories from which people must choose in a never-ending process. People make choices based on 'good reasons' which vary in form and according to context. Fisher describes good reasons as those we perceive as:

(1) true to and consistent with what we think we know and what we value,
(2) appropriate to whatever decision is pending, (3) promising in effects for ourselves and others, and, (4) consistent with what we believe is an ideal basis for conduct.

(1989a: 194)

Schrag (1991) describes good reasons as a gatekeeper role performed by humans. If warrants for belief or action in a narrative do not meet the criteria listed above, then narrative rationality, Fisher's final tenet, is moot. [. . .]

Within this framework, narrative includes 'traditional' forms such as novels or films, as well as non-traditional forms, such as the content of conversation, an interview or editorials and quotes printed by the media. Schudson notes the shaping of news through use of traditions in narrative, story telling, human interest, etc. This ties into the historical nature of culture.

All of this work recognizes that news is a form of literature and that one key resource journalists work with is the cultural tradition of storytelling and picture-making and sentence construction they inherit, with a number of vital assumptions about the world built in.

(Schudson 1991: 155)

Within the ritual view of communication (Carey 1989), news stories are seen as culturally constructed narratives. Within this framework, news still has the power to inform, but Bird & Dardenne (1988) explain that the information audiences receive is not facts and figures, but a larger symbolic system of news narratives. As a method of communication, news can take on qualities like the myth. Both convey culture. New stories, like myths, do not 'tell it like it is', but rather, 'tell it like it means'. [. . .] In this case study, news illustrates cultural narratives about inclusive education.

Fisher's framework has proven useful by enabling scholars to interpret reality, establish connections between people's stories and behaviour, and judge the narratives presented by others for completeness and consistency (Hollihan & Riley 1987; Foss 1989). When applied narrowly, as in the case of this study, the standards for narrative probability and fidelity are useful; 'not so much for testing the argument in a story but for testing its potential credibility with a particular audience and as a test of informal logic' (p. 52). Thus, several of Fisher's concepts offer an interpretive and humanistic approach to the study of communication phenomena. [. . .]

Fisher's narrative paradigm offers a suitable method to interpret and analyse the narrative themes in the news media coverage of the Hartmann v. Loudoun case, as well as editorials, commentaries and letters to the editor.

Evaluation of themes

Narratives contain key themes that display humans' experiences, as well as their values. Through stories we explain our actions and beliefs, as well as lend meaning to our lives. The stories told in the Hartmann v. Loudoun tale illustrate the tellers' 'good reasons' for supporting inclusion or opposing the practice. In composing stories to explain their life/reality, the tellers make choices based on their 'good reasons'. [. . .]

This section presents brief narratives and the good reasons embedded in themes drawn from press coverage of the Hartmann v. Loudoun case. In an effort toward brevity, this paper examines eight themes that evolved from the inclusive education debate in the Hartmann case. Themes were embedded in the stories told by the actors in this social drama. They expressed 'something that people believe, accept as true and valid; it is a common assumption about the nature of their experience' (Spradley 1979: 186). [. . .]

Offered here are themes that were chosen and created in keeping with interpretive, social-constructionist practices (Gergen 1985; Larkin 1986; Kohler Reissman 1993). No doubt others gathering data from the same stories might create different themes to describe and characterise the Hartmann v. Loudoun case. The process of identifying narrative themes began after more than 90 news stories, editorials, commentaries, letters to the editor and three radio transcripts about the case were gathered and analysed. The media stories came from a variety of sources, but most prominent were *The Roanoke Times*, *Richmond Times Dispatch*, *The New York Times*, *The Washington Post*, National Public Radio's (NPR) 'Morning Edition' and 'Talk of the Nation'. After achieving an understanding of the case, the social/moral arguments surrounding inclusion, and examining the narratives over time, the narrative themes began to reveal themselves. After common ideas and experiences were highlighted within the narratives, categories were created to characterise the narratives likely to increase readers' understanding of the moral arguments.

The themes are divided into those that support the Hartmanns or inclusion, and those that support the Loudoun School District or are against inclusion. (Four narrative themes each.) This division over-simplifies the nature of the public discussion about inclusion; there are more than two sides to this complex issue. However, this division provides a more concrete, linear way to discuss the narratives and themes. The themes found in narratives told by the Hartmann's and inclusion supporters include:

Narrative theme 1: Everyone wins with inclusive education

This narrative connects to an overarching theme imbedded within the IDEA legislation – that inclusive education benefits disabled children in the short run with better learning and, in the long run, with more employment and post-secondary educational opportunities. The benefit of inclusive education for non-disabled children is the ability to understand and cope with a more diverse society and people who are different from themselves.

For example, a *New York Times* analysis piece on inclusive education embraces the narrative of IDEA that it benefits all children, not just those with disabilities:

> Many educators and parents believe that segregating children with disabilities is bad, both educationally and morally. They say such a policy undermines the development of both disabled children, by failing to give them a chance to develop the skills and relationships that they will need as adults, and other children, by preventing beneficial contact with the full range of people in their communities.
>
> (Lewin 1997: 20)

Mark Hartmann's mother, Roxana, most often provides this 'everyone wins' narrative, in both her quotes to media and her *Roanoke Times* commentary on her son's case. In the following narrative from her commentary, she explains the benefits of inclusive education for all children:

> . . . (Mark) has demonstrated that there are no long-term harmful effects on the classmates of a disabled child. In fact, full inclusion gives them an opportunity to embrace diversity and grow in compassion and understanding – honorable goals that will serve our children well through their lifetime. In sum, through inclusion, we can make our communities a better place for people with disabilities one child and one family at a time, if we work together. It's the best thing to do for our future together.
>
> (Hartmann 1998: A7)

Roxana Hartmann's quotes for the newspaper explain also the difference inclusion made for Mark in terms of his less volatile behavior specifically:

> 'He understands language. I can talk to him like I can talk to you. I don't have to speak differently,' Hartmann explained.
>
> The other day it was raining and I didn't feel like taking him swimming, so I said to him that I didn't want to go. He just waved his hand a little, saying we didn't have to go. There was no screaming, no tantrums.
>
> (Lu 1998: A1)

Joseph Hartmann, Mark's father, presented this same narrative nationally when he was part of an NPR 'Morning Edition' story on inclusive education:

> JOSEPH HARTMANN: He's becoming able to cope in society as society is, with his peers in the classroom. He knows when his teacher says: 'OK, class, everybody be quiet' that it is his job to be quiet. He knows when the teacher says: 'OK, class, it's time to go to lunch,' – 'OK, I've got to get my lunch box and stand in line with everybody else and go on . . .'
>
> If you have him in an autistic class, three or four other autistic kids, and they sit around and play with blocks all day, you don't take them out into the world except to visit.
>
> (Abramson & Chadwick 1997b).

The news media also relied on prominent pro-inclusion sources, which made the narrative compelling. In articles about the broader inclusive education topic, such as the following *New York Times* article, Judith Heumann, an assistant secretary in the Office of Special Education and Rehabilitative Services at the US Department of Education, who is herself a wheelchair user, explains the 'everyone wins' narrative in a national community context:

> 'Education is academic, but it's also social, learning how to live in a community, learning about differences,' she said. 'I tell parents who are afraid to send a child with disabilities into a regular setting that overprotection does no service when that disabled child becomes an adult. If your child was out of sight, out of mind, that doesn't change. People who might have become their friends in school won't know them.'

Academically, too, she said, all children can benefit from inclusion.

> 'The methods that teachers learn from working with the disabled and individualizing instruction, are useful with other students, as well,' Ms. Heumann

said. 'In a way, you can see every child as having special needs. So the ideal is a system in which every child gets an individualized education.'

(Lewin 1997: 20)

The narrative takes on even more strength when adults with disabilities, who were the product of inclusive education, enter the discourse. The following was a letter to the editor in *The Roanoke Times*, written after a commentary disparaged the benefits of inclusive education:

> I have cerebral palsy and a hearing impairment. I spent most of my school years in 'regular' schools in Connecticut in the 1960s and 1970s, so I am a product of inclusion. I shudder to think what I would have become had I not been given the challenges and intellectual and social stimulation I received. It motivated me to get a good education and to try to make a difference in the world.
>
> The parents of children with disabilities in Montgomery County only want what I was given. These children are more likely to learn appropriate behavior if they are 'included' in regular classes. Able-bodied children learn about acceptance, tolerance and compassion toward those who are 'different', and perhaps something about 'the power of the human spirit'. Not all education is gained from books and facts. Holladay's misconceptions tell me we still have a long way to go toward understanding and accepting people with disabilities.
>
> (Vass-Gal 1998: A7)

These letters to the editor from disabled people fit with Swain & Cameron's notion of 'coming out' for disabled people (1999). They say that when people embrace their social identity as disabled persons, they begin challenging oppression and 'campaigning for equal opportunities to access education, employment, transport, housing, leisure facilities and control over personal lives' (Swain & Cameron 1999: 76). The narratives from disabled people who are proud of their identity have even stronger resonance because their success demonstrates the potential for Mark Hartmann to grow into an adult with a positive self-concept.

Narrative theme 2: Inclusion is cheaper

This narrative appears in two ways. One implied theme is that society benefits in general from inclusive education because well-educated disabled children mean future contributing, tax-paying members of society, rather than tax burdens. However, typically, the narrative was more overt: inclusive education costs less than institutionalisation of severely disabled children.

Roxana Hartmann makes the argument that institutionalisation is expensive and has long-term costs for society.

But the commonwealth does support large institutions. A large chunk of your tax dollars are spent in institutions. It costs more than $80,000 per year to support a person in an institution, and it's getting more expensive all the time. By the year 2000, the national average will reach $113,000 per person in an institution. There are 189,000 Virginians with mental retardation alone – the greater majority housed in institutions. But why is this relevant to the education of a disabled child?

We know from experiences of our sister states that it all begins with decisions focused on educating the disabled child. Early-intervention strategies and an inclusive education posture are proven as an effective approach to integrate our disabled citizens into the community with jobs that they can be trained for and normal home settings to live in. Community-based living and care works better than institutions, and costs far less.

(Hartmann 1998: A7)

The message from the US Department of Education about IDEA is similar. It estimates that educating students in neighborhoods, who would previously have been institutionalised, saves $10,000 per child (US Department of Education, 2000). Consistent with notions of American pragmatism, this narrative ties to capitalistic notions of 'the bottom line', in which citizens embrace policies that reduce taxes or give the most benefit for the least amount of tax dollars.

Narrative theme 3: Human rights should apply to everyone in a civilized society

Typically, this narrative is tied to every American's right to a free public education. The right to an education is presented as a human right available to all equally. Roxana Hartmann puts it succinctly:

After contemplating this response, I have decided to review some facts that may be overshadowed by accusations (real or imagined) and that may not be obvious to a casual observer.

First of all, public education is the right of all children. The Individuals With Disabilities Act guarantees access for disabled students into the 'least restrictive environment.' The only measure is that the school must demonstrate that the disabled child is able to learn in the LRE with appropriate support, services and accommodations.

. . . In all our debate, we should remember that each and every child in our community, including the disabled, is a valued human being who has a basic right to opportunity – whether we are talking work, education, housing or access to public buildings. To consider it otherwise will take us back to the 1860s.

(Hartmann 1998: A7)

Several members of the local southwestern Virginia community continue the free and public education narrative in a number of letters to *The Roanoke Times*:

> How does Holladay justify saying that his daughter has more of a right to an education than my brother? Holladay is concerned about students who 'can learn algebra and Spanish, children for whom the schools are intended, and whose futures will depend on what they learn now.' All children's futures are determined by what they learn. This is a public school system, and everyone has a right to an education.
>
> (Greenberg 1998: A7)

> Our community has chosen (inclusion) for more than 10 years, with all its pitfalls, challenges and magic, because we care about children. All children have a future, and, in America, schools are intended for everyone.
>
> (Bickley & Bickley 1998: A7)

> Public schools aren't for the learning elite. They are public schools, and by law must provide an appropriate education in the least restrictive environment for all children. There is no such thing as separate but equal.
>
> (Eaton 1998: A7)

Although an explicit link is not made in the statements, the theme within these statements is reminiscent of the education reforms that African Americans fought for in the 1950s and 1960s to bring about integrated public education for black and white children. The inclusion movement puts forth the same notion, that separate but equal does not fit with American ideals.

Narrative theme 4: Inclusive education has proven itself

Specifically, this narrative tied into Mark Hartmann's success in an inclusive education environment before moving to Virginia and, broadly, the success of such programmes nationally and in Blacksburg, VA, where Mark Hartmann was placed early in the case. For example, Jamie Ruppman, an education consultant who works with disabled children, saw Mark's success back in Illinois destroying the case of Loudoun County. Educators from Illinois did testify that Mark was successful in their inclusion program before the family moved to Virginia (DeVaughn 1995a).

As Roxana Hartmann explained: 'All you have to know about this case is that Mark was successfully included in Illinois and in Montgomery County. The only place he could not be successfully included was Loudoun County, and that's clearly because the school system did not have the commitment to do it' (Benning 1997). Hartmann continued this argument by explaining why she chose to move to Montgomery County: '[That county] is one of the few school districts in Virginia to honor and abide by IDEA – the law. Among other states, Virginia is ranked 46th in its support of people with disabilities and their families' (Hartmann 1998: A7). Others made similar arguments.

'I have heard nothing negative about having this child stay,' the president of the Montgomery County Council of PTAs said. 'What I have heard is: Why did the school system take a negative stand against this child in the first place? From a parent standpoint, this woman did everything she could for her kid (in Loudoun County), then set out to find what she could for him somewhere else.'

. . . We need to show that it works so other school systems can try to do the same thing.

(DeVaughn 1995b: A1)

The successful inclusive education program narrative is also connected specifically to Mark's educational growth. Roxana Hartmann says: 'He has blossomed in a very nurturing environment here with people who are dedicated and understand him and his disability. He'll stay here until he finishes school' (Lu 1998: A1). The Timmy Clemens case also bolsters the narrative of inclusive education 'proving itself':

Four years ago, Timmy Clemens could not walk near a classroom without becoming so scared he couldn't enter the room. His autism required a full-time aide and much patient coaxing to get him through a day.

By his senior year last year, Timmy could walk to classes in Blacksburg High School on his own. With the help of his aide, Marc Eaton, and a special board that lists the alphabet and short words such as 'yes' and 'no', he did homework and took tests in courses such as algebra and honors history. Today, as a postgraduate, he works with an aide in a job at Blacksburg's Municipal Building.

'Some truly believe in it; some think it's a waste,' said Judy Clemens, Timmy's mother. But other people's opinions don't matter, she said, because she can see the improvements in her son.

I don't think inclusion is perfect. But I think it's going to get better and better, and I'm proud of Montgomery County.

(Applegate & Lu 1998: A1)

Although these narrative themes in the Hartmann case advanced the cause of inclusive education, many who opposed the Hartmann arguments and/or inclusion were included in media coverage or wrote commentaries against the issue. Their oppositional narratives suggested the following themes:

Narrative theme 5: Not in my kid's school

This narrative presupposes that inclusive education will always have a disruptive effect on non-disabled children in the classes and therefore should not be allowed. It is based on some anecdotal reports that a few severely disabled children, such as those with autism, have been disruptive. However, there is also much anecdotal evidence of disruptive non-disabled children, which is rarely mentioned in anti-inclusion narratives. One parent, Steve Holladay, a Blacksburg, VA, parent, stated this narrative through his commentary piece in *The Roanoke Times*. The Virginia Tech professor claimed to quote his daughter, whose words were 'shocking':

> Many of these children (inclusion students) are uncontrollable. They enter your classroom in the middle of a class, and it may take 15 minutes for their aide to return them to the classroom they are assigned to. They break into loud crying fits or other noise making episodes regularly, at unpredictable times and without apparent cause, bringing a halt to teaching until control is re-established.
>
> They wander around the class while the teacher is trying to teach, sometimes selecting a student to sit with and engage in an up-close, face-to-face staring contest. They may unexpectedly slap you in the forehead when you walk by them in the hall . . .
>
> It cannot be denied that many of these children are extremely disruptive. And if they have been found to be too disruptive for normal classrooms in other school districts, why do we place them in our classrooms where our children have their only opportunity to learn many foundational concepts? Do they magically behave better here? . . . Montgomery County has become an island that will accept highly disruptive children into our schools, children impaired to the point of being totally oblivious to the educational process going on around them, children incapable of learning in any way marginally related to the original intent of the school's programs, or to the expectations placed on other children in the classrooms.
>
> (Holladay 1998: A7)

Other parents present this narrative of the disruptive effect of inclusive education. Even the mother of an autistic child wrote:

> I am the mother of an autistic child, and I agree with Steve Holladay . . . I do believe in mainstreaming, where the child is placed in a regular classroom for short periods of time and gradually works up to a full class period. With mainstreaming, 'normal' children get the education they deserve and need without disruption by our 'learning-challenged' children.
>
> (Kingery 1998: A7)

A teacher continued the narrative of disruptive inclusion kids.

> 'Our biggest problem is putting up with emotionally disturbed kids when they are disruptive and distracting to other children,' she said. 'That's a waste of time and that's where we're losing ground.'

Hall, [a] language arts teacher, also resents having to design different tests and notes and other material for some students and fears it inevitably watered down the lesson for all students.

(Applegate & Lu 1998: A1)

Narrative theme 6: Protect the sensitive 'normal' students

Those who question inclusion also argued that it may be traumatic for non-disabled children to be in the presence of severely disabled children:

> Beyond lost education, what effect might this have on the sensitive child who isn't yet ready to experience this type of behavior and instability?
>
> I am sincerely sympathetic for Ms. Hartmann and her situation, and very thankful that my own children are healthy. I further admire her obvious determination to provide what she believes to be the best growing and learning environment possible for her son. However, she and others who move here to take advantage of our inclusion policy seem to have little concern about the effect their children may have on other children in the classrooms.
>
> . . . Does Ms. Hartmann care about the boy or girl who sits in front of the inclusion child during the uncontrollable screaming fit? What about the child whose personal space is invaded by stares or inappropriate touching? Or my own daughter, who receives a stunning slap on the forehead out of the blue?
>
> I asked other adults for their views about our inclusion policy. Not one spoke positively about it. One individual told of a girl whose earring was torn off by an inclusion child, and who subsequently was terrified of going to school. Another said her son quit Scouts because an inclusion child had selected him to shadow and touch.

(Holladay 1998: A7)

The mother of an autistic child adds to the narrative, believing her son's behaviour might upset other children. 'He couldn't tolerate all the activities and stimulus, nor would it be fair to the other children in the classroom' (Kingery 1998: 7A).

Narrative theme 7: School is about academics

In contrast with the inclusive education argument that it benefits children in many more ways than just academics, those opposed to the practice argue schools are to provide an education in reading, writing, arithmetic, etc. The attorney for Loudoun County illustrates this narrative in her comments to NPR's Morning Edition:

KATHLEEN MAYFOUD, ATTORNEY FOR LOUDOUN COUNTY, VIRGINIA, SCHOOLS: Socialization is part of that, but academic and educational instruction is obviously the primary responsibility. So, Loudoun would have had to totally overlook the educational requirements in favor of a minor goal.

(Abramson & Chadwick 1997b)

Holladay ties the idea of a proper learning environment with this narrative and argues that inclusive education is its antithesis.

Doesn't it seem obvious that loss of teaching time to disruptive or ongoing distractive behavior isn't conducive to learning?

Similar to Ms. Hartmann, we (the other parents) are also determined to provide our children the best possible learning environment. As an educator myself, I don't like our inclusion policy. I would never tolerate such disruption in my classrooms unless, as has become the case in Montgomery County, I was mandated to do so by law.

I truly do care about Mark. However, I care more about his classmates who can learn algebra and Spanish, children for whom the schools were intended, and whose futures will ultimately depend on what they learn now.

(Holladay 1998: A7)

Narrative theme 8: Attendance is not the same as integration

This narrative questions definitions of inclusive education. It also re-interprets various aspects of inclusive education as having a negative effect. For example, Richard Schattman, a Vermont principal who believes in inclusion, explains how inclusion, when poorly implemented, gives those opposed to inclusive education fodder to urge for its dismantling.

'A student can be more isolated and segregated in a normal classroom than in special education,' Mr Schattman said. 'Inclusion isn't about placing the kid. It's about making the placement successful both for the kid and for the rest of the class. And it's not easy. You need small classes, lots of planning time, and staff that believes in it.'

Some special education experts worry that the inclusion movement may lead to dumping children with special needs into classes where they will be ignored or taunted, and eliminating the special services and support that they receive in settings intended just for them.

'It has not been demonstrated that regular classrooms, even fortified regular classrooms using the best practices can accommodate all children all the time,' said Douglas Fuchs, a professor of special education at Vanderbilt University. 'The full inclusionists honestly believe that creating a situation in which teachers individualize instruction for each student is a terrific goal we should all dedicate our lives to. So we should kick away the crutch of special education. But that's a high stakes game, and I'm not sure it's realistic.'

Nor are all parents and advocates for children with disabilities convinced that it is the correct goal.

(Lewin 1997: 20)

This narrative supports those opposed to inclusion by noting that it may not be the right accommodation for every disabled child. This type of theme turns inclusive education on itself, i.e. because it may not be appropriate for all disabled children, maybe it should not be used at all. *The New York Times* story above continued this narrative by explaining that because of disruptive, abusive, and violent children, Vermont, the premier state for successful inclusive education, is placing such children in separate settings (Lewin 1997).

Conclusions and discussion

As noted in this analysis, narrative themes were divided into those that support the Hartmanns/inclusive education and those that do not. This reflects a problem that is imbedded within the debate itself, by creating a division that oversimplifies the nature of inclusive education. The public discussion about this case reflects standard news coverage of a controversial issue – 'either-or' dichotomy, debate rather than discussion (Tannen 1998). When the news narratives follow lines of 'yes' or 'no' about inclusive education, they miss an opportunity to critically assess the issue for all children in US public school systems. When the focus is on a two-sided debate, rather than a multi-faceted discussion, the news media are also more likely to drop coverage of the topic if one side of the debate tires of presenting their narratives.

The media stories and commentaries, and the themes they illustrate about inclusive education, lend insight into the participants' beliefs, actions and world views, as well as their conflicts of opinion and perception relative to the setting (Hollihan & Riley 1987). Although this paper touched on just a few of the prominent themes about inclusive education in the news, we believe the themes offered in this paper dominate the discussion. Furthermore, we conclude that even though some parents of non-disabled children are vehemently opposed to inclusive education, it was the more numerous and more vocal parents of severely disabled children, educators, and proponents of IDEA who set the tone of the debate and framed inclusion as a workable approach to educate disabled children. We conclude that though the Hartmanns lost their case against Loudoun County, the narratives they inspired actually won in the court of public opinion.

It has taken almost 25 years for pro-inclusion narratives to take hold. As programmes in Montgomery County, VA, Illinois, and Vermont show, school districts need not only well-trained faculty and well-financed programmes to succeed, but public support as well. For example, when parent Steve Holladay wrote to criticise inclusive education in Montgomery County, VA, his criticism was met with seven letters to the editor positively endorsing inclusive education. In the pro-inclusion environment of Montgomery County, VA, the local newspaper, *The Roanoke Times*, seemed to present the proponents' narratives wholeheartedly. Even when the Hartmanns lost their case, the newspaper published a family-provided colour photo of Mark Hartmann on its front page (Lu 1998). In the photo, Mark Hartmann, wearing T-shirt and shorts, grins broadly as a picture-perfect 'average' kid. The image alone provides a 'good reason' that Mark should be in a regular classroom because he is presented visually as a 'regular kid'. Earlier, the newspaper published a large 2-page spread on inclusive education in the county, providing a location for thoughtful discussion of the issue and primarily 'good reasons' for inclusive education.

Some opponents of inclusive education fear the public and policymakers may be swayed by an underlying message of pity for the 'poor, little disabled children'. The conservative *National Journal* feared during the re-authorisation of IDEA in 1997 that:

> Overhaul of the Individuals with Disabilities Education Act is tailor made for policy decision by anecdote. The facts and figures are sparse and conflicting; the horror stories are stark and vivid. And the interest groups are well organized, disciplined and loaded with heart-tuggers or spine-chillers, depending on their legislative goal.
>
> In the past, organizations representing the disabled could count on their substantial political clout in Congress. 'Politicians are terrified of them – that they'll trot out people in wheelchairs,' a lobbyist for an education organization said enviously. 'It's very easy for a Member to feel virtuous voting for their issues'.
>
> (Stanfield 1995)

Yet the findings from this narrative analysis illustrate that proponents of inclusive education have no need to trot out hackneyed, pity images of disabled children. They rely on much stronger and more salient narratives: inclusion is a win-win situation for everyone; public education is every child's right; inclusion is cheaper than institutionalisation; and inclusion has proven itself successful nationally. These 'good reasons' hold the most persuasive power because they appeal to the audience's general understanding of equality and humanity, which most Americans embrace. As one woman with cerebral palsy and a hearing impairment explained the good reasons from her personal inclusion experience: Disabled 'children are more likely to learn appropriate behavior if they are "included" in regular classes. Able-bodied children learn about acceptance, tolerance and compassion toward those who are different, and perhaps something about "the power of the human spirit." Not all education is gained from books and facts' (Vass-Gal 1998: A7).

These themes/stories in support of inclusion are consistent with American values of equality – the country has determined that schools cannot be separate and truly equal. Furthermore, the effects of inclusion, while perhaps detrimental to a few students, largely have promising effects for both students with and without disabilities. Inclusion represents Fisher's notion of a powerful narrative being representative of an ideal basis for conduct. While many of the stories against inclusion suggest pragmatic or traditional bases for educational policy, readers of the narratives are likely to find the rationality of the pro-inclusion arguments more consistent with US history and culture. For example, the 1960s civil rights movement, which successfully dismantled separate but unequal educational systems for blacks and whites, suggests the type of ideal conduct to which Fisher refers. The civil rights movement forced the United States to acknowledge once again the central narrative of its founding that all citizens are created equal and deserve equal opportunities in all aspects of US society, including education.

Although the narratives evaluated in this study were only linked to the media coverage of inclusive education, we believe another area of inquiry could involve comparing coverage of this movement for disabled children with narratives reported in media about desegregation of US schools in the 1960s and 1970s. Would narratives from both movements support the same or similar themes? US history tells us that some of the same arguments and cultural values were employed during that period of change in US educational policy. For example, some of those who were against the integration of black children into predominantly white schools made some arguments parallel to those opposed to inclusion: that desegregation would be disturbing to both black and white children, that it would be disruptive to the academic process, that schools were for academics not socialisation, and that some students were not served by desegregation. Our conclusion is that just as these anti-integration narratives proved less persuasive in the 1960s, the narratives against inclusion are becoming less effective today.

After the loss of her son's case, Roxana Hartmann said she will continue to lead national discourse about inclusive education:

'This is the end, but it's not going to stop me from talking about inclusion,' Roxana said. 'No, if anything, it's made me more of a believer than ever' . . . 'This is not about winners and losers; this is about schools doing the right thing for the children,' she explained.

(Lu 1998: 1A)

Widespread media coverage of Hartmann's narrative and those of other supporters of inclusion should also prove to help make others believers in the movement's aims.

References

Abramson, L. and Chadwick, A. (1997a, Nov. 6) Disabilities. *Morning Edition* (transcript # 97110611–210).

Abramson, L. and Chadwick, A. (1997b, Nov. 7) Mark Hartmann: Part II. *Morning Edition* (transcript # 971101709–210).

Applegate, L. and Lu, K. (1998, February 1) Seeking best place to learn. *Roanoke Times*, p. Al.

Benning, V. (1997, July 10) Court backs decision to remove autistic boy from regular class. *Washington Post*, p. D1.

Bickley, S. and Bickley, P. (1998) Community supports inclusion policy [Letter to the Editor]. *Roanoke Times*, p. A7.

Bird, S.E. and Dardenne, R. W. (1988) Myth, chronicle, and story. In J. W. Carey (ed.) *Media, Myths, and Narratives*, pp. 67–86. Newbury Park, CA: Sage.

Carey, J. (1989) *Communication as Culture*. New York: Routledge.

Corker, M. and French, S. (1999) (eds) *Disability Discourse*. Buckingham: Open University Press.

DeVaughn, M. (1995a) Autistic pupil not welcome. *Roanoke Times and World News*, p. Al.

DeVaughn, M. (1995b, February 17) Judge hears from autistic boy's mom, school board. *Roanoke Times and World News*, p. B l.

Eaton, M. (1998) Inclusion can help all students [Letter to the Editor]. *Roanoke Times*, p. A7.

Fisher, W.R. (1984) Narration as a human communication paradigm: the case of public moral argument. *Communication Monographs*, **51**, 1–22.

Fisher, W.R. (1985a) The narrative paradigm: 'In the beginning'. *Journal of Communication*, **35**, 74–89.

Fisher, W.R. (1985b) The narrative paradigm: an elaboration. *Communication Monographs*. **52**, 347–67.

Fisher, W. R. (1989a) *Human Communication as Narration: toward a philosophy of reason, value, and action*. Columbia, SC: University of South Carolina Press.

Fisher, W. R. (1989b) Clarifying the narrative paradigm. *Communication Monographs*, **56**, 55–8.

Fisher, W. R. (1993) When teaching 'works': stories of communication in education. *Communication Education*, **42**, 279–81.

Foss, S. K. (1989) *Rhetorical Criticism: exploration and practice*. Prospect Heights, IL: Waveland Press.

Gergen, K.J. (1985) The social constructionist movement in modern psychology, *American Psychologist*, **40**. 266–75.

Greenberg, L. (1998) Everyone has a right to go to public schools [Letter to the Editor]. *Roanoke Times*, p. A7.

Haller, B.A. (1999, July) *News Coverage of Disability Issues: a final report for the Center for an Accessible Society*. San Diego, CA: Center for an Accessible Society.

Hartmann, R. (1998, February 16) My son's right to an education doesn't hurt others. *Roanoke Times*, p. A7.

Holladay, S. (1998, February 7) Learning-challenged kids shouldn't be in regular classrooms. *Roanoke Times*, p. A7.

Hollihan, T. A. and Riley, P. (1987) The rhetorical power of a compelling story: a critique of a 'Toughlove' parental support group. *Communication Quarterly*, **35**, 13–25.

Hynds, E. C. (1989) Survey finds large daily newspapers have improved coverage of education. *Journalism Quarterly*, 692–6, 780.

Kingery, D. (1998) Mainstreaming can be done gradually [Letter to the Editor]. *Roanoke Times*, p. A7.

Klagge, J. and Morton, F. (1998, March 13) Balancing the needs of special and regular students *Roanoke Times*, p. A9.

Kohler Reissman, C. (1993) *Narrative Analysis*. Newbury Park, CA: Sage Publications.

Larkin, T.J. (1986) Humanistic principles of organizational management. *Central States Speech Journal*, **37**, 36–44.

Lewin, T. (1997, December 28) Where all doors are open for disabled students. *New York Times*, p. A1.

Lu, K. (1998, January 14) Autistic pupil loses fight to be 'included'. *Roanoke Times*, p. 1A.

Pae, P. (1994, December 16) Loudoun can take autistic boy out of regular class. *Washington Post*, p. C1.

Rosen, M. and Jones, R. (1994, October 17) Odd child out. *People*, p. 113.

Schrag, R. (1991) Narrative rationality and 'first stories': pedagogical implications for children's television. *Communication Education*, **40**, 313–23.

Schudson, M. (1991) The sociology of news production revisited. In J. Curran and M. Gurevitch (eds) *Mass Media and Society*, pp. 141–59. London: Edwin Arnold.

Spradley, J. (1979) *The Ethnographic Interview*. New York: Holt, Rinehart & Winston.

Stanfield, R. (1995) Tales out of school. *National Journal*, **27** 33–4.

Suarez, R. (1997, November 17) Inclusion. *Talk of the Nation* (transcript # 97111701–211).

Swain, J. and Cameron, C. (1999) Unless otherwise stated: discourses of labelling and identity in coming out. In M. Corker and S. French (eds) *Disability Discourse*, pp. 68–78. Buckingham: Open University Press.

Tannen, D. (1998) *The Argument Culture*. New York: Random House.

US Department of Education (2000) Overview of IDEA. [Available on-line]. http://www.ed.gov/offices/OSERS/IDEA/

Vass-Gal, S. (1998) Parent's worries reflect misconceptions [Letter to the Editor]. *Roanoke Times*, p. A7.

Washington Post (1998, January 14) Loudoun disability case won't be heard, p. B3.

Wilgoren, D. (1994a, August 16) Loudoun wants autistic boy out of class. *Washington Post*, p. B1.

Wilgoren, D. (1994b, October 28) Mother says regular school is crucial for autistic boy. *Washington Post*, p. B3.

Wilgoren, D. (1994c, December 8) Ruling due on boy's schooling. *Washington Post*, p. VI, Virginia Weekly section.

Wilgoren, D. (1994d, December 27) In autism case, hearing is over, but battle isn't. *Washington Post*, p. D1.

Wilgoren, D. and Pae, P. (1994, August 28) As Loudon goes, so may other schools. *Washington Post*, p. B1.

The narrative analysis contained in this chapter clearly identifies the way in which the meaning of inclusion is being contested. The competing narratives carry with them different 'truths' about what inclusion is and the values underpinning it. By illuminating these narratives Dorries and Haller provide a thought-provoking tool for analysing 'the inclusion debate' and also a means for reflecting on one's own beliefs.

CHAPTER 24

Unequivocal acceptance – lessons for education from the Stephen Lawrence Inquiry
Robin Richardson

In this article, Robin Richardson draws attention to what many in education deny. He asks us to question the levels of institutional racism that exist within education and the teaching profession. Richardson requires us to be pro-active in our response to this issue. As he said in the original version of this article, we must become antiracist. We must demonstrate '(1) robust refusal even to reflect, let alone to reproduce, "racial" inequalities, (2) vigorous commitment to listening and attending to black experience, stories and perceptions, (3) relentless review of "laws, customs and practices" in education, including those which are sanctioned or promoted by the DfEE, QCA and Ofsted, (4) equally relentless review of occupational culture, not least in the attitudes implicit in staffroom cultures towards black boys and towards non-"Western" traditions and heritages, particularly Islam.'

'There must be an unequivocal acceptance,' declares the report of the Stephen Lawrence Inquiry, 'of the problem of institutional racism and its nature before it can be addressed, as it needs to be, in full partnership with members of minority ethnic communities.'

(Paragraph 6.48)

A number of commentators on the report have pointed out – though the report itself does not say this – that there is institutional racism in the education system in much the same way that there is in the police service, and in the criminal justice system more widely. [. . .]

Backlash

This article was written less than a fortnight after the Macpherson Report was published [in 1999]. [. . .] The early signs are that the police service will indeed take the report seriously. In society more generally, however, a vicious backlash has already started. It is in addition ominous that the first reactions of the teachers' unions have been essentially defensive.

It would be 'extraordinarily unfair', said the National Union of Teachers (NUT), to condemn the education system: 'The teaching profession has done more than any other institution to counter racism. It is true that we need to see a greater representation of ethnic minorities on the staff, but this doesn't represent racism' (*The Guardian*, 24 February). The National Association of School Masters and Union of Women Teachers (NASUWT) said teachers would resent being blamed for the underachievement of black pupils: 'Many of these problems arise not just because of issues of race but also because of poverty and social class' (*Daily Express*, 8 March). The secretary of the National Association of Head Teachers (NAHT) said that he rejected 'the accusation that schools are guilty of institutional racism' (*Today Programme*, 10 March).

These defensive reactions from the teaching profession need to be seen within the context of the wider backlash in society as a whole. The flavour of this was captured in a letter to the press by a Conservative councillor in Haringey:

> The Lawrence inquiry report is a biased, politicised smear . . . The report . . . [shows] . . . little evidence that racism – rather than simple human error – was the source of police failings in the murder investigation . . . There was 'institutionalised racism' in Nazi Germany, South Africa and the American South, but the only institutional racism – properly defined – in the British police is the racial quotas the Government is proposing to introduce. In addition to being racist, these quotas smear successful Black officers . . . The report should be put where it belongs – in the bin.
>
> (*The Independent*, 3 March)

Polly Toynbee in *The Guardian* on 3 March . . . [described] a racist cartoon in the *Daily Mail* (2 March) but reserved her principal criticisms for the *Daily Telegraph*:

> From the day the Lawrence report appeared it has rubbished and condemned its every finding. If you want a perfect model for institutional racism, buy the Telegraph for a whiff of Britain's conservative establishment. In its leaders and columns the racism is witting and unremitting, proud and disgraceful. It revels in it, rolls in it, abominating politically correct non-racists.

Such strong words will not, let us hope, be applied to the NUT, NASUWT and NAHT! By the time this article appears, the teachers' unions will perhaps . . . have acknowledged that the education system – *including the teaching profession itself* – has a case to answer . . . They will have to engage in three main tasks: (a) elucidate the history and meanings of the term 'institutional racism'; (b) listen attentively and respectfully when it is alleged and argued that the term institutional racism accurately describes significant realities throughout the education system; and (c) come up with some practical ways forward.

History and meanings of the term

The term 'institutional racism' was coined by Stokely Carmichael and his co-workers in the 1960s. Officially, racism was no longer part of American law – it was no longer institutionalised. But racist attitudes, assumptions and beliefs were still, Carmichael argued, embedded in American institutions and in white American culture. Therefore it could be said that not only individuals but also institutions can act in racist ways – i.e. if they treat Black people less favourably than white people, and if they therefore perpetuate and exacerbate inequalities between white people and Black in relation to goods such as health, education, property and power.

Further, Carmichael's point was that institutions can act with racist effects even when individuals in those institutions neither realise this nor intend it. Racism could only be eliminated, it followed, if there were significant institutional changes. The term 'institutional racism' was a deliberately provocative way of saying that major changes were still required throughout American society.

The term quickly crossed the Atlantic and was applied to British situations. There was no recent history of segregation as official government policy but nevertheless the concept made sense to campaigners. Here too it gave voice, in a convenient shorthand way, to people's feelings and perceptions. Here too it was a shorthand way of evoking a political programme. In the field of employment law it was translated into the legal term 'indirect discrimination' and incorporated into the Race Relations Act. However, the term 'indirect discrimination' was by no means a complete translation of what Carmichael and other campaigners had in mind.

In 1981 Lord Scarman referred to institutional racism in his report on the Brixton disorders. He is widely believed to have said that there is no institutional racism in Britain. His exact words are worth quoting, however, for in certain respects he has been misrepresented.

> It was alleged by some of those who made representations to me that Britain is an institutionally racist society. If by that is meant that it is a society which knowingly, as a matter of policy, discriminates against Black people, I reject the allegation. If, however, the suggestion being made is that practices may be adopted by public bodies as well as by private individuals which are unwittingly discriminatory against Black people, then this is an allegation which deserves serious consideration and, where proved, swift remedy. [. . .]

Stephen Lawrence Inquiry

Subsequently a number of academics argued that the concept of institutional racism, in Lord Scarman's second sense, is not clear enough to direct policy or to underpin research. The term was nevertheless retained by campaigners, as a shorthand term to articulate their perceptions and outlook. It came again into prominence in 1998 . . ., as is now well known, when it was used by a range of witnesses at the Stephen Lawrence Inquiry, in allegations against the Metropolitan Police. [. . .]

In the Macpherson Report the Commission for Racial Equality is quoted as saying:

> Institutional racism has been defined as those laws, customs and practices which systematically reflect and reproduce racial inequalities in society. If racist consequences accrue to institutional laws, customs and practices, the institution is racist whether or not the individuals maintaining those practices have racial intentions.

The report quotes also an elucidation by Professor Simon Holdaway:

> The term institutional racism should be understood to refer to the way institutions may systematically treat or tend to treat people differently in respect of race. The addition of the word 'institutional' therefore identifies the source of the differential treatment; this lies in some sense within the organisation rather than simply with the individuals who represent it. The production of differential treatment is 'institutionalised' in the way the organisation operates.
>
> (Paragraph 6.32)

A fuller and stronger definition would stress that an institution is racist in so far as it is not antiracist – i.e. if it fails to combat and reduce racism both in its internal structures and in its dealings with other bodies. [. . .] Antiracism involves a refusal, an explicit and energetic refusal, even to reflect inequalities let alone to reproduce them. Such antiracism involves addressing, to cite the terms which Scarman himself used, three interlinked but separate realities: (a) racial disadvantage, i.e. the social exclusion of Black people, (b) racial discrimination, and (c) 'poisoned minds and attitudes'. Also, of course, it involves combating racist violence and harassment.

Application to education

The definitions cited above can be rewritten so that they more directly and more challengingly refer to the education system. Here, then, are the allegations which the teachers' unions, amongst many others, have to consider:

> In the education system there are laws, customs and practices which systematically reflect and reproduce racial inequalities . . . If racist consequences accrue to institutional laws, customs and practices, a school or a local education authority or

a national education system is racist whether or not individual teachers, inspectors, officers, civil servants and elected politicians have racist intentions ... Educational institutions may systematically treat or tend to treat pupils and students differently in respect of race, ethnicity or religion The differential treatment lies within an institution's ethos and organisation rather than in the attitudes, beliefs and intentions of individual members of staff. The production of differential treatment is 'institutionalised' in the way the institution operates.

Similarly the oral evidence given by the Black Police Association can be interestingly and challengingly modified (and expanded slightly) in its wording, so that it refers to teachers rather than to police officers:

The term institutional racism should be understood to refer to the way a school may systematically or repeatedly treat, or tend to treat, people differentially in respect of 'race', ethnicity, culture or religion. So we are not talking about individual teachers, but about the net effect of what they do ... A second source of institutional racism is our culture, the culture of the teaching profession as a whole and the culture of each individual staffroom. The occupational culture within the teaching profession, given the fact that the majority of teachers are white, tends to revolve around white experience, white beliefs, white values.

The officer who presented these views on behalf of the Black Police Association, Inspector Paul Wilson, strikingly stressed that the white occupational culture of the police service fashions the outlook and behaviour of Black officers as well as white. Again, his words can be adapted slightly so that they apply to education as well as to policing:

Interestingly I say 'we' because there is no marked difference between black teachers and white. We are all consumed by this occupational culture. Some of us may think we rise above it on some occasions, but generally speaking we tend to conform to its norms. It is all-powerful in shaping our views and perceptions of a particular community.

Quotations

The quotations in Box 1 are all connected with the Stephen Lawrence Inquiry, and all can be used to illustrate or unpack points in this article. [. . .] Readers may also be interested to consider the diagram which appears as Box 2, 'the iceberg structure of institutional racism'. [. . .] The term 'racial inequalities' [. . .] is unpacked in further detail in Box 3.

Box 1 Racism in Britain today – voices and perceptions

Every Black person	The level of racism	Procedures and a culture
The death of Stephen Lawrence and the heroic struggle for justice waged by his family stands as a tragic epitaph to the racism that deeply poisons the British criminal justice system and the utter failure of the police to take such crimes seriously. The failure to deliver justice to Stephen's family is a denial of justice to every Black person in Britain. *Dave Weaver, Bandung Institute*	A public inquiry is a form of theatre. But the theatre is not itself a judicial instrument. What this inquiry gains from being staged, even in edited form, is that it forces us to confront the level of racism in Britain today – far worse, according to Neville Lawrence, than when he first came here in the 1960s. *Michael Billington, The Guardian, 14 January 1999*	Any long-established, white-dominated organisation is liable to have procedures, practices and a culture which tend to exclude or disadvantage non-white people. The police service in this respect is little different from other parts of the criminal justice system, or from government departments … and many other institutions. *Speech by the Home Secretary, House of Commons, 24 February 1999*
Didn't know before	**All of us**	**Civil rights movement**
Edmund Lawson QC: You referred to the victims of the assault, Stephen Lawrence and Duwayne Brooks, as the two coloured lads? **Detective Inspector Bullock**: Yes. **Edmund Lawson QC**: Do you understand that using the expression coloured is regarded as offensive? **Detective Inspector Bullock**: I didn't know that before, sir. *Transcript of the Inquiry*	To tackle institutional racism means saying that all of us in the organisation from the very top to the bottom are part of the problem. *Herman Ouseley, Commission for Racial Equality*	The inquiry has opened many people's eyes to the reality and extent of police racism. We now have to build on this awareness and develop a civil rights movement, which will work in a united, non-sectarian manner. If the momentum is to continue we need to develop monitoring groups as an integral part of the process. We cannot ask the Lawrences to lead the movement for another five years. *Southall Monitoring Project*
Not enough	**Every**	**More than this**
Most of all *The Colour of Justice* demonstrates the role played in our society by unconscious racism. It isn't about a few bent coppers. It's about how white Britain treats black Britain. As a black woman said to me in the interval: 'It's not enough for a white person to say 'I am not a racist'. You have to ask yourself if other people find you racist.' *Review in Independent on Sunday, 17 January 1999*	Every nigger should have their arms and legs chopped up and left with fucking stumps. *One of the youths suspected to have committed the murder*	It doesn't matter how much a black person tries to explain his or her feelings in a racist society, those who are listening will continue to believe that there is no such thing as racism and that everyone is treated the same. Their reasoning is 'we have Black friends, and we have Black neighbours, so we are not racist'. It takes more than this to show whether you are racist or not. *Doreen Lawrence, on the last day of the inquiry*

Source: *Inclusive Schools, Inclusive Society: race and identity on the agenda*, by Robin Richardson and Angela Wood, published by Trentham Books for Race On The Agenda (ROTA), summer 1999, reprinted with acknowledgement.

Box 2 The iceberg structure of institutional racism in education – the case of African-Caribbean pupils and students

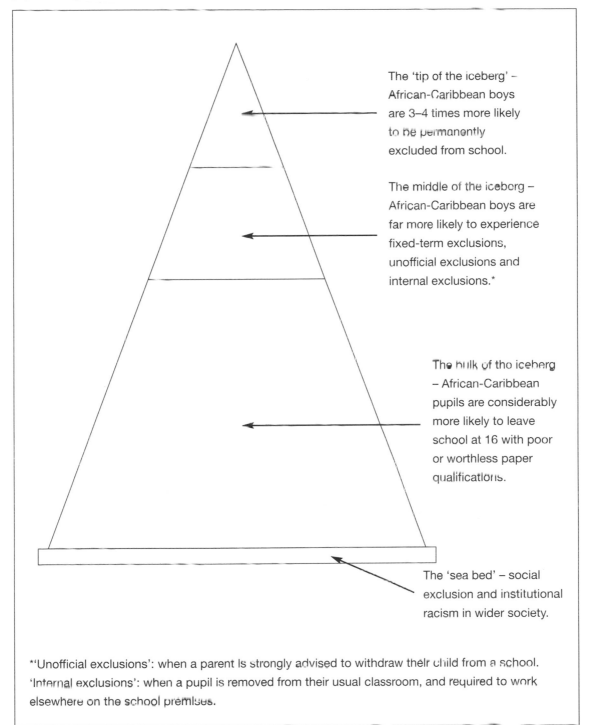

The 'tip of the iceberg' – African-Caribbean boys are 3–4 times more likely to be permanently excluded from school.

The middle of the iceberg – African-Caribbean boys are far more likely to experience fixed-term exclusions, unofficial exclusions and internal exclusions.*

The bulk of the iceberg – African-Caribbean pupils are considerably more likely to leave school at 16 with poor or worthless paper qualifications.

The 'sea bed' – social exclusion and institutional racism in wider society.

*'Unofficial exclusions': when a parent is strongly advised to withdraw their child from a school. 'Internal exclusions': when a pupil is removed from their usual classroom, and required to work elsewhere on the school premises.

Source: Inclusive Schools, Inclusive Society: race and identity on the agenda, by Robin Richardson and Angela Wood, published by Trontham Books for Race On The Agenda (ROTA), summer 1999, reprinted with acknowledgement.

Box 3 Racial inequality in institutions – dimensions and examples

Dimensions of inequality	Examples of inequality in the criminal justice system	Examples of inequality in the education system
OUTCOMES – (a) 'Goods' White people receive more benefits than black, and racial inequality is therefore perpetuated.	Crimes against white people are investigated and cleared up more effectively than crimes against black people.	White pupils leave school at 16 or 18 with substantially better paper qualifications than black pupils.
OUTCOMES – (b) 'Bads' Black people receive negative results more than do white people and in this way too inequality is perpetuated.	Black people are far more likely than white to be stopped and searched by the police.	Black pupils experience punishments, particularly permanent and fixed-term exclusions, more than white pupils.
STRUCTURE In senior decision-making and policy-making positions there are proportionately more white people than black, and in consequence black interests and perspectives are inadequately represented.	There are few black officers at or above the rank of inspector, and also few black people in the rest of the criminal justice system.	There are few black headteachers or deputy heads, and few black education officers, inspectors, teacher trainers and textbook writers.
CULTURE AND ATTITUDES In the occupational culture there are assumptions, expectations and generalisations which are more negative about black people than about white.	Black people are more likely than white people to be seen as criminals or potential criminals.	Black pupils are more likely than white pupils to be seen as troublemakers, and to be criticised and controlled.
RULES AND PROCEDURES Customary rules, regulations and practices work more to the advantage of white people than black.	Throughout the criminal justice system black people are treated less favourably than white people.	The national curriculum reflects white interests, concerns and outlooks and neglects or marginalises black experience.
STAFF TRAINING Staff have not received training on race and racism issues, and on ways they can avoid indirect discrimination.	Police officers have not been trained to identify and investigate racist attacks.	Neither initial not inservice training pays sufficient attention to race and racism issues.
FACE-TO-FACE INTERACTION Staff are less effective in communication with, and listening to, black people than they are in interaction with white people.	Encounters between white police officers and black members of the public frequently escalate into needless confrontation.	Encounters between white staff and black pupils frequently escalate into needless confrontation.

Source: Inclusive Schools, Inclusive Society: race and identity on the agenda, by Robin Richardson and Angela Wood, published by Trentham Books for Race On The Agenda (ROTA), summer 1999, reprinted with acknowledgement.

Arguments

At this point, in the context of the iceberg diagram (Box 2) and the tabulation of dimensions and examples (Box 3), it is appropriate to stand back and consider critically the arguments which have been advanced so far in this article. How might the leaders of the NUT, NASUWT and NAHT respond to the arguments, and – for example – to the claim that the iceberg shows realities over which the education system has control, and for which it is therefore culpable? I imagine them replying along some such lines as the following:

> Well, if you insist on defining institutional racism as 'reflecting and reproducing inequalities' between black people and white, maybe schools are guilty. But that is not the definition which the Macpherson Report itself puts forward. Anyway, the facts summarised graphically in your iceberg diagram do not necessarily mean that schools are reflecting and reproducing inequality. It could be that schools are in fact *reducing* inequalities. The progress is slow, admittedly, but nevertheless steady. There is a huge legacy of history to dismantle. Black people are more involved in British society – there is more social inclusion of black people – than 30 years ago. Or even ten years ago. The education system must be given some, indeed much, of the credit for this.

That is the first point in a possible reply. A second point might be about causality, or, rather, about the alleged absence of causality, and might be developed as follows:

> But supposing it is true that schools are reflecting and reproducing inequalities, you cannot argue back from this to institutional racism as the cause. You cannot validly claim that there is an occupational culture in the teaching profession which excludes and legitimises negative views of Black pupils, and which causes the unequal outcomes which appear (we stress, again, *appear*) to arise. By the same token you cannot claim that the unequal outcomes are caused by 'laws, customs and practices'. There *may* be a causal connection, of course, but you have not demonstrated it.

Response to the response

The responses imagined above were considered by the Macpherson team in relation to the police service. For they too were faced with an argument, advanced on behalf of several police officers, that it is invalid to argue back from racist outcomes to racist causes. 'Yes,' the argument for the police ran, 'we did not behave as efficiently as usual in our investigation of the murder. Yes, one or two of us were perhaps less thoughtful and sensitive towards Mr and Mrs Lawrence than we usually are in our dealings with members of the public suffering from trauma and bereavement. It could be said, yes, that we were not as fully professional as is customary. But that does not mean that we were racist, either as individuals or as an institution.'

The Macpherson team gave this argument careful attention. The team was led, after all, by someone with an expert legal mind, trained to examine arguments about causality, and the relevant evidence, with considerable rigour. 'Incompetence does not,' says the team's report, quoting a legal judgment made in 1991, '… become discrimination merely because the person affected by it is from an ethnic minority.' They explain that a key legal concept in this context is 'inference'. What can reasonably be inferred from the facts? What other reasons might there be for the facts? How do those involved explain the facts? (For example, how do police officers explain why they behaved so unprofessionally in the Lawrence affair? … How do teachers explain the underachievement and high exclusion rates of black and Muslim pupils?) What can be inferred from the way people talk in the witness box? These are basic questions which the inquiry team asked. They quote at one point (paragraph 6.41) from a legal judgment dating from 1996:

> The process of inference is itself a matter of applying commonsense and judgement of facts, and assessing the probabilities on this issue of whether racial grounds were an effective cause of the acts complained of or were not. The assessment of the parties and their witnesses when they gave evidence also form an important part of the process of inference.

Their conclusion is that 'mere incompetence cannot of itself account for the whole catalogue of failures, mistakes, misjudgements and lack of direction and control which bedevilled the Stephen Lawrence investigation.' The catalogue was caused, they infer, not by incompetence but by institutional racism.

Could a similar inference be drawn about the education system? In the education system is there a 'whole catalogue of failures, mistakes, misjudgements and lack of direction and control' bedevilling what happens to black and Muslim children and young people? Yes, say several of the people quoted in the grid in Box 1. And if teachers, headteachers, union leaders, education officers, civil servants, inspectors and elected politicians refuse to listen and attend, then this refusal is itself a powerful piece of evidence from which inferences may be validly drawn.

Robin Richardson reminds us, as did Norman Kunc in chapter 4, that just because we think we are doing good does not mean we necessarily are. The nature of our social structures both reflects and creates the assumptions that underlie our social actions. If our systems are inherently divisive then however much we may make claims of being inclusive we will always fail to achieve the goal. Achieving inclusion is an active process requiring us to search for barriers, old and new, and then to find the ways to dismantle them.

Index